EARL R. BECK

A Time of Triumph and of Sorrow

SPANISH POLITICS

DURING THE REIGN OF

ALFONSO XII

1874-1885

SOUTHERN ILLINOIS UNIVERSITY PRESS

Carbondale and Edwardsville

FEFFER & SIMONS, INC.

London and Amsterdam

Library of Congress Cataloging in Publication Data

Beck, Earl Ray, 1916–
A time of triumph and of sorrow.

Bibliography: p.
Includes index.
1. Spain—Politics and government—1875–1885.
I. Title.
DP 232.B42   320.9'46'08   78-23282
ISBN 0-8093-0902-5

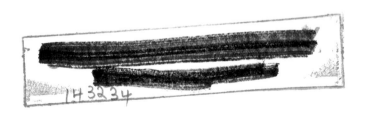

CONTENTS

P R E F A C E

T HIS BOOK is being written at a most propitious time—a young
and appealing monarch has just taken over the throne of Spain
and, both at home and abroad, observers are waiting to see
whether he can bring a thrust toward the modernization and
liberalization of his country. A hundred years ago another young
and appealing monarch ascended the throne of Spain and observers of that era raised the same question—could that king,
Alfonso XII, aid in the modernization and liberalization of his
country? That the answer was to be a little yes and a larger no
was not due to the king's lack of intelligence, lack of good intentions, or lack of goodwill and courage. To some degree it was
due to his youth, to some degree to his ill health, and to a much
larger degree to the effect of entrenched customs, traditions, and
political usages. The author sincerely hopes that the present
monarch, older and more mature than Alfonso XII, may be able
to accomplish more than did his predecessor. But he also hopes
that he shares the intelligence, the goodwill, and the ability that
Alfonso had begun to display before his untimely death.

The research for this book has bound together the author's
twin interests in the histories of Germany and of Spain. Alfonso
XII was a fervent Germanophile. He was an ardent admirer of
Kaiser Wilhelm I and his Iron Chancellor, Otto von Bismarck.
They, on their part, learned of the Spanish monarch's admiration from the careful and detailed reports of their ambassadors.
Both Melchior Gustav Paul, Graf von Hatzfeldt-Wildenburg,
who was the German envoy until late in 1878, and Klaus Eberhard Theodor, Graf zu Solms-Sonnenwalde, who replaced him,
followed Spanish politics closely and fully. The latter became a
close friend of the king, who often poured out to him his frustrations with events at home. Through Solms's reports come an
intimate view of a complex period of Spanish history.

Alfonso shared much of his reign with his own Bismarck, Cánovas del Castillo. Like Bismarck, Cánovas brought peace and stability to his country after a period of internal unrest. He had Bismarck's self-esteem and self-confidence, but governed a much weaker and less resolute nation. Like Bismarck he was a pragmatist, much more so than he has been represented by his biographers. Although he failed to make Spain a first-rate power, did not succeed in providing it with a genuinely parliamentary government, and lacked the energy and vision for progressive social reform, he probably accomplished as much as could be achieved under existing conditions. If the young monarch had lived longer, if Cánovas had come to know him better and to realize his true potential, more might have been accomplished.

But this study does not seek to be a biography of either Alfonso XII or Cánovas. Both men moved within a complex pattern of politics and were hemmed in by circumstances and traditions. And none of Cánovas's opponents displayed much initiative, let alone charisma. Sagasta played the political game with the same cynicism as did Cánovas. The parade of lesser personalities—Serrano, Posada Herrera, Martínez Campos, Alonso Martínez, León y Castillo, Pi y Margall, Ruiz Zorrilla, and so forth—finds no one bearing the banner of political greatness. This was a period in which the motif was the search for peace and quiet after governmental instability and civil war. It was a time of triumph for the king, who returned to the throne of his ancestors; for Cánovas, who guided his nation into a path of conciliation; and even for Sagasta, who retained a role of political significance. But it was also a time of sorrow for that same monarch, who saw frustration added to personal tragedies; for Cánovas, whose cynicism reflected his realization that he had not really moved Spain to greatness; and for the great majority of the Spanish people afflicted with floods, earthquakes, and cholera and still suffering under a government unresponsive to their needs.

ACKNOWLEDGMENTS ARE DUE to many for assistance in the preparation of this book—to the Department of History of The

Preface

Florida State University for making possible two lengthy research periods in Spain; to the officials of the municipal hemeroteca and the Biblioteca Nacional in Madrid; to the officials of the British Public Record Office, who were always kind and cooperative; to the innumerable booksellers and especially Gabriel Molina Sucesores, who have helped in the acquisition of personal and library resources over the past twenty years; to the Strozier Library of The Florida State University, which has been most cooperative in the acquisition of microfilm materials from the United States Department of State and the German Foreign Office, the Cortes debates, and the microfilm files of *La Epoca*, and whose interlibrary loan office helped in the acquisition of needed sources from libraries throughout the country. A special debt is owed Judy Greaves, who helped to complete research in the British Public Record Office on the last years of this study. And above all the author owes an incalculable debt to his family for their support and encouragement.

Grateful acknowledgment is also made of the Duke University Press for permission to use material from my article "The Martínez Campos Government of 1879: Spain's Last Chance in Cuba," *Hispanic American Historical Review*, May 1976, Copyright 1976 by Duke University Press.

EARL R. BECK

Tallahassee, Florida
September 2, 1978

Note on Spanish Names and Titles

THE AUTHOR has followed the normal usage of the Spanish names in the text. The spelling of some names varies—for example, Balmaseda and Valmaseda. So far as appropriate, names have been used in as simplified a form as possible, but both the paternal and maternal names are commonly joined in some cases —for example, Romero Robledo and Calderón Collantes.

Spanish titles have been anglicized in the text; the Spanish forms are commonly used in the notes.

A Time of Triumph

and of Sorrow

I

Revolution and

Restoration

HAT A STRUGGLE! What a struggle!" he murmured a few minutes before he died.[1] He referred to his own last painful gasps for life, but the words portrayed the whole reign of King Alfonso XII of Spain. Not that it was a long one—he died a month before the end of his eleventh year on the throne. But those eleven years saw the reestablishment of Spain's traditional royal family, the adoption of a constitution which survived for more than fifty years, the exclusion of the military from the dominant role it had played in politics, and the achievement of greater political stability than Spain had known for a century.

The king was not the prime mover in these accomplishments —like his contemporary William I of Germany he placed his confidence in his chief minister, Antonio Cánovas del Castillo. Cánovas in Spain, like Bismarck in Germany, held the center of the stage during most of the reign of Alfonso while the king remained in the background. But in both cases the position of the ruler was necessary to support that of the minister. And in both cases the ruler's personality made possible the accomplishments of the minister. On occasion both monarchs also exercised more influence on the course of events than has been commonly assumed.

Alfonso XII has been labeled "the king without good fortune" by one of his biographers.[2] And, indeed, his brief life was one filled with personal tragedies—the untimely loss of a first wife whom he had married for love over the protests of ministers and family; the loss of a favorite sister; the constant evidence of the foolishness and willfulness of a wayward mother; and the losing battle with a progressively virulent tuberculosis. In his brief reign he saw his country beset by civil war, ravaged by earthquakes and floods, and haunted by the specter of radical political movements. Received rather coldly at the outset of his reign, Alfonso had established much rapport with his people before it closed. His goodwill, sincerity, and honest concern were manifested in times of suffering. In the long line of Spanish sovereigns he holds a place worthy of respect and sympathy.

The country whose throne he assumed early in 1875 had a chaotic political heritage. Under Napoleon the Bourbons had temporarily lost their throne while Napoleon's well-meaning but bumbling brother Joseph ruled. With the fall of Napoleon the Bourbons returned in the person of the cynical and realistic Ferdinand VII. In 1820 Ferdinand confronted the first of the military coups which troubled Spanish politics for half a century. At his death he added strength to the role of the army by a disputed succession. The Bourbon family had held to the succession of the nearest male relative, which in this case would have been Ferdinand's brother, Carlos (Charles). But Spanish traditions had never excluded female succession and Ferdinand's will named his daughter Isabella as his successor, under the regency of her mother, María Cristina. The consequence was a bitter civil war not suppressed until 1839.

The opponents of the ruling monarchy were designated the Carlists after the first pretender to the throne, who would have been Carlos V if he had been able to establish his claim. They were strongest in the northern part of Spain. The Basque provinces of Álava, Guipuzcoa, and Vizcaya, and the adjacent province of Navarre were the stronghold of what became the Carlist "Tradition." The tough and picturesque adherents of the cause of the male line of Bourbons in Spain fought resolutely within the mountain fastnesses they knew so well. Their monarchism was reinforced by a stern and unbending Catholicism, which resented the moderately liberal tendencies which developed under Queen Isabella II. They defended also the traditional rural interests of their region and its claim to autonomous rights and privileges. But the Carlist cause also found adherents in Catalonia and in Valencia, where the rugged area of the Maestrazgo was the scene of desperate struggles. Defeated in 1839, the Carlists remained true to their lost cause and were quick to seize later opportunities to defend it.

Meanwhile, the reign of Isabella II continued to be chaotic. Both sinned against and sinning, the monarch was one of the tragic figures of Spanish history.[3] Her marriage to an effeminate cousin, Francisco de Asís, reputed to be impotent, was one of the scandals of the nineteenth century, a marriage designed to rob her of offspring and turn the throne over to the descendants of her younger sister, Luisa Fernanda, who married the French duke of Montpensier, a member of the Orleanist branch of the French Bourbons.[4] Isabella was reported to have said that on her wedding night her consort wore more lace on his underthings than she did.[5] But Isabella found a long line of favorites willing to make up for her husband's deficiencies.[6]

The influence of the military in politics had been enormously enhanced by the First Carlist War. Under Isabella the army became to a high degree the arbiter of the destinies of the nation.[7] Four generals dominated the course of politics—Baldomero Espartero, Leopoldo O'Donnell, Ramón María Narvaez, and Juan Prim. Different in personality and in political orientation, each played the role of a military *caudillo*, who combined leadership in arms with an influence on governmental policies. Military *pronunciamientos*, proclamations of political revolt, were issued in 1820, 1836, 1854, and 1868. With the exception of Narvaez the disposition of the generals had been vaguely liberal, but the fluctuations of political forces and the vagaries of the queen had prevented the development of any sound political tradition.

The last of these military pronunciamientos, that of 1868, cost Isabella II her throne. All in all, she had governed badly, never quite gaining the maturity, the wisdom, and the willpower that a Spanish monarch required. Although her impulses were generous, she frequently deserted her most loyal supporters. She tolerated a court camarilla engaged in unconcealed corruption. Late in her reign her religious feelings led her to maintain a close relationship with a fanatically religious and narrow-minded ex-nun, Sor Patrocinio, who became the symbol of the queen's unwillingness to heed the sober counsel of friendly political advisers.[8] In the end Isabella had used up whatever stock of political favor she once had. The Revolution of 1868 was hailed as "la gloriosa"—the harbinger of saner and more sensible government. As Isabella left Spain in its wake, there was no real likelihood that she could return to the throne unless imposed by force of arms and with a repressive government. Her misfortune had also left her shaken mentally—there were to be evidences of a complete inability to comprehend the depth of her own disgrace within the land she had governed.

The future Alfonso XII was eleven years old when he, along with his mother and sisters, left Spain as a result of the Revolution of 1868. His childhood portraits seem to predict the tragedies of later life. Large and staring eyes in a sad and smileless countenance divert the viewer's attention from the Catalan costume in which the mother had dressed him to gain the goodwill of one of Spain's least monarchist regions.[9]

For the young prince exile must have been something of an adventure. In Madrid he had often been lonely and neglected and his education by all reports had been deficient. One account has the young prince being told in couplet form that he must wash his feet every two or three months.[10] Undoubtedly this was a fabrication, but the level of education for princes in Isabelline Spain was apparently quite low.

The royal family installed itself in a sort of hotel-palace in

Paris. Although Isabella christened it the "Castilian Palace," it was more commonly designated after its former Polish proprietor the Basilewsky Palace. Although it was small for a monarch accustomed to luxury and display, its purchase, the maintenance of a still considerable staff of attendants, the pensions distributed to loyal supporters who accompanied her into exile, and the numerous subsidies for newspapers and potential supporters back home placed an insupportable strain on the queen's finances. By 1873 she was in serious financial difficulty.[11] Apparently her style of life did not greatly change—she continued to have a series of "favorites" while in exile.[12]

In Paris the fiction of the royal marriage was abandoned and Isabella and Francisco de Asís formally separated. Francisco considered himself free to follow his own inclinations, going so far as to hold meetings with members of the Carlist camp and display sympathy for the cause of the pretender.[13] On the other hand, he badgered Isabella to provide him with a generous pension, adding to her financial embarrassment.[14] Although Isabella sought to preserve Alfonso's respect for "Papá," efforts to bring about even an outward reconciliation of the couple failed.[15] Francisco was to live the remainder of his life in France, dying there in 1902.[16]

Throughout the six years between the Revolution of 1868 and the restoration of Alfonso XII late in 1874, Isabella maintained a desperate round of negotiations directed toward her own return to Spain. From her correspondence and her conversations in exile it is clear that she never comprehended her own responsibility for the downfall of the monarchy. Still a relatively young woman—only thirty-eight at the beginning of her exile—she had visions of regaining the throne and recovering its perquisites (had she succeeded, she might have ruled to her death in 1904). But her hopes were to be disappointed. The Spanish Cortes adopted a liberal constitution in 1869 and sought a new constitutional monarch. The abortive invitation to Leopold of Hohenzollern-Sigmaringen triggered the Franco-Prussian War of 1870–71. The Cortes then called an Italian Prince, Amadeo of Savoy, to the throne in 1870. Just before that choice had been made in

Spain and with quite apparent reluctance and obvious later second thoughts, Isabella completed a formal act of abdication in behalf of her son, whom she now proclaimed Alfonso XII.[17] But throughout the interim period until the actual Restoration and even on several occasions thereafter, Isabella gave evidence that she would not be averse to reconsidering her action.[18] And the legality of the act, signed abroad and not ratified by a Spanish Cortes, was to constitute an early problem for the Restoration government.

Meanwhile, Isabella had found a generous supporter and Alfonso something of a substitute father in the marquis of Alcañices, the duke of Sesto. In the years of exile the patron's wealth helped to tide over the former monarch in her financial difficulties. In many encounters it is clear that he also won the genuine affection of the young prince.[19]

Alfonso spent four years in the Collège Stanislas in the Latin Quarter. He was still accompanied by his former tutor, who bore the unlikely Spanish name Guillermo Morphy.[20] In these years the government of Amadeo of Savoy ran into increasing difficulty, beset by jealous political leaders of factious parties unable to form reliable coalitions. Early in his reign the conservative government of Gen. Francisco Serrano, duke of la Torre, had given away to the much more liberal government of Manuel Ruiz Zorrilla, to be the leader of a radical republicanism after the Restoration. He, in turn, was succeeded by Práxedes Mateo Sagasta, already displaying the practical and somewhat ruthless political maneuvers to be characteristic of him, only to be replaced briefly by Serrano and then by Ruiz Zorrilla, still loyal to Amadeo, but unable to allay the frustrations of a monarch who never won the respect, let alone the support of the Spaniards, and who voluntarily relinquished the crown.[21]

Before Amadeo reached the unfortunate end of his reign early in 1873, Alfonso had been sent to Vienna to continue his education in the quasi-military academy, the Theresianum. Apparently his education was well managed, because Alfonso began to display the precocity which was to aid his early assumption of responsibilities. He also came into contact with the excitement, splendor, and high culture of one of Europe's most glittering cities. From later evidence it is clear that his stay in Vienna marked the beginning of a genuine and strong Germanophilism.[22]

It was also while he was in Vienna that Queen Isabella became guilty of one of her most egregious indiscretions. Although her hated brother-in-law, the duke of Montpensier, had been one of the backers of the Revolution of 1868, she now agreed in January 1872 to his leadership of the Alfonsist cause. The young prince had serious reservations but accepted his mother's decision. His uncle paid him a brief visit in Vienna. There is no evidence that the uncle gained his nephew's respect, but the two posed for a joint photograph which was widely distributed in Spain. Within a year the duke had wasted 1,700,000 francs supplied by Isabella without any real accomplishments. And at that point he decided to give up the cause.[23] The only real outcome of this brief period of family cooperation was one that had not been anticipated. On a visit to his relative's house at Christmastime 1872 Alfonso met María de las Mercedes, the daughter of Montpensier, and began the first stage of an ill-fated royal romance.[24]

Montpensier's decision to surrender the leadership of the Alfonsist cause was due in part to his well-founded suspicion that Isabella was planning to replace him with General Serrano, who had once been her favorite.[25] But *el general bonito* strongly rejected any commitment, and the queen's followers, aware of the increasing influence of Antonio Cánovas del Castillo, pressured her to accept him as leader of the Bourbon cause.[26]

When the Revolution of 1868 broke out, Cánovas was already a well-known political figure.[27] Born in Málaga in 1828, the son of the master of a secondary school, Cánovas moved to Madrid in 1845. There he took courses both in philosophy and law and received degrees in each, although he never actually practiced law. He wrote poetry, took part in the publication of several newspapers, and began the career of historian, which was to be one of the most notable aspects of his life's work.

During this early period in Madrid he had powerful patrons who assisted him financially, socially, and politically. His mother's cousin, Serafín Estébanez Calderón, was a famous writer of the period under the pen name of "El Solitario." He was also assisted by his fellow Malagueño José de Salamanca, the most prominent financier of the day, made wealthy and powerful by the collection of government salt taxes and railroad and real estate transactions. Both were involved in the first major railroad built in Spain from Madrid to Aranjuez and Cánovas held a sinecure with that company for ten years. Apparently his only obligation was to pick up his paycheck once a month.

Other literary people, however, received similar favors. And Cánovas quickly moved into this classification. He wrote for the notorious and illegal newspaper, *El Murciélago*, and for the more staid daily *La Patria*, founded by Joaquín Francisco Pacheco, the leader of a section of the Moderado party called "the Puritans." In 1850 Pacheco entrusted him with the direction of the newspaper. A year later Cánovas was able to bring his family to Madrid, buy a house, and provide space for the beginning of an extensive private library.

Cánovas's entry into politics was facilitated by a friendship growing out of the café society of the day. A chance meeting had led to intimacy with the nephew of Gen. Leopoldo O'Donnell, one of the great politico-military leaders who dominated so much of the history of Spain during the nineteenth century. Cánovas was the author of the Manifesto of Manzanares issued by O'Donnell as he initiated the Revolution of 1854. It advocated "the preservation of the throne, but without the camarilla which dishonors it," the rigorous enforcement of the fundamental laws of the state with improvements affecting those of elections and the press, governmental economy and reduction of taxes, the merit system in civil and military employment, centralization in government with safeguards for local interests, and a national militia. In its measured tones it heralded Cánovas's later advocacy and presumed authorship of O'Donnell's Liberal Union, a combination of the moderate and liberal groups behind a more responsible monarchy. Twenty years before the Restoration Cánovas had developed the basic principles which he would seek to follow, although in both cases some of the high ideals remained literary expressions rather than practice.

From this time on Cánovas was continually involved in political activity. Although he was disillusioned by the consequences of the Revolution of 1854 and tended toward a more conservative course thereafter, he remained a close associate of O'Donnell. He served in the Constitutional Cortes of 1855. He had become a few months earlier a third-class official in the Ministry of Foreign Affairs and early in 1855 was promoted to second-class status. Later in the year Gen. Juan de Zabala y de la Puente, the minister of foreign affairs, appointed him to the position of director of the Spanish Agency of Prayers in Rome, a governmental agency established to further the petitions of Spanish Catholics at the papal court. This was a position both of prestige and profit. It disposed of a very significant revenue—Cánovas's private fortune apparently dates from this period. Cánovas was Spain's only official representative in Rome, since the Papacy had denounced seizures of church property by the Spanish state, declared the Concordat of 1851 disrupted, and broken off diplomatic relations. In 1857 Cánovas returned home, became briefly civil governor of Catalonia in 1858, then director general of administration and subsecretary of the Ministry of the Interior before becoming in 1864 minister of the interior under Alejandro Mon and in 1865 minister of overseas territories under O'Donnell.

In these varied experiences Cánovas learned much of practical politics. His participation in the Revolution of 1854, where his political ally O'Donnell was outmaneuvered by his associates and social unrest threatened, left Cánovas with a deep aversion to revolutions. His administrative experience convinced him that there was little real concern in governmental spheres for political morality. José Posada Herrera's "management" of the election of 1858 showed Cánovas the potentialities of control over the electoral process. His service as minister of overseas territories began his confrontation with Spain's nineteenth-century dilemma—the contradiction between an anachronistic national pride and the realities of national power. And closer acquaintance with the affairs of the royal family led him to the conviction that Isabella II had revealed her incompetence for the crown.

As a consequence, the Revolution of 1868 found Cánovas voluntarily sitting on the sidelines of politics. Approaches to obtain his support gained the retort that he would neither erect nor tear down barricades. Although he defended Isabella II and her mother from charges of wrongfully making use of funds obtained from the sale of the royal jewels, he distanced himself from her cause and was among those who had exerted pressure upon the queen to abdicate in behalf of her son in 1870. He played a relatively minor role in the Constitutional Cortes of 1869, opposing the articles granting universal suffrage and complete religious freedom (although the constitution did preserve state maintenance of the church). Cánovas opposed the choice of Amadeo I as Spain's first elected monarch and accurately predicted that the Italian prince would be unable to rally the support of the nation. When the republic came with its alternation of presidents, the growing strength of the federalist movement, and the splintering of left-wing forces, Cánovas became the outstanding spokesman in behalf of the return of the Bourbons in the person of the future Alfonso XII.

By 1872 Cánovas was already exercising a primary role in behalf of the Alfonsist cause within Spain. Close advisers of the queen, including the duke of Sesto, urged her to give official support to his efforts. But Cánovas's unconcealed criticism of the queen's past role and of her existing life-style led her to seek alternatives. Only when Montpensier and Serrano had proved their lack of reliability did the queen finally turn to Cánovas.[28] Very probably it was at his instance that her designation of his leadership was accompanied by a formal ceremony in the Basilewsky Palace on August 4, 1873. In the presence of her son, other members of the royal family, and her most loyal advisers the queen conferred upon Cánovas full powers in the representation of her son's cause. The ceremony was confirmed by a letter signed by her and the prince, and Cánovas began the difficult task of creating a broad coalition of support for Alfonso in the midst of deep party divisions, unbridgeable personal differences, and the continuing machinations of the queen.[29]

By this time, of course, Amadeo had left and Spain had begun its chaotic and tragic first trial of republicanism. The brief period from February 1873 to January 3, 1874, saw a kaleidoscope of events. Four presidents came and went. The Carlist cause which had revived after the Revolution of 1868 took on new momentum. A federalist and cantonalist movement added the dissidence of Catalonia and considerable portions of southern Spain to that of the Basque provinces. And there were in Spain some significant reflections of the social unrest and terrorism connected with anarchist movements and the First International. Emilio Castelar, the last of the elected presidents of the First Republic, sought to reestablish unity and order; he accomplished much, but only at the price of dictatorial rule and the suspension of constitutional guarantees of personal liberties.[30] Foreign problems added to domestic difficulties. There was bitter controversy over proposed reforms to allay the existing revolution in Cuba and a harsh confrontation with the United States over the seizure of a supposed American vessel, the *Virginius*.

By January 2, 1874, it was clear that Castelar would fail to get renewed support from the Cortes when it reconvened. The major source of criticism was the severity of the measures he had taken to reestablish order and unity. Among these measures had been the return to their commands of a number of conservative generals displaced during the more radical phase of the republic, and they watched with concern as it appeared that the republic was about to be returned to the leadership of the more radical, federalist, and socialist personalities of the Cortes.[31]

It was the captain general of Madrid, Manuel Pavía, who took action. As the Cortes voted against Castelar early in the morning of January 3, 1874, and before it named his successor, Pavía's troops surrounded the parliament building, entered the chamber, and with a few shots fired in the air sent home the deputies who had professed themselves willing to die for their principles. There had been no pronunciamiento—Pavía had neither personal ambitions nor a clear program of action.[32] Spanish historians named his low-keyed coup "the Paviada," giving it a somewhat humorous cast and separating it from the earlier line of military revolts, although it illustrated once again the transcendent role of the military in Spanish history.[33]

Pavía met with party leaders representing a broad spectrum of opinion, from the Alfonsists on the right to the moderate republicans on the left. Castelar, whom Pavía had strongly supported, did not attend, denouncing Pavía's action as illegal and brutal. Cánovas and his followers announced their refusal to support any government which did not proclaim its intention to restore the Bourbons under Alfonso. Those who had accepted Pavía's invitation to consult in respect to the course to be followed recommended that a "Government of the Executive Power" be constituted under Francisco Serrano y Domínguez, duke of la Torre, regent of Spain following the Revolution of 1868 and president of the executive power pending the arrival of King Amadeo.[34] With this action the First Republic passed into its final stage of dissolution.

It was, indeed, debatable whether the First Republic still existed. The liberal constitution of 1869, which had been preserved, with minor changes, during the republican era was continued, as was also the title president of the executive power. Pavía had hoped that his coup would bring all parties together to preserve a national and unitary republic. But within a few months of its formation Serrano's government drifted strongly into the hands of the Constitutionalist party of Sagasta.

What Serrano himself anticipated for the future remains a question. His inclinations were vaguely monarchist. Some of his followers believed that he regarded his government only as an *interinidad* awaiting the propitious moment for the restoration of the Bourbons. Others were quite sure that his intentions centered on the more liberal Orleanist duke of Montpensier. Still others were convinced that the duke of la Torre was lured by the example of Marshal MacMahon in France. MacMahon was also a duke (of Magenta), and although he was supposed to be leading the Third French Republic toward a monarchical restoration, there were indications that he enjoyed his personal authority.[35]

In Spain there were widely held suspicions that Serrano thought of heading a lifelong grand dukedom. His wife, Antonia Domínguez y Borrell, was more ambitious than her husband. The only daughter of the count of San Antonio, she was twenty years younger than her husband. A beautiful reincarnation of Lady Macbeth, she enjoyed her husband's high position and her own resultant social prestige. She had been semi-ostracized from the high society of Madrid as a result of the duke's role under Amadeo and bitterly resented the slight. Although Isabella sought to soften her antipathy by sending her "a rich brooch of *fleur de lis* set in diamonds," the duchess had no intention of giving up her position as first lady of Spain. During the Restoration she was to give ample evidence of her resentment of her husband's loss of position.[36]

Serrano confronted a complex of grievous problems. Most of the cantonalist movement in the south had been broken up by General Pavía during the presidency of Castelar; the remaining stronghold, Cartagena, was taken by Serrano's nephew, Gen. José López Domínguez, shortly after the new government got underway.[37] But the continuing danger of federalist ideas forced the government to keep extensive garrisons in the cities of the south while it was confronted by the most serious threat yet posed by the Carlists.

The Carlists controlled the entire northeastern part of Spain from the Basque provinces across to Catalonia and extending into Aragon and Valencia. Intercourse between France and Spain by land had to run through Carlist territory. The pretender had been anointed Carlos VII by the bishop of La Seo de Urgel. He had an effective government with a postal service and an official newspaper, was well supplied with money and provisions, and exercised a strict and sometimes ruthless control over the territories in his power. Some 60,000 armed men were under his command. His kingdom was predominantly rural, but within it were liberal urban strongholds. These cities the Carlists held under siege, seeking to force their surrender by cutting off supplies and by devastating bombardments.[38]

The heart of liberal resistance in Carlist territory was the city of Bilbao, around which were gathered some 18,000 of the best Carlist troops, well provided with artillery. After Serrano's commanding general of the Army of the North, Domingo Moriones, ill-provided with troops and artillery, met defeat in his efforts to relieve the city, the duke of la Torre took a personal hand. With additional forces and considerable artillery he hastened northward, but accomplished little. Not until still more reinforcements under the command of the marquis of the Duero, Manual de la Concha, arrived did the Carlist forces desert their now untenable positions. The relief of Bilbao on May 2, 1874, added to the prestige of Concha, one of Spain's ablest generals but a pronounced Alfonsist.[39]

Prompt action at this point by the government forces assembled to break the siege would have brought the rapid dissolution of the Carlist cause. Arthur Houghton, one of the closest observers of this Second Carlist War, never ceased to wonder at the reluctance of the government forces to proceed with dispatch and energy against their Carlist opponents.[40] With the possible exception of Moriones, there were no Shermans or Grants among the government generals, and they never replied in kind to the raids and sackings of the Carlists, never imposed stern discipline in the regions conquered, never took action against the clergy who often deserted priestly duties to support the Carlist armies. Perhaps Serrano was rightly concerned with the possibility that complete victory, if associated with the name of Concha, would be followed by the immediate proclamation of Alfonso. On the other hand, he also lost his best opportunity to emblazon his own name on the pages of Spanish history and to solidify his rule, if that was his ambition.

At any rate Serrano returned to Madrid in a vain effort to cope with the growing political dissent there. After a long delay, Concha finally led his forces toward Estella, the Carlist capital. But the delay had given the Carlists ample time to reorganize their armies, reestablish the morale lost with the failure at Bilbao, and fortify the commanding heights surrounding the capital. In these operations General Concha was killed by a Carlist bullet on June 27, 1874, an event depriving the government forces of their best strategist and the Alfonsists of their best hope for an early restoration. The military defeat was not all that serious, reported Count Hatzfeldt, the German envoy. But Serrano's regime had been, he said, "seriously weakened in its own camp." The general had no prestige left, had displayed little energy, and his wife was close to prominent Radicals.[41]

Instead of taking personal command, Serrano made another error in choosing Concha's successor. Passing by younger, more imaginative officers, he named Juan de Zabala y de la Puente, already seventy years of age, cautious, and not very competent. Through the summer and well into the fall the Carlists continued unhampered in their control of the northeast. A daring raid led by the pretender's brother, Alfonso de Bourbón, and his wife captured and pillaged the city of Cuenca, less than a hundred miles from Madrid.[42] Not until the snows lay deep across the mountain areas of combat and the cold of winter storms sapped the strength of government forces did Marshal Serrano finally decide again to take command of the armies in order to gain the long-awaited victory.

Government action against the insurgents in Cuba was also less than inspiring. The republican reform projects were discarded, and the armies in Cuba received little reinforcement during this period of trial at home.

Meanwhile, the coalition of forces brought together by Pavía had divided and the Constitutionalist party of Práxedes Mateo Sagasta moved to take control. By May 13 the government was predominantly Constitutionalist, and on September 3 Sagasta took complete control. During the remainder of the Serrano period Sagasta governed sternly, engaging in political deportations of federalist Republicans and Carlists, censorship of newspapers, and rigid controls over university students.[43]

Sagasta had begun his political career in 1854, combining a quest for revolutionary change in the regime of Isabella II with considerable personal ambition.[44] A critic of the political general

Leopoldo O'Donnell, he had cast his fortunes with General Prim and alternated effective opposition in the Cortes with periods of flight and exile abroad. Early in the Revolution of 1868 he had joined with Serrano, supported the monarchy of Amadeo I, served as minister of the interior and foreign minister during the rapid alternation of cabinets, and had been one of the major authors of the liberal constitution of 1869. Originally a "Progressive," he had come to head the Constitutionalist party after 1871 with the newspaper, *La Iberia*, as its major party organ. Sagasta's career revealed a sense of idealism heavily tempered by cold practicality. Never an intellectual, he had "never read a book," and he presented a diametric contrast to his later rival, Cánovas del Castillo. In his view the "liberalism of fire and torch" must be transformed into a more disciplined and political liberalism. The party he headed made use of the opportunity provided by the Serrano regime to establish control of local administration throughout Spain and create an impressive political machine. By the time of the Restoration the Constitutionalists were well on the way to the consolidation of a genuine grassroots support.[45]

In spite of its hesitations in dealing with the Carlists, the Serrano regime had also won recognition and goodwill from a number of foreign governments. The move in this direction had derived from a rather unexpected source, the government of Imperial Germany. Although there were renewed rumors of Machiavellian Bismarckian policies designed to establish yet another Hohenzollern on the Spanish throne, or, failing this, to negotiate an offensive-defensive alliance with Spain, the German effort had much more restricted objectives. Both the German and the English Foreign Offices were being fed reports that the Carlists were receiving extensive aid from France. Although Bismarck, as will be seen, did not lay much weight on potential Spanish assistance or alliance, it would obviously be of advantage if the chaotic conditions to the south of his recent enemy were stabilized.[46] The German initiative was rapidly followed by Great Britain, Austria, and France.[47] Only Russia remained aloof. There was, of course, in the recognition by Germany and Austria an area of anomaly—it was directed to the government of the duke of la Torre, not to a republic, and stressed the hope that the duke would continue to defend "conservative principles."[48]

The need for internal stability was emphasized by the difficulties which German and English commerce had undergone during the cantonal period and continued to confront in respect to commerce directed toward the northern shore of Spain. Late in 1874 came a new issue involving the shipwreck of a German ship off a Carlist-held port with the seizure of the vessel and the confiscation of its cargo by the Carlists. The Germans raided and temporarily occupied the port of Zarauz in reprisal. This was not meant to be hostile to the Serrano government. Indeed, after the Restoration there was an offer of cooperation of German naval forces with the Spanish naval forces in the area. But both Serrano and his successors were concerned with foreign naval action in Spanish territorial waters and the offer was refused. As will be seen, Spain paid an indemnity to Germany for the Carlist action.[49]

Meanwhile, Alfonso left the Theresianum in Vienna to visit England, where he was to enroll in still another school. But an exploratory visit to England was followed by a round on the Continent, where he visited Germany in September 1874, seeing the sights of Berlin, spending some time in Cologne, observing the Krupp factories at Essen, and being royally entertained in Munich by Prince Adalbert of Bavaria, who was married to the sister of Francisco de Asís. He was, of course, not received officially by any of the high officers of the German government. This could scarcely have been expected when Germany had recognized the regime of Serrano. A lieutenant colonel accompanied him to explain military affairs and, presumably, to carry back reports of the young prince's character to his superiors.[50]

The reports must have been favorable. Within a month after this visit the German Foreign Office informed Hatzfeldt in Madrid and Schweinitz in Austria that German favor for Alfonso was strong—Montpensier was unacceptable as being French and Carlos was the tool of papal forces, and since Germany favored a monarchical solution, Alfonso was the only choice.[51] And

Schweinitz was directed that if Alfonso appeared at the Austrian court, he should seek an opportunity to see him and tell him he had "the highest authority" to deal with him in a friendly fashion.[52] This was followed shortly by a note to the German ambassador in St. Petersburg along similar lines with "the highest authority" clearly identified as the kaiser himself.[53] Both Austrian and Russian responses were favorable—the Alfonsist cause was the "desirable" and "most natural" solution to the Spanish question.[54]

The dispatches concerned emphasize the falsity of the absurd rumors that Bismarck was during this period about to embark on another adventure in order to bring Prince Friedrich Karl of the house of Hohenzollern, the hero of Sadowa, Metz, and Orléans, to the throne of a united Spain and Portugal. The young prince received news of this rumor with more common sense than did many of his elders, writing to his mother, "Nor do I believe in the candidacy of a Hohenzollern in Spain, because it seems to me that Bismarck is too capable to seek an impossibility, of which he has proofs in Maximilian of Mexico and in Amadeo in Spain." And he added that the idea of an offensive-defensive alliance with Spain might be more likely on the part of Germany and that if such an offer were made, Spain would do well to accept it, exploit it, and then breach it when France gained enough strength internationally to be stronger than Prussia. In this he felt he was following a line set by Ferdinand the Catholic.[55] He was, of course, to discover later that Bismarck would be less than lukewarm in respect to an alliance with Spain. He did not, of course, visit the court of Vienna to get the message sent to Schweinitz, but probably received it indirectly from Morphy, who was acquainted with the German ambassador, Count Hatzfeldt, and had earlier been invited to dinner by the diplomat.

Although Cánovas was later to show himself less anti-German than has often been supposed, it was his inspiration that sent Alfonso for a brief schooling in England at the military academy in Sandhurst. To Isabella's objections, he answered that by this trip the English would see "the most intelligent prince of his age in Europe, without any doubt, and the most suited to be a good constitutional monarch."[56] As a consequence, Alfonso left Paris on August 11, 1874, spent that month and the first days of September in England visiting port installations, military encampments, and arsenals, as well as the more traditional tourist attractions before returning to the continent and making the German tour mentioned above. In October he returned to England and enrolled at the Sandhurst military academy, where he remained until the end of December only shortly before the unexpected pronunciamiento at Sagunto.[57] It was, of course, from England that Alfonso issued the so-called Sandhurst Manifesto in which he signed the proclamation sent to him by Cánovas promising to be a constitutional monarch when he returned to the throne. The proclamation was in the form of an impersonal response to birthday congratulations on the occasion of his seventeenth birthday, which could well be taken as a sign of his reaching his majority.[58] In the long run the brief stay in England had more significance in Spain than in England itself—it identified Alfonso with the English type of monarchy, winning the adherence of some Spanish liberals. Apparently he did not make the kind of impression on English ruling circles that he had on those of Germany and Austria. English diplomatic dispatches show little sign of real warmth for the Spanish monarch.

As the prince signed the Sandhurst Manifesto and shortly thereafter returned to Paris for the vacation period, neither he nor Cánovas knew how close was the moment in which the promises which had been made would have to be redeemed. Cánovas had, indeed, worked diligently for the Alfonsist cause. And he had accomplished much. Against the queen's own inclinations he had welcomed the adherence of many who had been strongly aligned with the revolutionary movement of 1868.[59] Perhaps one of the most startling acquisitions was that of Francisco Romero Robledo, who had lost his liberalism when projected reforms in Cuba threatened family properties there. Romero Robledo had already begun to display his skill as a political manipulator, which was to make him, perhaps more than Cánovas himself, responsible for the early consolidation of the

Restoration.[60] There were also some conditional adherences to the Alfonsist cause of those who had been members of the so-called Radical party. Five of the most prominent newspapers of Madrid, *La Epoca*, *El Tiempo*, *El Diario Español*, *El Eco de España*, and *La Política*, as well as several provincial newspapers became Alfonsist organs.[61] Cánovas's strategy was the propagandization of the cause of the young prince to a point at which a constitutional cortes could be called and the restoration of the Bourbon heir proclaimed. And this action should be carried out under civilian, not military, auspices.[62]

The Serrano government tolerated the Alfonsist propaganda. It allowed the printing in Spain of the Sandhurst Manifesto. It exercised little surveillance over known Alfonsist sympathizers, either civilian or military. But its own position in respect to the cause of the prince remained uncertain. In the middle of November the German ambassador in Lisbon reported that he had learned from "secure and completely confidential sources" that the candidacy of Alfonso had been discussed in the cabinet with about half of the ministers favoring Alfonso and the other half a republic under Castelar and his party and Serrano not taking a stand.[63] But prominent government adherents continued to advocate the candidacy of Montpensier,[64] and confidential sources indicated that Serrano's strongest concern was that the Carlist War should be brought to a triumphant solution before he relinquished power. Apparently at that point he would be quite willing to sponsor a constitutional cortes which would decide for a monarchy, but whether that monarchy would be firmly in the hands of the prince and his existing advisers—especially Cánovas—might be very dubious.[65]

Accordingly, at long last Serrano departed from Madrid for the battle front on December 8, 1874, arriving in Logroño in the snow on the 10th. Proceeding some four days later to the front at Castejón, he met with various generals, most significantly Moriones. The latter responded to Serrano's late-won impatience for action by convincing him that an active campaign in the snow and the cold would be impossible and that the season of bad weather should be used for reinforcing the troops confronting the Carlists by reducing the size of the garrisons no longer needed so urgently elsewhere in Spain. Serrano hesitated once more—he was still watching the horizon and the barometer when the news of Sagunto arrived.[66]

Cánovas's plans had meant to bypass the military. Although the political wisdom of this may seem apparent, the realism of his planning seems faulty. In the midst of the Carlist War when the strength of the military was vital to the Alfonsist cause, what did Cánovas expect from the generals? Did he expect them to follow a path of self-abnegation, leaving the course of events completely in civilian hands? Did he expect them to continue to risk their lives and those of their men and leave all claims to gratitude from the restored monarch to the caprices of fate? Did he anticipate that after more than half a century in which the military had played so prominent a role in Spanish politics, it would now accept a place on the sidelines, particularly when military prestige was so much at stake not only in respect to the Carlist War but also in Cuba? What did Cánovas expect from General Serrano, from Sagasta, and from their associates? Did he anticipate that Serrano would yield the center of the stage without protest? Did he believe that a practical politician like Sagasta would step aside in the midst of a rapid consolidation of party machinery and organization? Did he anticipate that remnants of republican and federalist movements would jump on the Alfonsist bandwagon? How did he anticipate exerting the firm hand of control without a close partnership with the military? How could he realistically contemplate an arrangement with the Carlists which would end the fighting at the price of a large-scale entry of Carlist officers into the regular armed forces?

A little over five years later Cánovas and Gen. Arsenio Martínez Campos were to confront one another in a great debate in the Senate semicircle. On that occasion Cánovas was to say in retrospect that the worst misfortune he had confronted in 1874 was the necessity of having the general at his side. For the general's pronunciamiento at Sagunto had ignored his wishes and undercut his plans. But it might also be argued that there was a very good chance that without Martínez Campos the Cánovas era might never have got underway.[67]

Martínez Campos was born of a military family in Segovia on December 14, 1831.[68] It was natural for him to enter upon a military career and his family connections along with his own ability gave him entry into Spain's general staff school. Action in the turbulent political events at home was accompanied by combat experience in Africa in 1860, in Mexico in 1861, and in Cuba from 1868 to 1872. During this period he rose to the rank of brigadier and obtained considerable prestige for military prowess.

In 1873 he served as captain general in Valencia and followed this with his first experience in the Carlist wars in Catalonia. His style of military leadership began to develop the characteristics of dash and daring which were to make him a popular figure in a period not very rich in romantic leaders, but his superiors found him a difficult subordinate, inclined to precipitate action and unwilling to accept superior authority when it contravened his own judgment. But he was successful and his prestige continued to increase.[69] When the first Spanish republic came under the more disciplined leadership of Emilio Castelar, Martínez Campos was named captain general of Catalonia.

In this position, civilian administration as well as military command was involved and it seems clear, contrary to some later judgments, that Martínez Campos had considerable administrative ability. Here, as later, he displayed a quest for conciliation and moderation which was to become the hallmark of his career. Misfortune befell him on this occasion, however. After General Pavía's coup, described above, the Serrano regime had promised that it would represent all parties and Martínez Campos, on his part, promised the Catalans that all parties except the rebellious Carlists and Cantonalists would be represented in the new administration to be established there. This promise was not kept and Martínez Campos not only resigned in protest but accompanied his resignation with an open proclamation of his disappointment with the new regime. An order of arrest was issued against him and he underwent a relatively brief period of incommunicado incarceration in the military prison at Las Palmas.[70]

Martínez Campos, however, had powerful friends among the military and they interceded for him. Probably it didn't require too much pressure to convince Serrano that he could ill afford to leave the popular general in prison at a time when the Carlists were a significant threat in Spain's northern provinces. In April 1874 Martínez Campos was assigned to command the second division of the Marshal del Duero's Army of the North.[71] But Martínez Campos became during the months which followed one of the most prominent Alfonsists and one distrusted because of his well-known proclivities for precipitate action. As a consequence, he was removed from command and placed in a reserve status (*en cuartel*) in Madrid. He would probably have been placed under precautionary arrest if the military governor of Madrid, Gen. Fernando Primo de Rivera, had not vouched for his security.[72]

By this time the personal rivalry of Cánovas and Martínez Campos was already well known. Both men had a strong sense of *amor proprio*. And the impatience of the general convinced him that Cánovas's prohibition against military action in behalf of Alfonso was leading to a fatal delay. He believed that he was the only person who could rally the generals behind Alfonso and felt that his prestige was declining while he sat inactive in Madrid.[73]

As a consequence, Martínez Campos once again disobeyed superior authority—that of Cánovas—and slipped away from Madrid to Valencia, and on December 29, 1874, in a field near the tiny town of Sagunto with two brigades "borrowed" from a close friend, Gen. Luis Dabán, proclaimed Alfonso king of Spain.[74]

And once again insubordination paid off! Lost in the excitement of the news from Sagunto was a similar pronunciamiento on the part of General Blas Villate y de la Hera, count of Valmaseda, at Ciudad Real.[75] Although Valmaseda had also had a brilliant military career in Cuba and Africa, he was apparently willing to take second place in this political action to Martínez Campos. The pronunciamiento was adhered to by the other generals, most importantly by Gen. Joaquín Jovellar, next to Serrano the highest commander in the field.[76]

In Madrid Cánovas suffered a brief and not unpleasant arrest (he enjoyed dinner in state with his jailer and received hundreds of visitors while under arrest).[77] Sagasta and his cabinet found that Gen. Fernando Primo de Rivera, who had guaranteed the security of Martínez Campos, was no more reliable than the man he watched over and he now informed them that the garrison troops in Madrid were heavily committed to Alfonsism and could not be relied upon to resist the coup.[78] After a lugubrious telegraphic conference with Serrano, who counseled against resistance, Sagasta and his cabinet surrendered authority without bloodshed.[79]

The minor melodrama at Sagunto had cut through a web of uncertainties. The army staked its claim for the gratitude of the new monarch and the continued respect of the nation. The Sagasta government made a show of yielding to force. And Martínez Campos signaled a new era by disclaiming all personal ambitions and recognizing the full authority of the civilian, Cánovas del Castillo, who now stepped to the fore as the unquestioned leader of a new political experiment.[80]

In all of these events the young monarch-to-be had played no role except that of the docile executor of Cánovas's wishes. News of his restoration came to him in Paris on the evening of December 30, 1874. He had just returned from England.[81] By some incredible accident the newspapers of Paris had not been previously informed. The new king received the news in a note from a female acquaintance and kept the secret to himself until after the evening's theater performance.[82] Cánovas, later to be labeled "the omnipotent papa," apparently did not think to telegraph the news to the monarch until the following morning.[83] And it was the minister not the monarch who ruled during the first years of the Restoration.

2

Cánovas: Pacification
and Conciliation

T HE NEWLY-PROCLAIMED KING left Paris on January 6, 1875, to be met at Marseilles by representatives of the new government back home—the marquis of Molíns, minister of the navy; General Valmaseda representing the army; the count of Heredia Spínola in behalf of the grandees of Spain; and Ignacio José Escobar, the director of the most prominent Alfonsist periodical, *La Epoca*.[1]

The monarch's reception in Barcelona was a favorable one. Visiting the institution there devoted to the advancement of industry, he responded positively to spokesmen for Catalan industry—"If I should succeed in making all of Spain a Barcelona, I am sure I would have made my country a great nation." After a brief visit to Valencia he arrived in Madrid on January 14. The capital turned out en masse to welcome him. The triumphal parade was a brilliant one. The monarch in the uniform of a captain general was accompanied by those generals who had assured his return. The king's appearance had greatly improved during his exile. The thin face of the prince had filled out somewhat. The haunting eyes were less prominent. The beginnings of a moustache were apparent. The prominent Bourbon nose and the weak Hapsburg chin reflected his ancestors, but if not handsome, the new king at least made a very attractive impression.[2] But the full judgment of many Spaniards awaited the accomplishment of the peace and stabilization which had been promised.

The monarch found Cánovas firmly in control of the course of events. The full powers granted him in 1873 had been employed to establish a ministry-regency awaiting the return of the king and Cánovas and his colleagues moved rapidly and decisively to establish their authority.[3] If one can criticize some of Cánovas's planning during Serrano's *interinidad*, one can scarcely fault him for the management of the most difficult period of the Restoration, that first year when new guidelines had to be established, with an effort for the balancing of extremes and the revelation of the firm hand of authority cushioned by a temperate attitude toward opposition.

Cánovas's political position was extremely difficult. He had hoped for before Sagunto, and continued to seek, a virtual consensus of opinion behind the new monarch. This would require an artful conciliation of liberal and conservative viewpoints, reflected in Cánovas's designation of the party he now created as the Liberal-Conservative party.[4] He had set a portion of the pattern in the words of the Sandhurst Manifesto which he had composed for the young king to send to his future subjects, as noted above. This message, dated December 1, less than a month before Sagunto, emphasized both an "hereditary" and a "constitutional" monarchy, the reestablishment of "legal order and political liberty," the guarantee of the rights of all "from the working classes to the most advanced" members of society, and parliamentary procedures "when all Spaniards are accustomed to them." He was, said the prince, "a good Spaniard," "a good Catholic," and "as a man of this century, truly liberal."[5]

But now high-flown phrases must be transformed into reality. A cabinet must be established, but every Spanish politician with experience had a political background easily faulted by opponents. The line between tolerance of criticism and opening a road to revolution was not easily drawn. The compromise between anticlericalism and ultramontane reaction would not be easily found. And there were, besides, the enormous tasks of winning the war against the Carlists, ending the rebellion in Cuba, and then coping with the staggering financial burdens thrust upon Spain by these wars and a long period of maladministration.

Cánovas moved rapidly and effectively to cope with these problems. His actions were marked by decisiveness and firmness. Some of his decisions were unwise and on occasion he found a way to reverse them. His manner and appearance reflected a natural sense of leadership. When he stood before the Cortes he gave a somewhat less aristocratic impression than he did in maturity. The stiff white collar and black bow tie were already the main sartorial feature and the spectacles worn on a black string provided the professorial note. The dark hair was well groomed but the somewhat scruffy moustache and the peculiar minuscule double pointed beard undercut the atmosphere of elegance. This, accompanied by a nervous tic or twitching of his eyes and an imperious manner in dealing with both associates and opponents, was to give him the nickname of "the Monster." But he was never ruffled or discomposed by opposition. And eventually some of his severest critics lauded his achievements, although they had opposed his methods.

His cabinet, quickly confirmed by the king upon his return, sought to represent varying points of view.[6] There was a relatively significant component labeled *Moderado*, a term connoting attachment to the cause of Isabella II and hence opposed to the Revolution of 1868 and also a favoring of "Catholic unity," the reestablishment of the unchallenged dominance of the church. Those most prominently classified in this fashion were the minister of foreign affairs (*Estado*), Alejandro Castro; of grace and justice, Francisco de Cárdenas; and of development (*Fomento*), the Marquis Manuel de Orovio y Echagüe. Also Moderado was the mayor of Madrid, Francisco de Borja Queipo de Llano y Gayoso de los Cobos, the count of Toreno, destined to play a significant role in later Cánovas governments. Closely aligned with these but not outright Moderado was Mariano Roca de Togores, the first marquis of Molíns, minister of the navy.[7]

Among the former liberals were Pedro Salaverría,[8] who took on the awesome task of minister of the treasury, and Francisco Romero Robledo, who became minister of the interior (*Gobernación*). Romero Robledo had become very much identified with the early stages of the Revolution of 1868—to him had been attributed the phrase, "the spurious race of the Bourbons has fallen forever." At first an adherent to the cause of Amadeo, he came to recognize the Italian king's shortcomings and moved to the Alfonsist position in 1872. As noted above, his marriage to the daughter of the prominent Cuban financier, Julián Zulueta, had made him a critic of reform policies in Cuba, which threatened the perquisites of plantation owners.[9] By the close of the republican era he was by far the most dramatic of the monarchists represented in the Cortes. His identification with the leadership of Cánovas at this time, apparently so strong and secure, was once again to be interrupted in 1886. Perhaps the most genuinely liberal of the Cánovas ministers was Adelardo López de Ayala, the minister of overseas territories, known as one of Spain's most able poets and who was extended felicitations even by the Constitutionalist newspaper *La Iberia*.[10]

As minister of war Cánovas chose not the hero of Sagunto, who had disobeyed his instructions in carrying out the coup d'état, but Gen. Joaquín Jovellar, who had commanded the Army of the Center at the time of the coup. There was, of course, a justification in the choice of a more senior general and Martínez Campos did receive his rewards. The first official act of the new regime promoted him to the rank of lieutenant general with retroactive seniority to August 8, 1873, professedly related to his actions in respect to the cantonal uprising in Valencia, thus avoiding a contradiction with the general's statement that his action at Sagunto had no personal ambitions or motives. Martínez Campos was also appointed to the command of the Army of Catalonia and the captain generalcy in that region.[11] He still had, as a consequence, opportunities for military achievement and prestige and was to take full advantage of them.

"Don't call the Restoration a counter revolution but conciliation," Cánovas had said, and had taken as his motif, "there are neither victors nor victims." Although the great Spanish philosopher José Ortega y Gasset was later to find these words "muddy principles," the new government was, in contrast to previous regimes, most generous to those identified with opposing political philosophies.[12] Serrano, the duke of la Torre, had gone across the frontier into France after Sagunto, but with the king's personal intervention very quickly received permission to return without molestation. In a personal interview after his return he assured the king of his loyalty to the dynasty, but was critical of the Cánovas government and distrusted by it.[13] His wife, as talkative and self-esteemed as ever, was the source of virulent comments on the course of events and of unfounded rumors of plans for political action.[14]

Conservative republican Emilio Castelar, the last of the presidents of the First Republic before the anomalous regime of Serrano, continued political participation and was to take a seat in the Constituent Cortes when it was elected. There his long, somewhat diffuse, and rhetorical orations against the government and in behalf of political liberalism were to become a highlight of the new regime. Since his opposition was much more largely philosophical than political and never really dangerous, he was not only tolerated but somewhat welcomed as a kind of showpiece, demonstrating the regime's willingness to allow open criticism within reasonable limits.[15]

Less moderate republicans such as Cristino Martos were to find political activity hampered at the outset, although Martos was a close friend of Cánovas.[16] Likewise, Francisco Pi y Margall, one of the few seminal figures of the republican period, played little part in the politics of the early Restoration period. Pi y Margall had been the major advocate of the federalist concept, advocating regional autonomy. The divisive cantonal movement which resulted was not what he had expected. He had also advocated factory relationships involving contracts between owners and workers looking toward social justice. His name became a symbol of the combination of social and political aims. Although he exercised little influence during the reign of Alfonso XII, the concepts he advocated awakened fears on the part of conservatives, admiration on the part of liberals.[17]

Perhaps the main enemy of the regime was Manuel Ruiz Zorrilla, who was the source of republican agitation from outside Spain and was hounded from Paris by pressure from the Spanish government in July 1877. Ruiz Zorrilla had been offered a guarantee of personal security if he remained in Spain, but became the leader of an intransigent republicanism which refused to accept the restored monarch and constantly plotted for his overthrow.[18]

Cánovas and his cabinet took rapid command of the situation. The initial period of the Restoration has been labeled the *Dictadura*, the "dictatorship." Its beginning is indisputable—the first decrees of the government began a course of firm action resolutely pursued. Less certain is its ending. Not until seven years later did Cánovas relinquish the reins of power taken up with Sagunto and his critics never relaxed their criticism of his harshness with the opposition.

The first and most dramatic action was the establishment of a stringent control of the press. Temporarily all of the left-wing journals were suspended—*La Política*, *La Civilización*, *La Prensa*, *El Gobierno*, *La Iberia*, *La Bandera Española*, *La Discusión*, *El Orden*, *La Igualdad*, *El Pueblo*, and *El Imparcial*. Within a day's time, however, suspension of all of these except *La Discusión*, *El Orden*, and *La Igualdad* was lifted. *El Gobierno*, apparently voluntarily, ceased publication.[19]

On January 30 the government issued a decree establishing guidelines for the press. Throughout the period which followed press control remained an ever-present aspect of the political scene. There were seasons of severity and periods of relaxation. But under the Dictadura liberty of the press remained a slogan of the government executed with severe limitations not always clearly expressed.[20] Not until the last day of 1875 did the government seek in a new press decree to clarify the regulations imposed. There was, of course, criticism of arbitrary judgments both before and after the proclamation of this second decree.

It was obvious that attacks on the monarchical system would no longer be tolerated. The inclusion of the word "indirect" in the press decree relating to attacks on the form of government reflected the broad latitude already assigned press courts in determining what were attacks. Similarly the press law forbade "injuries" to senators, deputies, and governmental officials. Although this was not intended to stop review of their actions, the line between criticism and "injury" was difficult to draw. Likewise prohibited were articles causing discord in the army. As *El Imparcial* pointed out, even praise of one general might occasion the jealousy of others and therefore promote discord.[21]

In perspective, of course, press regulation had been an almost constant aspect of the Spanish political scene. Barely a month before Sagunto *El Imparcial* was criticizing the severity of press censorship under the Constitutionalists and *La Iberia* was defending it.[22] This did not, of course, prevent both liberal newspapers from screaming to the heavens at the severity of Cánovas's actions, but probably made many observers view them somewhat philosophically.

With similar speed and decisiveness the government moved to establish control over local government. Between January 1 and 21, 1875, the civil governors of the Spanish provinces were replaced and the provincial deputations and municipal *ayuntamientos* throughout Spain were suspended.[23] This was, of course, the prelude to widespread and thorough action against all republican groups throughout Spain and also against the numerous Constitutionalist officeholders who had assumed their places during the *interinidad* of Serrano. The cries of dismay that echoed in the Constitutionalist press are a clear indication of the scope of Constitutionalist activity in the period preceding the Restoration.[24]

The architect of the government's internal policies and of the system of controlled elections under local political bosses (*caciquismo*) which resulted was Cánovas's minister of the interior Romero Robledo. Romero Robledo was, along with Cánovas, younger than most of the other members of the cabinet. His broad, square chin, thick blonde hair and beard, languid but expressive eyes above a sardonic smile which emphasized his resolute appearance conveyed a sense of self-assurance and inflexibility equaled only by that of Cánovas himself. Later events indicated that in accepting the leadership of Cánovas he did not give up his sense of independence; he remained his own man. Next to Cánovas he was the most able orator in the Restoration government, less eloquent and not always as fully in possession of his temper, but with the same tightly reasoned logic, the same lightly veiled cynicism, the same equanimity in the face of criticism. Like Cánovas he spoke easily on every subject—one of his most famous *discursos* was on the state of the navy when the only sea he had seen was the little lake in the Retiro Park![25]

Romero Robledo did not, of course, create the system of "made" elections which dominated the rest of the century. The nickname, "the Great Elector," had already been attached to the name of José Posada Herrera for his manipulations from the post of minister of the interior of the elections of 1858. The exact mechanism of the system of *caciquismo* remains, and probably will always remain, a subject of speculation on the basis of relatively scattered evidence.[26] The debates on the validation of seats in the Cortes and the charges of opposition newspapers reveal the devices used for electoral manipulation, although the assumption of "holier than thou" attitudes by the critics is hypocritical. Changes in the lists of electors, alterations of electoral districts, and direct interference with voters accompanied patronage and political favors. That *caciquismo* was particularly different from or worse than "bossism" in the United States is doubtful. But it underscored the hypocrisy of the regime and reduced its appeal to those who were not a part of the political game.

Whether one can speak of "popular opinion" in a country like Spain during this period is debatable. Undoubtedly the great masses of people both in town and country had no real opinion —the concerns of daily life, a respect for the church, a desire for peace and stability predominated over the desire for voting rights and political participation. Very probably the majority of those who could read and write leaned toward republicanism.[27]

For the illiterate and depressed classes there was already a strong sympathy for anarchist ideas. Early socialist movements in Spain identified with the anarchist approach sponsored in the First International by Bakunin. But by the 1870s socialist leaders arose who rejected the terrorism associated with anarchism. On the other hand native anarchism continued to be a vital force in the rural South and in Catalonia. Proclamations were issued. Regulations for anarchist organizations were drawn up. And the government worried over each new manifestation of this disruptive philosophy.[28]

But significant as republican and anarchist movements were, they remained minority movements. The great majority were passive, grateful for quieter times, and still preserved a vague respect for monarchical traditions and clerical authority. Active support for the monarchy, however, rested in a relatively restricted segment of the population drawn from the middle classes and the aristocracy. Knowing their own weakness, Restoration governments counted heavily upon repressive measures to control overt opposition.

The first step was the removal of many of the justices named during the preceding period and the revocation of the right to trial by jury.[29] How much this was accompanied by arbitrary arrests and imprisonments is debatable. Government circulars early in February instructed new public officials to take stern action to avoid new disorders and required government sanction for public meetings of more than twenty persons other than religious processions.[30] Censorship prevented any real exposé by opposition journals. When charges of illegal deportations and hardships in prison colonies in Ceuta, the Marianas, and Fernando Po began to appear, it soon became clear that a considerable portion of these deportations and imprisonments had been initiated under the Constitutionalists.[31]

As noted above, the most prominent deportee was Manuel Ruiz Zorrilla, who had issued calls for republican meetings to both civilian and military figures. The mildness of the regime's action was underscored in his ceremonial departure attended by a number of the leaders of the former republic. But when his *viva* for the republic as he departed was answered by three republican generals, their fate was not so mild—deportation to the Grand Canaries.[32]

Ruiz Zorrilla's action was contrary to the government circular of February 3, mentioned above, forbidding political meetings without government authorization. This was to be eased before the close of the year in preparation for Cortes elections but accompanied by a differentiation between legal and illegal parties based upon an acceptance of the Bourbon monarchy.[33]

With these steps Cánovas had secured the monarchy against any potential revolutionary change. By the late summer of 1875 he began to look forward to the last stage of political pacification, the elections for a Constitutional Cortes which would crown these efforts with a new monarchical constitution. He had been, of course, an open and pronounced opponent of the principle of universal manhood suffrage. In a lengthy speech in the Constitutional Cortes of 1869 he had protested the inclusion of that principle in the Constitution of 1869, declaring there was "no despotism worse than that of the masses" and defending conditions of capacity, intelligence, public interest, and a reasonable support of the government as qualifications for voting. He was later to say that "universal suffrage means the dissolution of society" and to characterize it as "the negation of the popular will and the parliamentary regime."[34] But in this period of conciliation he was unwilling to force a change from the existing voting procedures by the simple fiat of the monarch. As a consequence, Cánovas decided to allow arrangements for the elections to proceed under the voting arrangements he had opposed so strongly, but to place the responsibility for that decision in the hands of another person. This resulted in the brief substitution for Cánovas of the ministry of Gen. Joaquín Jovellar from September 12 to December 2, 1875. Obviously, Cánovas continued to dominate policy during that interim period.

Along with these efforts to reduce the danger of republicanism Cánovas sought also to reestablish good relations with the Papacy. There was an obvious strategy in Cánovas's church policy. If the breach of relations resulting from the republican era could be healed and the good will of the Spanish clergy and of the Papacy could be rewon, the new regime stood the chance of dividing Carlist forces and their supporters. The religious motif of those who followed the pretender would be greatly weakened. And non-Carlist conservatives would find it much easier to give support to a Restoration which still sought to break with the traditions of the prerevolutionary monarchy and to preserve at least a semblance of parliamentary government. There remained, however, a major problem—the price of good relations with the church could not extend to an endorsement of Ultramontane control over the Spanish church or the complete liquidation of all "modern" and "liberal" thrusts toward principles of religious toleration.

From the first Cánovas found himself under considerable foreign pressure to maintain religious toleration. That this pressure came strongly from liberal Protestant states such as England and Sweden was to be expected.[35] That it was strongly echoed from conservative states such as Germany, Austria, and Russia is somewhat more surprising. Germany was, of course, at this time involved in the throes of the controversy between the state and the Catholic church known as the *Kulturkampf*. Early in the Restoration period came German warnings that the new monarch should not be allowed, as had his mother, to fall under the excessive influence of the clergy. Similar concern on the part of the tsar was reported.[36] Only the liberal United States represented by the very conservative Caleb Cushing refrained from any indication of interference in the internal affairs of Spain![37]

Assurances in respect to the maintenance of religious toleration came from several sources. Private guarantees came from both Cánovas and the king,[38] and the duke of Sesto stated that he had taken the position of the king's chief steward to prevent excessive clerical influence on the monarch.[39] There was, however, no overt interference from abroad—a phrase in the draft of the German envoy's speech presenting his credentials to the king contained a reference to the matter, but this was deleted in its final version.[40]

At home, of course, the new government was under another

kind of pressure—that of mollifying the church and its Moderado supporters to gain the broadest possible popular support. As noted above, some of the Moderados had joined Cánovas's Liberal Conservative party, but a considerable portion of them remained independent. At the outset they were called the "Historical Moderados," indicating their hold to the past traditions of the monarchy and the church. In ideology they were not widely separated from the Carlists, although they held to the legitimate branch of the dynasty, but with their sympathies directed more to Isabella than to Alfonso.[41] They were to have an impressive list of newspapers favoring their cause including *La España Católica*, *La Fé*, *La Paz*, *El Eco de España*, *El Pabellón Nacional* and *El Siglo Futuro* (the latter two verging on outright Carlism), but the effectiveness of this press was much reduced by futile dogmatic controversies. Most observers believed that the Moderados had considerable strength among the ladies of the capital and that some of the prominent generals, including Martínez Campos, were committed to their cause. The German ambassador frequently expressed concern about the possibility of their leading a new revolution of the right.[42]

Early in January 1875 the new government began its efforts to reestablish relations with the pope. On the 15th the support budget exising in 1868 was reestablished. On January 20 the formula for the oath of the archbishops was revised so that they swore loyalty to the king, not to the laws or the constitution. Three days later the archives, libraries, and artistic objects of the church held by the state were returned along with vacant benefices and other positions. Back pay for bishops was also provided and the papal nuncio was given a solemn and formal reception.[43]

Accompanying these direct moves in behalf of the church were actions directed towards restoring church dominance over education. The motive force behind this move was the minister of development, the marquis of Orovio. Orovio had held the same position prior to the revolution. Strongly Moderado in his sympathies, he had clearly joined the Cánovas government with the impression that the clock was to be turned back seven years.

After appointing a new supervisor of public instruction, Joaquín Maldonado Macanaz, Orovio moved to reverse the virtually unlimited freedom of a full professor to determine the content of his courses, which had been one of the results of the Revolution of 1868. On February 26, 1875, a royal decree reestablished the requirement that professors adopt and submit to state inspection specific textbooks and programs for the courses they taught with the criterion of acceptability involving complete religious orthodoxy as well as respect for the constitutional monarchy and freedom from "baneful social errors."[44]

The move occasioned a storm of protest from the *catedraticos* of the Central University, as the University of Madrid was then known. Most prominent was Francisco Giner de los Ríos, professor of law, who addressed a letter of protest to Orovio himself. Others in Madrid and elsewhere joined in the protests, most notably Gumersindo de Azcárate and Nicolás Salmerón y Alonso. Governmental reprisals were severe. Giner de los Ríos was arrested and taken from a sickbed to prison in Cádiz with members of his family forbidden to accompany him. The rectors of the Universities of Madrid, Barcelona, and Seville were replaced. The three professors named above were removed from their posts along with others in Santiago, La Coruña, Los Palmes, Valencia, and Osuna.[45] From these expulsions was to result the creation of the *Institución Libre de Enseñanza*, the "Free Educational Institute" founded by Giner de los Ríos, one of the most creative institutions of a dull and uninspiring period, but one for which neither Cánovas nor his ministers could lay claim to fame.

It must, in justice, be noted that the Constitutionalist regime of Sagasta had already complained of the problems of the universities and a politicized faculty, and the American minister, Caleb Cushing, who claimed he had studied both sides of the question, found the removals justified.[46] But the controversy did embarrass both Cánovas and the king and Orovio was to leave his post as minister of development in September when Cánovas temporarily gave way to General Jovellar.[47]

By this time also the debates had begun over the proposed Article 11 of the new constitution, dealing with the relationship of church and state, destined to be the most controversial portion of that constitution. Heralding the later controversies, the Moderados began an intensive campaign for "Catholic Unity," that is for the suppression of all non-Catholic religious activities. By the middle of September this controversy had been further inflamed by the publication of a circular directed to all the bishops of Spain (even to the bishop of La Seo de Urgel, who had taken part in the crowning of Carlos VII) issued by the papal nuncio to the court of Spain, Juan Simeoni, the archbishop of Calcedonia. This action contradicted the established principle of *pase regio*, set forth in previous concordats with the Papacy, that church directives inspired from outside Spain—its origin was attributed to Cardinal Antonelli, the papal secretary of state—should not be circulated without government authorization. Part of the language of the circular also seemed to threaten the Spanish government.[48] Cánovas, of course, escaped the necessity of responding to the circular by the government crisis in which Jovellar replaced him. But he was to confront the issue quite directly in the controversy over the constitution noted in the following chapter.

The early months of the Restoration were also marked by several incidents in which Protestant activities in Spain were disturbed by local authorities. Of minor character at this point and quickly reversed by the central government, these incidents indicated the continuance of widespread popular intolerance and the difficulty confronted by the government in imposing the principle of religious toleration in a country where it still encountered much hostility.[49]

Meanwhile, the Restoration government had moved toward stabilization of Spain's chaotic financial condition. The complexities of the Spanish treasury both before and after the Restoration defy all efforts for rational explanation. The chaos of the preceding period was underscored by the rapid turnover of treasury ministers—five during the period 1854–56; six during the short reign of Amadeo I; and seven during the republican period.[50]

Several conclusions are patent in the complicated financial

manipulations which followed. First and most importantly, the level of public debt exceeded the capabilities of Spain's existing taxation system.[51] It combined public bonds with treasury notes of various dates both of which carried interest requirements placing serious strains on the Spanish treasury and allowing little opportunity to care for their amortization. Obviously the expenses of the wars with the Carlists inside Spain and the insurgents in Cuba added to the vagaries of internal politics and accompanying economic disruption had overburdened the public treasury.

Pedro de Salaverría, Cánovas's first treasury minister, found himself confronted by a *fait accompli* in the form of a Spanish convention with her foreign creditors signed in December 1874, just before the pronunciamiento of Sagunto. In his view the Restoration government could not afford to weaken its credit status by seeking to renegotiate this settlement (such a renegotiation would have been the third in the last five years). Accordingly Salaverría assumed all existing exterior debts as contracted in good faith and issued new bonds to pay for these. In the relevant proclamation he noted that those who held interior debts were placed at a disadvantage, but that the treasury level did not at that time allow a stabilization of these obligations.[52]

But tax revenues were insufficient and financial difficulties were to be endemic during most of the period which followed. The ordinary revenues of the Spanish government derived largely from land and industrial taxes distributed in a complex and inefficient manner. Special taxes were levied on tobacco and sugar. A tax on personal identity papers, which had been fairly moderate when adopted in 1874, was considerably increased in 1876. Other major revenue sources were the tariffs and the state royalties on the sale of the products of the Rio Tinto mines. Trends toward tariff reduction under the preceding government were immediately reversed, with Salaverría pointing out in justification that the protectionist policies of France and Germany had pushed Great Britain toward protectionist measures and Spain could follow no other course. But all of these measures were to prove insufficient to meet the heavy expenditures of the state and deficit financing remained the motif.[53] On some occasions, as in respect to the 1876 loan for the Cuban war, as noted below, the terms were extremely unfavorable.

As noted more fully below, the economy of Spain expanded rapidly during this period. Industrial growth and railroad expansion were impressive, but government financial procedures put heavy burdens on real estate and the level of indirect taxes was excessive. The continuance of poverty in the rural regions is indicated by the high figure of emigration continuing until the end of the century.[54] The entire picture of the economy during the early years of the Cánovas era is, of course, darkened by the existence of colonial warfare and the expenses resulting from the Carlist War. The effect of internal profiteering and self-interested economic policies is difficult to assess. Some reflections of these are found in the debate over Cuban reform which is dealt with extensively later in this book.

One of the most vital problems of the Restoration regime was that of concluding the Second Carlist War. As has been noted, the sympathies attached to the cause of the pretender, Carlos VII, had already begun to decline during the period of the Serrano-Sagasta regime.[55] Neither of the two pretenders around whom the Carlist wars had centered possessed high qualities of leadership let alone a genuine charisma. A self-seeking and unrealistic coterie of pompous advisers surrounded both and neither of them displayed a strong sense of loyalty to the generals who furthered their cause. There was rivalry among the second pretender's most prominent generals, Antonio Dorregaray, Rafael Tristany, Francisco Savalls y Masot, and Carlos's brother Alfonso de Borbón y Austria de Este, as well as among the lesser *cabecillas*, or chieftains, who directed local operations. Savalls was probably more effective than Dorregaray, a veteran of the First Carlist War, but also fiercer and crueler in dealing with prisoners of war and the inhabitants of occupied territory. Eventually after a conference with Martínez Campos in 1875 Savalls was to be hailed as a traitor, court-martialed, and relieved of his command. Dorregaray had lost his command earlier.[56]

Another significant general of the Carlist cause also deserted during the early days of the Restoration. This was Gen. Ramón

Cabrera, known in the earlier conflict as the "Tiger of the Maestrazgo." Living comfortably in England in exile between the two conflicts, he had grown old, weary, and disillusioned and assumed no significant role in the second conflict. But his name still carried weight and the government was able to negotiate an agreement by which the former guerrillero recognized the accession of Alfonso XII in exchange for a confirmation of his military titles and his position as count of Morella. As a consequence Cabrera issued a manifesto explaining his defection from a cause he considered hopeless. He was also brought to Spain in the hope that he might encourage other Carlist leaders to come over to the Alfonsist side.[57]

Although Cabrera's example found little immediate response, it emphasized the willingness of the new regime to deal moderately with the former rebels, with the possibility of Carlist officers transferring their military titles and employment to the Alfonsist forces. The censorship of the day veiled the extent to which this process was carried, but details surfaced in Cortes debates at the end of the year. Gen. Manuel Salamanca y Negrete, often to be a thorn in the side of the Restoration government, produced facts and figures casting considerable doubt on the "heroism" displayed by Alfonsist forces.[58]

Even with division in the Carlist ranks, negotiation for the transfer of allegiance of Carlist officers, new expenditures for armaments, and new levies of troops, the end of the Carlist War was not achieved easily. Early in February 1875 Carlist forces surprised and routed Alfonsist forces at Lácar and placed the young king, who had joined his armies in the North, in some peril.[59] Through the months that followed the process of pacification proceeded painstakingly and haltingly. There was considerable mention abroad of the possibility of constituting two Spains—a Carlist and an Alfonsist one.[60] Some critics suggested that the government moved slowly because of the enormous profits which were being made by some army contractors.[61] More probably it was the inherent caution of the Alfonsist generals which delayed things—they had experienced too many surprises from their wily foes in the past.

Of all the Alfonsist generals Martínez Campos was the only one to conduct a somewhat daring campaign. This gained its first fruits in Catalonia with an impetuous attack on La Seo de Urgel.[62] The taking of this Carlist stronghold was the first decisive victory gained by government forces and an enormous boost to their morale. In the period that followed, although the government exploited this victory to the hilt for propaganda purposes, there was concern for Martínez Campos's self-willed action, and the general did, indeed, continue to go his own way, leading his forces all the way up to the French border and again getting the headlines, although critics regarded his action as rash and potentially highly dangerous.[63]

Martínez Campos emerged from the war as the only charismatic army leader. At this point he was commonly considered a Moderado. Although it was supposed that he opposed the government's prohibition of the return of Isabella II, this was not entirely true. He was in communication with her, but pointed out in a letter of May 13, 1875, that her return would be contrary to Alfonso's order as well as Cánovas's although he criticized the "band of iron" which the prime minister had placed around the young king. A second letter called Cánovas "a man proving himself fatal for Spain" and hoped for her early return. There were some rumors of potential new coups, but the general's loyalty to the monarch was never really in question and no coups or plans for coups ever eventuated.[64]

The end of the war was heralded by the campaign of the same General Primo de Rivera who had captained the garrisons of Madrid and been the final key to the fall of the Serrano regime. As the Carlist forces fell into disarray, he led the government troops in the capture of Estella, the capital and stronghold of the Carlists. Not until February 28, 1876, did the pretender Carlos VII with some 10,000 followers cross the border into France, while Alfonso XII made a triumphal tour of the North to return to Madrid as the great "Peacemaker" on March 20, 1876.[65]

But Carlism remained as the cause of "the Tradition" for much of the North and still had many sympathizers in other parts of Spain. The Basque provinces in the period that followed suffered from the "agony" of the loss of their *fueros*, their special legal privileges, and although Catalonia received somewhat better treatment in the first years of the Restoration, she, too soon had occasion to complain of mistreatment.[66]

Meanwhile, the necessities of the Carlist War had taken precedence over the problems associated with the insurrection in Cuba. Not until the Carlist War was concluded could the new government turn its full attention to the civil war on the other side of the Atlantic. Events there were once again to place the personal fortunes and careers of Cánovas del Castillo and Arsenio Martínez Campos in rivalry.

The king's role in these events had been minimal. Perhaps his greatest contribution had been his success in conveying to Sagasta and to the diplomatic representatives at the court his intention to pursue a liberal course. He qualified this statement with the comment that he could not, of course, take a significant role until his position had been confirmed by the Cortes, but indicated that he would thereafter exercise greater influence. His statements aided in bringing the adherence of the Constitutionalists to the monarchy, as noted in the next chapter, and blunted the edge of foreign criticism of the government's religious policy.[67]

He did not take a significant role in the military effort against the Carlists. The first visit to the battle front at Lácar had almost been a disaster and Cánovas had been criticized for exposing the new-made monarch to such peril. It was later to be alleged that the first onset of the king's eventually fatal tuberculosis had manifested itself at this time.[68] If so, it was well concealed. But the government could not afford to risk an accidental death of a sovereign upon whom so much depended. As a consequence the king took no real part in the campaigns and there were critics of the government's effort to give him an aura of heroism.[69]

In Madrid the king began the nightly escapades which became the subject of much gossip during his reign. At the age of seventeen it was not surprising that he would seek relief from the boredom of palace associates. His amorous adventures were to become notorious and there were to be some embarrassing consequences.[70] Perhaps, however, there was also some relief at the king's evident *machismo*, much in contrast to his putative "papa," Francisco de Asís.

From a distance "Mama" was a more serious problem. Queen Isabella II was clearly emotionally incapable of coping with her new situation in life. She had wanted to accompany her son on his return, but was stopped by government intervention.[71] Through the early months of 1875 she barraged the government back home with pleas to be allowed to return—pleas answered by Cánovas in a series of letters combining an effort to convince her of respect and affection while maintaining the prohibition.[72] In Cánovas's eyes she was the only real danger to the throne.[73] Isabella sought also, with little success, to convince governments abroad that if she returned, she would not seek to influence events.[74] The German consul in Bayonne reported rumors that she was contemplating coming back unannounced.[75] On one occasion she suggested to the German ambassador in Paris that she could mediate the end of the war with the Carlists.[76] Carlos VII, while still in possession of much of northern Spain, had written to her with the invitation to return to his part of Spain, and she had threatened to do so if her son did not call her back to Madrid.[77] In November 1875 she sent her current favorite, the former minister and then palace superintendent Carlos Marfori, back with letters to her son and, when he was arrested, threatened that she might revoke her abdication and return.[78] But a month later she had found a new favorite, one Ramiro de la Puente, who became a new obstacle to her return and a new embarrassment for the crown.[79]

Isabella was a cross borne by Alfonso throughout his brief reign. The detailed story of her intrigues and maneuvers emphasizes the wisdom of Cánovas's insistence on her absence from the Spanish scene.

Cánovas was much concerned to provide the constitutional basis for the new monarchy. He had led Spain through a difficult year of transition. The time was now ripe to create a permanent regime. Spanish historians have dealt with the Cánovas era as though each step along the way was carefully planned and executed by Cánovas. A close examination of the details and complexities which surrounded the transition period suggest that much was accidental and fortuitous. This is not to belittle the role of Cánovas—like Bismarck he considered politics the art of effecting the possible and brought to the tasks of the new state a strong will and inflexible purpose which carried him through an arduous period marked by opprobrious criticism of both a political and personal nature.

3

Constitution, Cortes, and Controversy

I N SPITE OF Cánovas's wishes the Restoration had come with a pronunciamiento, implying insurrection or coup d'état. Cánovas had hoped to avoid this element of illegality, to wait until a Cortes was convoked and had issued a call for the return of Alfonso. As has been seen, the probability of such a course of events was relatively obscure. The action of Martínez Campos had converted uncertainty into reality, but it left Cánovas with the dilemma of a search for legality.

The situation was alleviated somewhat by the fact that the government it replaced was similarly illegal. It, too, had come into existence by process of coup d'état and its actions had been quite as dictatorial as those taken under Cánovas. Furthermore, its goal of a return to legal government was less clearly stated. The Cánovas regime began with the employment of the full powers in representation of their cause confided into his hands by Alfonso and his mother. Under these powers Cánovas established his first ministry and engaged in the initial acts of stabilization noted above. The return of Alfonso, his confirmation of the Cánovas ministry, and his affirmation of his legal claim to the throne as opposed to the illegality of the Carlist cause provided some first steps toward legality. But Cánovas still confronted a question without an answer—which of Spain's constitutions now applied—that of 1845 or that of 1869? The Constitution of 1869 derived from revolution against the throne could not be upheld; the Constitution of 1845, identified with the thoroughly discredited Isabelline regime, could not be used without tarnishing Alfonso. And how could a new constitution be established in the midst of civil war and without a clear definition of the existing regime?

Cánovas's solution of the dilemma was the establishment of a brazenly maintained fiction set forth in scholarly language and supported with ironic eloquence and complete equanimity in the face of criticism. This fiction was that Spain had an "internal constitution," one which existed by virtue of its monarchical system. The lace and ruffles were not embroidered on this specious fiction until the debates on the new constitution, but the initial steps had been taken with the king's Sandhurst Manifesto asserting his intention to be a constitutional monarch and setting forth his claims on the basis of Spain's historical heritage. In the words provided by Cánovas the young king referred to "the *reestablishment* of the Constitutional monarchy," to the difficult task of "*reestablishing* in our noble country, along with peace, *legal order and political liberty*," to "representative institutions *confirmed by all historical precedents*," which, he said, had never ceased to function during his mother's reign. He added that Spanish princes had never solved their problems without the cooperation of the Cortes, and in his conclusion once again linked Spain's history with a declaration of liberalism. The king also asserted that if the Constitution of 1845 was, and he apparently assumed it was, de facto void, then that of 1869, created when the monarchy did not exist, was also de facto void.[1] As a consequence, it was implied, the new regime was now free to create a new constitution which would comport with Spanish traditions but also take note of recent history. Thus Cánovas had cleared the way for a path of compromise while maintaining the full right of the monarch (and his representatives) to determine the limits of compromise to be allowed.

[47]

During the early days of the Restoration Cánovas talked much of conciliation, "a policy of attraction," and "legal community."[2] The formation of a party around him and the restored monarch was virtually automatic and spontaneous. As *La Política*, one of the organs of the political group of dissident Constitutionalists, phrased it, some welcomed the return of the king with joy, some with benevolence, others with resignation.[3] But behind the celebrations with which the people had welcomed the monarch lurked a wide variety of expectations. Most importantly, Alfonso XII symbolized a hope for quieter times and stability. As *La Política* summed up a broad area of popular opinion, "It is now time to close the era of disturbances, of revolutions, and of reactions. The country is weary of upsets."[4] The prospect of peace strongly reinforced the concept of legitimacy.

Nevertheless, the continued maintenance of a quasi dictatorship without constitutionally defined authority was clearly impossible. Cánovas moved in May 1875 to demonstrate the broad adherence to the regime and to lay the basis for the drafting of a constitution. At his invitation three hundred and forty-one political leaders who had served as deputies or senators under the monarchy met in the Senate hall on May 20 to express their support of the new monarchy and to elect a Committee of Thirty-Nine Notables to prepare a draft constitution. Strongly represented were the Moderados, who had the largest share of the delegates held by a single party.[5] Next most numerous were former members of the so-called Liberal Union, which formed one of the basic components of Cánovas's Liberal Conservative party. These were strengthened and aided in the process which followed by some forty-one members of the Constitutionalist party who had separated from its ranks to give support to the new regime. Some of these were shortly to take up membership in the Liberal Conservative grouping. The other dissidents were to be part of the ill-fated and much abused Spanish Center party. They were to maintain that their action at this time and through the constitutional debates which followed did not carry with it a surrender of their liberty of individual action. Between them and their former party colleagues raged a bitter controversy during the summer and fall of 1875.[6]

The division of the Constitutionalist party had begun with a debate within the directing junta of the party in respect to its attitude toward the new regime. The issue was complex and involved emotional as well as rational aspects. First and most important was the question, "What had been the long-range intentions of the Serrano government when the Constitutionals exercised a leading role?" No single, clearly agreed upon answer was available. The Constitutionalists were professed monarchists but gave fervent devotion to the liberal Constitution of 1869, which had served the republic as well as the monarchy of Amadeo. Many of them had favored the cause of Montpensier as likely to be more liberal than Alfonso. Many of them had a deep sense of loyalty to Serrano, whom they believed had been betrayed. Although the guarantees of individual liberties in the Constitution of 1869 had been suspended for emergency conditions, they did not wish to see them lost. Nor did they wish to surrender religious freedom, trial by jury, and universal suffrage.

The Constitutionalists had, therefore, entered the Restoration period with a deep sense of grievance. Their period in power had been interrupted in the midst of urgent efforts to defeat the Carlists. The credit for that accomplishment, for which they had laid the groundwork, would now go to those who had conspired against them. The Constitution of 1869, which was their *bandera*, their rallying point, was being dismissed as a dead letter. The Restoration had come without them, indeed against them, but they could not oppose Alfonso's claim to the throne. At the same time they were forced to stand by helplessly while Romero Robledo destroyed their control over local administration and the political apparatus which accompanied it. Under these circumstances Sagasta and many of his close associates were almost apoplectic at the suggestion of some prominent party members "that the defeated should on the evening of that occurrence sing in the chorus of the victors."[7]

Although the controversy over the attitude to be taken by the party had begun at least as early as February, it did not surface publicly until late April. The house of Francisco Santa Cruz witnessed the decisive scenes in the struggle. Sagasta, Augusto Ulloa, and others of Sagasta's close followers advanced a formula by which the party would recognize the existing governmental authority and promise collaboration but with the proviso that the constitutional and parliamentary monarchy of Alfonso XII would retain the legitimate conquests of liberty achieved during the previous era.[8]

This formula did not satisfy a number of the party leaders. The most prominent of the dissidents, Manuel Alonso Martínez, proposed an alternate formula by which the party would declare its intention to follow a course of "loyal and noble cooperation in the consolidation of the throne of Alfonso XII." It would also offer the party's disinterested assistance in the termination of the civil war and the maintenance and advancement of liberty, order, and unity within the country although reserving its particular position and constitutional views until these goals had been achieved. Sagasta and his associates rejected this formula and compromise efforts proved unavailing.[9]

The height of the controversy was reached in May 1875. On May 3 the dissident Constitutionalists—nine in number—issued a call for a meeting on May 16 at the house of Santa Cruz looking to the union of all monarchical parties. The government on its part was reported to be threatening the removal of all officeholders adhering to the Sagasta formula and declaring the formula of Alonso Martínez the only acceptable one.[10]

The division of the party leaders was widened by a series of bitter letters. On May 2 Sagasta claimed a virtual one-man control of the party.[11] The directive committee of the party had, he said, at the end of 1873 given leadership of the party to himself, the duke of la Torre, and Adm. Juan Bautista Topete y Carballo. Since both of the other members of the triumvirate were military leaders, they were now prohibited from political activity by the regulations of the new regime. Sagasta had, as a consequence, resisted the pleas of some party members to pay court to the victors. This he regarded as inappropriate "for that time in which everything conspired to keep us shut up in our tents, firm in our principles, maintaining our program (*bandera*), without pretending to or seeking the power to which we were not called and which our patriotism obliged us not to oppose."

The response of the dissidents was set forth on May 17.[12] They denounced "the usurpatory character as sole director of the Constitutional Party" claimed by Sagasta, criticized his "spirit of domination and arrogance"—his claim that "el partido soy yo." Beyond the personal element their major criticism of Sagasta was directed against his insistence on the maintenance of the Constitution of 1869 which they regarded as completely unrealistic.

Sagasta in reply denied he sought to exercise a one-man control over the party and criticized his opponents' use of intemperate language, although his own had by no means been above reproach.[13] By this time, of course, reconciliation was impossible. The division extended to the party press. Sagasta sought to characterize *La Iberia* as the only authorized voice of the party.[14] Even before the development of personal divisions the party newspaper *La Política* had strongly supported a full accord with the Alfonsist government. It claimed the support of the duke of la Torre, who could not, of course, make public announcements.[15] *La Política* was to carry its support of the new regime to considerable lengths including fulsome praise of Cánovas himself.[16] The dissidents were also to have support from two other party organs, *Los Debates* and *El Parlamento*.

La Iberia launched a large-scale campaign to vindicate Sagasta's leadership of the party and its own position as the authorized party organ. Beginning on May 18 and continuing for three months thereafter *La Iberia* published an impressive list of letters of adherence to Sagasta from the provincial leaders of the party. In the end more than 30,000 signatures were obtained.[17] This formidable marshaling of Sagasta support gave evidence not only that he had a firm hand over the party machinery but also that the Constitutionalists had taken full advantage of their brief control of the government to establish themselves throughout the peninsula. While this accomplishment is impressive, it underscores the intention of the party to hold on to power indefinitely and makes it clear that the harsh approach of Cánovas and Romero Robledo to the administration of local government and the preparation for the elections was unavoidable.

Meanwhile, Cánovas and Romero Robledo took full advantage of the division within the opposing party. The dissidents were, as has been seen, strongly represented in the Assembly of Notables called by Cánovas. Eleven of them were chosen as members of the Committee of Thirty-Nine Notables charged with preparing a draft constitution. Four of these, Fernández de la Hoz, Pedro Nolasco Aurioles, Manuel Silvela, and Cristóbal Martín Herrera decided to become members of Cánovas's party and were to have considerable influence in its councils. Seven dissidents remained independent, still maintaining the liberal Constitutionalist point of view, although they were not recognized by their former party colleagues. Also a member of the committee but taking no stand for or against the dissidents was José Posada Herrera, whom the dissidents considered sympathetic to their position.[18]

The role of leadership among the dissidents of the committee lay with Alonso Martínez. He was the major spokesman in seeking to retain as much as possible of the liberal features of the Constitution of 1869.[19] The most serious point of division within the committee lay in the definition of religious toleration destined to become Article 11 of the Constitution of 1876. By July 20 it was clear that the constitution being drafted was going to adopt a compromise position on this question.

Although it might have seemed that the religious policy of the early months of the Cánovas regime should have satisfied the most fervent Catholic, the so-called Historical Moderados were insistent upon "Catholic unity," the end of all toleration of non-Catholics.[20] The issuance of the circular of the papal nuncio, Monsignor Simeoni, the archbishop of Calcedonia, closely coincided with a tactical change of government which allowed Cánovas to move to a slightly more liberal religious stance.

As has been noted, Cánovas, although opposed to universal manhood suffrage, was unwilling to dispense with it for the elections of a Constitutional Cortes designed to give the impression of the broadest possible support for a new constitution. His own resignation and replacement by Gen. Joaquín Jovellar was accompanied by the resignation of the Moderado ministers Alejandro Castro, minister of state; Francisco de Cárdenas, minister of grace and justice; and the marquis of Orovio, minister of development. Supposedly these were replaced by ministers of more liberal persuasion, although one of these, Fernando Calderón Collantes, who became minister of grace and justice, was later to show himself very close to the Moderado position.[21] The life of this ministry was, of course, brief, lasting only from September 12 to December 2, 1875, in order to confirm the principle of universal manhood suffrage. The debate over the proposed draft of the constitution highlighted the period.

The nuncio set the tone for the Moderados, opposing the proposed draft of Article 11 of the constitution as violating the Concordat of 1851, which he maintained was still in effect.[22] Moderado party leaders such as the marquis of Corvera had already begun their advocacy of simply returning to the Constitution of 1845.[23] In the midst of the controversy Moderado journals began to suffer as many press denunciations and suspensions as did the liberal ones. *El Pabellón Nacional*, perhaps the most extreme of the Moderado newspapers, was later to claim that it had been more severely treated by the government than any other newspaper.[24]

Although only eight of the thirty-nine notables supported the extreme position of the Moderados, the strength of popular sentiment behind this viewpoint was considerable. But the adhesion to this viewpoint by the Carlists made it untenable for the Alfonsists; and from the first Cánovas, and the king using Cánovas's words, had talked of the inappropriateness of this position in "modern times." Hence Cánovas had to adopt a stand which preserved the force of toleration without alarming moderate Catholics. The pertinent article read as follows:

The Catholic, apostolic, Roman religion is that of the state. The nation assumes the obligation to maintain the cult and its ministers.

No one shall be molested in Spanish territory for his religious

opinions nor for the exercise of his own religion except for the respect owed to Christian morality.

However, ceremonies or public manifestations other than those of
the religion of the state will not be permitted.[25]

Already within the Committee of Thirty-Nine Notables the
point was being made that the article was flexible and subject
to differing interpretations under different governments.[26] Although the most liberal newspapers continued to hold to the
clearer statement embodied in the Constitution of 1869,[27] the ire
of the Historical Moderados against the draft article tended to
undercut criticism by the liberals. On other issues of personal
freedom, however, and on press censorship the draft constitution was less than satisfactory and the dissident Constitutionalists
gave little evidence of opposition.[28]

Meanwhile, Cánovas continued to dominate proceedings in
spite of his temporary absence from the presidency of the cabinet. On December 2 he returned to that post with some cabinet
shifts which placed Calderón Collantes in the ministry of foreign
affairs and another Moderado-minded leader, the count of Toreno, in the ministry of development. It was this cabinet which
conducted the elections of January 20–23, 1876, which determined the composition of the Constituent Cortes. The Liberal
Conservatives and their allies won 333 seats; the Constitutionals
obtained 27 and the Moderados 12. As a consequence, the opposition to Cánovas's plans was reduced to a vocal but impotent
minority.[29]

By this time the Constitutionalists had met at the Circo del
Principe Alfonso on November 7 and proclaimed their willingness to accept the position of "the most liberal party within the
monarchy of Alfonso XII," although maintaining their adherence to the Constitution of 1869.[30] On December 12 Sagasta and
a number of party leaders, including Augusto Ulloa y Castañón,
Antonio Romero Ortiz, and Eduardo Alonso Colmenares, met
with Cánovas and the Constitutionalist party leader emerged
with Cánovas's recognition of Sagasta as the leader of His Majesty's Opposition.[31] This somewhat sudden acceptance of the
new regime by Sagasta puzzled *El Imparcial*, the powerful voice

of a liberal monarchism but critical of the Constitutionalists. *El Imparcial* felt the Constitutionalists had revealed their lack of devotion to principles, especially since they had not only accepted the role assigned them by Cánovas but guaranteed success in some electoral districts. They were, said *El Imparcial*, simply playing a game under government sponsorship.[32]

From this point on the dissident Constitutionalists were trapped in an untenable position—they were now committed to support the constitutional draft which they had helped to prepare, but were increasingly shunted away from any real influence. Presumably Cánovas might keep the door open for them to join his Liberal Conservatives, but this had not been their intention.

The Constitutionalists, in spite of their bargain with Cánovas, considered themselves free to join with other liberal groups in criticizing Romero Robledo's election procedures.[33] The English ambassador, Sir Austen Henry Layard, still a defender of Serrano and a bitter critic of Cánovas, reported in this regard, "Illegally and scandalously as all elections have been carried out since I have been in Spain, no government has shown so cynical and undisguised a contempt for representative institutions as that of Señor Cánovas del Castillo."[34] And in a later report when the Cortes was debating the validity of election results, stories emerged of 300 carabinieros being sent to preserve order in an electoral district with 900 voters, of the president of one of the election boards holding at the mouth of the ballot box "a blunderbuss with a mouth the size of an orange," and of Castelar's comment that it was less dangerous to raise a banner on a barricade than to vote.[35]

The managed elections, of course, assured approval of the Constitution of 1876. Presumably the draft originated by the Committee of Thirty-Nine Notables had simply given verbal form to the project developed by Cánovas himself. To a high degree it was his constitution and he gave it able support in the Cortes which met from February 16 to July 21, 1876.[36]

With unruffled eloquence he met on the floor of the Cortes the critical questions raised by opponents on both left and right, providing a new defense of the positions he had already taken. Was the Constitution of 1869 still operative? If not, did that of 1845 have validity? Was the dictatorship exercised by the government legal? If so, when would it be ended? Were the deputies in the Cortes inviolable? Could they go so far as to defame the government or the monarchy? Cánovas's answers were often specious but met the needs of the situation. The Constitution of 1845 had been voided by the Revolution of 1868 but that of 1869, drawn up in the absence of the monarch, was also invalid. All that remained was the unwritten constitution deriving from the unchallengeable sovereignty of the monarch. This had given legal force to the acts of the ministry prior to the adoption of the formal constitution. Deputies in the Cortes had freedom of speech so long as they did not fail in the proper respect to the basic institutions of the state—the monarchy and the church. The ordinary rules of the Cortes had, of course, allowed a deputy to be called to order if he used dangerous or offensive phrases. Cánovas was providing for the definition of dangerous the same formula used for illegal parties—those who refused to accept and conspired against the existing institutions of the state.

Even Cánovas's opponents recognized his oratorical ability, although they began to charge that he was the only member of the government party capable of defending the dubious positions taken so that the rest of the Liberal Conservatives became quiescent spectators of a one-man show.[37]

The constitution which emerged provided for a constitutional monarchy in which the sovereignty clearly rested in the monarch, although it was to be exercised only through responsible ministers and the Cortes.[38] The king's prerogatives were stated in a series of articles which Cánovas excluded from discussion in the Constitutional Cortes. He was proclaimed constitutional monarch "by the grace of God," his person was "sacred and inviolable," and his authority extended to "everything which conduces to public order at home and the security of the state abroad." The line of succession was determined very much as previously, following the custom of closest male descendant if available, failing which female succession was specified. All of the descendants of the legitimate line would have to die out before any Carlist succession became possible.

The election of this Cortes by universal suffrage was set aside and the vote for the lower house, the Congress of Deputies, was to be determined by later legislative action. Adopted two years later the regulations required voters to be male, over twenty-five, and to pay either twenty-five pesetas annually of real estate tax or fifty pesetas of industrial taxes.[39] Their effect was to reduce the number of eligible voters from almost four million to less than 850,000.[40] However, the number of voters in Spain never closely paralleled those qualified and the monetary qualifications were moderated by provisions extending the vote to various professional, artistic, military, and civil service groups.

There was also to be a Senate composed of three groups, senators by personal privilege, life senators named by the Crown, and elected senators. As will be seen, the composition of the Senate was to be the source of a major political crisis at a later period.

Temporarily lost in the constitution were the right to trial by jury and some of the provisions of the Constitution of 1869 guarding against arbitrary arrest.[41] These were major items of discussion in the Constitutional Cortes along with the article on religion, Article 11.

Perhaps second only to Cánovas in the defense of the constitution in the Cortes debates was Manuel Alonso Martínez. He and another dissident, Francisco de Paula Candau, had been elected members of the parliamentary commission charged with defending the draft of the constitution before the Cortes and Alonso Martínez, as president of the commission, spoke frequently.

In many respects Alonso Martínez was to act as the parliamentary leader of the dissidents during this period, although they were not, of course, at this time an organized group and there was to be evident rivalry among them. Too ambitious to be satisfied with a legal career, too cool and rational to be a good politician, Alonso Martínez was one of the best orators of his day but never attracted a personal following. Although respected, he was not capable of party leadership. Later the dissidents were to seek as their leader José Posada Herrera, but that well-known and highly respected political figure had accepted the presidency of the Congress of Deputies. This position, although supposedly honorary and politically neutral, was to be obtained only by the votes of the majority party. In accepting it Posada Herrera had in effect removed himself from any active political role. He obtained not only the votes of the majority Liberal Conservatives, but those of the Constitutionalists and the dissidents as well.[42]

Alonso Martínez's most effective intervention came in the later stages of the debate where he ably seconded Cánovas in defense of the controversial Article 11 against the attacks of the young firebrand of the Moderados, Alejandro Pidal y Mon, who gave vehement support to the cause of "Catholic unity."[43] In this debate Alonso Martínez was able to answer Pidal y Mon with the words of papal pronouncements and authorized interpretations of the Catholic position which made it clear that the Catholic church outside of Spain had accepted a much more liberal view of religious toleration than was being advanced in Spain. Arguing for Article 11, Alonso Martínez emphasized that Spain's economic development—the building of railroads employing foreign workers, the expansion of businesses with foreign capital—made religious toleration "a social necessity." "Without the emancipation of the individual conscience and the free flight of thought," Alonso Martínez concluded, "human progress is absolutely impossible."[44]

The article on religion was carried by a sizable majority with the dissident Constitutionalists joining with the government forces against their former party comrades and liberal republicans, who opposed the article because it was not liberal enough, and the Moderados, who considered it excessively liberal.

But Alonso Martínez and Candau also supported the provisions of the constitutional draft relating to the suspension of individual liberties against arbitrary arrest, portraying the Constitution of 1869 as having been too rigid and hence ineffective. As Candau noted, the government under it could not even arrest beggars and provide the necessary charitable care. The dissidents continued to support the government even after the adoption of the constitution.[45] On July 15, 1876, Alonso Martínez defended the continuance of Cánovas's dictatorship, this time with the support of the Cortes, for the period between its meetings. "We have," he said in behalf of himself and his colleagues, "loyally supported the government; we continue supporting it, always upon reasonable terms; we believe that it is not in the interest of the country that this ministry should disappear, and for these reasons are not disposed to give it a vote of censure."[46]

This cooperation of the dissident Constitutionalists and the Liberal Conservatives was rudely interrupted by unplanned events taking place during the hot summer vacation period. From the first Cánovas had sought to appease Moderado sentiment as much as possible. The severity of educational supervision by the Moderado marquis of Orovio had been given tacit support by Cánovas, and the Moderado members of his ministry who had left in September had been replaced by the quasi-Moderados Calderón Collantes and the count of Toreno when he returned in December. But Cánovas's defense of Article 11 in the Cortes had seemed liberal and awakened hopes for a more liberal attitude on the part of the government.

These hopes for a liberal interpretation of Article 11 were blasted by events taking place in Mahón on the island of Minorca beginning on the night of August 19, 1876. The sub-governor of Mahón, one Antonio de Castañeira, represented the strongly conservative Catholic position of many Spaniards on an island heavily influenced by foreign visitors and settlements. On this fateful night unidentified persons complained to Castañeira that the Protestants in the Methodist church of Mahón were disturbing them by the loud singing of psalms and the recitation of creeds with the windows of the establishment wide open. The sub-governor immediately proceeded to the locale, entered the establishment, and ordered services halted.[47]

In later discussions of the event it was revealed that the bishop of the island had been much concerned with the growth of Protestantism there. Various kinds of harassment preceded and followed the incident. The Protestant newspaper *El Bien Público* had been suppressed. Masters and custodians of Protestant schools had been forbidden to accompany their children on the way to school or on their way home afterward. The son of the American consul there had been expelled from the public school he had been attending and a Catholic suspected of being a Mason was deprived of burial in the Catholic cemetery.[48]

Confronted by a hail of criticism from Spanish liberals and protests from both the English and German diplomatic representatives, the government launched an investigation.[49] It ordered the governor of the Balearics to carry out an on-the-spot review, but when he pled illness, allowed him to send his secretary to review the actions of a superior officer. The secretary found nothing contrary to his task in taking up quarters in the sub-governor's house and accepting without question all of the statements of the most intolerant Catholic witnesses. In the end he agreed with the sub-governor that the building he had entered was a schoolhouse, not a church, although a portion of it had been made into a chapel. He did not interview any of the seventy to eighty adults who had congregated for an evening service. He concluded, as a consequence, that the sub-governor had been acting in the legitimate exercise of his authority as supervisor of schools![50]

The government followed this jaundiced decision with a circular defining Article 11 of the constitution in a very restricted fashion—no notice of any sort could be placed on the public way or an external wall of a non-Catholic church or cemetery; churches and schools must be licensed and separate establishments built for the two uses; directors of all church schools must be Spaniards and registered with the authorities.[51]

The Mahón affair provided the Constitutionalists and other liberal groups with a point of sharp attack on the Cánovas government. *La Iberia* was able to cull critical comments from German, English, Italian, Portuguese, Austrian, and Belgian newspapers.[52] It also reported continued actions by the bishop of Minorca with regulations for the baptism of illegitimate (non-Catholic) children, the exclusion of children of Protestants from public schools, and other acts of harassment against Protestants.[53] Actions against Protestant churches elsewhere in Spain with open doors or even with an open Bible represented on the exterior wall had been taken. Clearly, said *La Iberia*, Cánovas had now become himself a Moderado.[54]

These events left the dissident Constitutionalists in a difficult quandary. Alonso Martínez as president of the Commission for the Constitution of 1876 had given strong support to Cánovas in respect to Article 11. Although it had been stated by government deputies in the debates that the interpretation of that article might vary from government to government, the dissidents had obviously not expected the government to adopt so restrictive an interpretation. Alonso Martínez had suggested that signs should be allowed on Protestant churches and schools if for no other reason than to keep good Catholics from entering them.[55] But when the Protestants requested a legal opinion on the scope of the article, he admitted in his *dictamen* or formal statement that the question of signs remained uncertain. However, asserted Alonso Martínez, there was no doubt in respect to the article's guarantee of the inviolability of the temple, the cemetery, and the book.[56]

Confronted with what he considered a clear challenge of principle, Alonso Martínez initiated a series of conferences with his fellow dissidents. The leader of the dissidents felt that their agreement to cooperate with the majority had extended only to the period in which the Restoration was being confirmed and a constitution drawn up. The original agreement, he was to emphasize, had preserved freedom of action for those who cooperated with the government. Now, he felt, the government was departing from the principle it had placed within the Constitution of 1876 and it was the legitimate role of the dissidents to use their weight in the center of the parliamentary spectrum to moderate the trend of the government toward reaction. Although not using the label themselves, the dissidents were already being classified as the "Parliamentary Center."[57]

A number of Alonso Martínez's colleagues were disturbed by the possibility of being separated from the Cánovas fold. Early in November, Santa Cruz, who had been active in the move for the original separation from the Constitutionalists, called for a new meeting of the Constitutionalist dissidents. A personal invitation was extended to Alonso Martínez, but by meeting time he had decided not to attend. Some fifteen of the fifty-four parliamentary leaders identified with the group attended, including most notably Manuel Silvela, the duke of Tetuan, and Fernández de la Hoz. Clearly this group was determined to maintain its ties with Cánovas. In the period that followed most of the members took up full affiliation with the Liberal Conservative party.[58]

Meanwhile, Alonso Martínez and his followers did not completely break their ties with the government. On November 15, 1876, he joined with the Constitutionalists José Luis Albareda and Augusto Ulloa in speaking against the government decision supporting the sub-governor of Mahón. But he stated his position in a mild and conciliatory fashion, emphasizing the overriding importance of the toleration of religious dissent and still gaining from Cánovas respectful attention, recognition of his services to the government, and an acknowledgment of his right to freedom of action within the existing political framework.[59]

In the Cortes debates and in the period following the government's bête noire was Cristóbal Martín de Herrera, the minister of grace and justice. The brother of the archbishop of Santiago, Martín de Herrera had earlier been a Moderado but had joined the Constitutionalists and then had been one of the dissidents who decided at an early date to move into Cánovas's party. At this point he seemed to be reverting to Moderado sentiments. He would never have voted for Article 11, he declared, if he had thought it prevented penalties against Protestant propaganda.[60]

His speeches and government action at the same time aggravated the situation. In the midst of the debate over Mahón a professor of history of the Instituto de Noviciado in Madrid was halted in the middle of his lecture and shortly thereafter expelled from his position for the antireligious tone of the textbook he had written.[61] The secure government majority supported its actions in the vote on the interpellation on Mahón but the Constitutionalist dissidents voted with their former party colleagues in opposition and there was, therefore, a sizable group of 60 deputies now opposing the government's religious policy. Of the government's majority of 183, 90 were counted as Moderado in sentiment if not in name.[62]

The action in Mahón triggered religious fanaticism elsewhere. In December the directors of the Civil Hospital in Cádiz issued orders forbidding Protestant pastors to visit patients there. Protests of the German, English, American, Danish, and other consuls gained the reply from the civil governor that since this was a private institution, he could do nothing officially but would use his personal influence to get the order reversed.[63] Behind the scenes it was clear that Cánovas had not been happy with the events at Mahón and was even more disturbed with the incident at Cádiz.[64] He had no desire to arouse foreign criticism of Spanish religious intolerance. The incident at Cádiz had been followed by official protests of both England and Germany, the latter on the personal order of the kaiser.[65] On December 15 Hatzfeldt learned from Cánovas that he had sought to satisfy Layard on religious matters, which Layard confirmed, in particular that Protestant congregations could use the same buildings for churches and schools if the hours of religious worship were made known to the authorities.[66] A little later a government order directed that all public hospitals be open to Protestant clergy.[67]

Although these concessions helped to reduce diplomatic pressure, they were not publicly revealed. The year 1876 closed, therefore, with the opposition increasingly outraged by Cánovas's rapprochement with the Moderados. And Cánovas's critics continued to refer to his regime as the *dictadura*. From the first the term was debatable. Few political opponents were exiled or arrested. But the threat of arrest remained and the Constitution of 1876 had fewer safeguards of individual liberties than that of 1869. Most importantly, trial by jury was abolished. Opposition newspapers continued but so did government censorship. The actions of governmental officials in respect to the press were often capricious and suspensions threatened many newspapers with bankruptcy. The control of local administration was completely in the hands of the government party. This carried with it control over the election process. In turn Cánovas's and Romero Robledo's dominance over the Liberal Conservative party placed all governmental decisions within their hands.

Although the debates in the Cortes gave opponents the opportunity to have their say, the criticism could not change the course of events since the government maintained an overwhelming majority. The only possibilities of change were: 1) that the opponents would convince the ruling party of the unwisdom of its policies, a most unlikely possibility; 2) that the opponents would win away from the majority party enough members of the Cortes to reduce its strength, again unlikely in view of the government's control over patronage and the pressure for party unity; 3) that the opponents could convince the king that the ruling party was making serious errors, to be in the long run the only effective hope of criticism; or 4) to raise the threat of a hostile public opinion which might lead to revolution, a device constantly used but not too effective in the absence of any clearly expressed "public opinion."

There was, therefore, a sense of helplessness and hopelessness which aggravated the hostility of the opposition. Projects of law were never amended on the floor of the Cortes. The opposition proposed changes; the government deputies argued against them; the government votes rejected them. His Majesty's Opposition, therefore, functioned in something of a vacuum, providing an expression of the policies it would follow if the majority party grew weary or became convinced of the wisdom of turning governmental power over to its opponents. The adoption of the constitution, therefore, did not quiet the government's critics.

The real strength of criticism is, however, difficult to determine. Something like 3 percent of the country's population determined the course of politics. Among this group the similarities were more notable than the differences. The landed aristocracy, military leaders, bourgeoisie, and civil servants controlled the destiny of the state. They profited from a period of remarkable economic expansion during the entire reign of Alfonso XII. Industrial expansion was joined to agricultural progress. Although wheat production failed to prosper in this period, the production of grapevines and wines showed an enormous expansion and brought great profits. The production of olives, fruits, and sugar beets rose. This was also the heyday of the growth of iron and steel production. And, of course, the building of railroads went on apace, with the accompanying profits to the construction companies and political magnates who furthered the projects. Medium industry also progressed, particularly the textile factories in Catalonia, whose production quintupled in only a few years. Bilbao's population rose from 15,000 to 80,000, becoming Spain's principal industrial center and sharing with Madrid the major financial position. This was a time of "an obvious state of euphoria" in respect to foreign trade, the building of steamship lines, and the "gold fever" on the stock exchange, which made the years 1876–86 "a golden decade."[68]

There were, of course, dark shadows amidst the sunshine. State finances, in spite of the reform efforts of Cos-Gayón noted above and Camacho noted below, continued to run ever deeper into the red. This was the day of the "sick peseta" and depreciations and premiums for gold formed a continuing motif.[69]

Much of the financing of the economic expansion, therefore, rested in the hands of foreign investors. Foreign capital dominated the mining industry, utilities, municipal services, and many of the banking and insurance companies.

Nor was economic progress accompanied by social reform. Although some large landholdings, both civil and ecclesiastical, were broken up, many of them survived. The peasants in southern Spain lived in conditions of poverty which they survived only by the most frugal diet and primitive living conditions. They seldom ate meat—their diet consisted of rice and vegetables cooked with olive oil, bread, and occasionally a little fish.[70] The *latifundia* in the South, as a consequence, gave birth to an anarchist movement which gained considerable strength and worried the government throughout Alfonso's reign.

In the cities industrial expansion was accompanied by the exploitation of and economic pressures on the workers. Although wages rose, inflation outstripped the level of wage increases.[71]

The helplessness of the working classes made the most progressive cities the home of ardent republicanism. Socialist movements were born, gained followers, held congresses.

But neither anarchism nor socialism nor republicanism gained enough strength to threaten the established oligarchy in control of the state as long as that oligarchy itself did not lose its basic coherence. The year 1877 was to be marked by such a threat. Political excitement and anger threatened the whole framework of government. This was triggered by steps completing the organization of the Senate which seemed to preclude the possibility of the opposition's ever controlling its membership. Before dealing with these events, however, it is appropriate at this point to digress from the course of domestic events to examine the nature of Cánovas's management of foreign policy during the first years of the Restoration.

4

The Foreign Policy of

Cánovas del Castillo

 LTHOUGH CÁNOVAS had counted the creation of a favorable international atmosphere as one of the most important aspects of his work of preparation for the Restoration, his name was not well known in international circles at the outset. There was strong favor for Alfonso from the beginning, but it apparently derived more from the monarch's own personality than from any work of his chief minister.[1]

It is somewhat ironic that the most laudatory reaction to the new regime came from the American representative, Caleb Cushing. In February Cushing reported that Cánovas appeared "to be laboring anxiously and conscientiously to establish institutions of constitutional and parliamentary monarchical government like that of England." Four months later he characterized Cánovas as the "master spirit in the government . . . an accomplished writer; a superior parliamentary debater; and a serious practical statesman." By the time Cánovas had been in office a year Cushing was praising Cánovas in a thirty-seven-page dispatch in which he noted that although his government was a dictatorship, it had not been stained by a single act of bloodshed, "has been as liberal in fact as any of the so-called liberal governments have been in profession; it has respected individual rights to a degree of which the country has seen no previous example for many years; it has not trampled on personal security by sending off ship loads of its political enemies beyond the seas as they did; it suffers its opponents to walk the street unmolested, to write, to speak, to intrigue, with forbearance and toleration almost unexampled: in a word, it has been faithful to its programme of reconciling liberty with order, always of course on the premises of hereditary monarchy."[2]

Cushing's favor was so strongly expressed that it aroused the angry comment of the British representative, Sir Austen Henry Layard, who had had close relationships with the Serrano regime and was a bitter critic of the course of events under Cánovas. Layard felt that Cushing was simply striving for effect in order to lay the ground for the settlement of his country's claims negotiations. There were to be, indeed, charges that Cushing profited personally by the claims settlements noted below, but this remains unproved. Cushing's reaction was basically that of a man of very conservative temperament who knew previous Spanish history well and welcomed the changed course of events which he now encountered.[3]

Cushing's support was, as was to be expected, strongly echoed by the Austrian and Russian representatives.[4] The German envoy, Count Melchior von Hatzfeldt-Wildenburg, and his assistants reacted much more cautiously, expressing fears that Cánovas's position would be too reactionary, that he would throw in his lot with the Moderados, or that he would be unable to stabilize and secure the new regime.[5] As has been noted, he joined with the English and Swedish representatives in an effort to emphasize the need for political and religious liberalism.

A review of the course of diplomacy during the early years of the Restoration, however, reveals a rational and sensible management of foreign policy on the part of Cánovas. The major guidelines of Cánovas's foreign policy was caution and moderation. He recognized Spain's fairly minimal resources and potential in world affairs. He realized that Spain could not claim the role of a major power, particularly in non-European affairs. Cuba, however, presented a special case. Here neither he nor his foreign ministers had any real option—no sign of weakness could be shown. He sought to conciliate the great powers insofar as that was possible without a real loss of prestige—to convince the United States that the war in Cuba would be over quickly and that Spain would seek to make reforms there; to convince the great power on the European continent, Germany, that Spain recognized and applauded her accomplishments and looked to her friendship; to assure England that the Restoration monarchy would be moderate and support religious toleration; and to work patiently but persistently to obtain a more favorable attitude from France. It was from France that he saw the greatest potential dangers—at the outset from its apparent sympathy for the Carlists; later as the source of republican or anarchist propaganda.[6]

The new government confronted a congeries of inherited problems. One of the most serious, but also one of the earliest to reach a settlement, was the affair of the *Virginius*. The history of the *Virginius* affair is not one of the brighter sagas of American diplomacy. The steamer, flying the American flag and with American papers later alleged to be fraudulent, had been overtaken November 5, 1873, by the Spanish warship *Tornado*, captured, and taken into the port of Santiago de Cuba. Arms and munitions were aboard and a number of the personnel of the ship had been identified with the Cuban revolutionary cause. In Santiago military courts acting at the orders of one Brigadier Juan de Burriel y Lynch condemned the entire crew to death and within a week fifty-seven persons were shot. Some of these were American, some British citizens, and both countries were involved in the reparations demands which followed.[7]

Spain narrowly escaped war in the immediate aftermath of this incident. That diplomatic procedures were followed was partially due to Cushing, not yet minister to Spain, who was consulted by the United States Department of State and who counseled moderation.[8] Part of the credit was due to Emilio Castelar, then president of the first Spanish republic, who warned against the "madness" of going to war against the United States at a time of civil war at home and in Cuba over the capture of a foreign ship on the high seas—the *Virginius* had been taken in waters near Jamaica.[9] Throughout the negotiations there continued to be extremists in both countries—in the United States maintaining that the fraudulence of the ship's papers provided no excuse for Spanish actions; in Spain denying the justice of providing indemnities for the families of those who were obviously Cuban revolutionaries.

The return of the ship and surviving passengers had been agreed to under Castelar. An indemnity for those who had suffered imprisonment in Cuba and for the families of those who had been executed was drawn up in terms by which Spain did not fully accept imputations of wrongdoing and had been signed under the Serrano government. Confronting this *fait accompli*, the Cánovas regime proceeded to honor the terms already agreed upon and to pay 225,000 pesetas as aid to the families of victims of the incident.[10]

Cuba remained, of course, a continuing source of difficulty between the United States and Spain. The war then going on in Cuba had broken out in 1868 after the revolution of that year in Spain. The Ten Years War which followed had greatly altered the character of revolutionary action on the island. Although it was always difficult to assess the actual number of insurrectionists, they never exceeded 20,000 men under arms, but they had much assistance from the civilian population. Guerrilla tactics continued to predominate, but there were some encounters of sizable armies and in some of these Spanish forces came to disaster. Black and mulatto fighters were considerably augmented in numbers, a formal revolutionary government established, and revolutionary military leaders with real élan and considerable ability appeared. Increasingly the focus of the revolt rested on independence rather than autonomy or reform, although the support for these alternative solutions of Cuban problems remained divided.[11]

Spain confronted, therefore, a real and pressing challenge in Cuba as the Restoration began. The captain general then in command, one of Spain's most prestigious generals, the marquis of la Habana, was quickly replaced by the more politically conservative count of Valmaseda.[12] Valmaseda found the situation in Cuba beyond his capabilities. In the earlier stages of the fighting a fortified line, a ditch or *trocha*, had been drawn across the center of the island to guard the more prosperous western portions of the island from the depredations of the insurgents in the east. But Valmaseda confronted the incursion across the *trocha* of the forces of one of the most daring of the revolutionary leaders, Máximo Gómez. And his fiscal administration came under such challenge from a royal financial commission under Rodríguez Rubí that he relinquished his post late in December 1875, to be succeeded early in the following year by General Jovellar, who had held at the outset the post of minister of war in the first cabinet of Cánovas and then had temporarily replaced Cánovas as the president of the cabinet during the election of the Cortes.[13]

Jovellar's appointment came shortly after the creation of a Hispanic-Colonial Bank formed to facilitate a new loan of 200 million pesetas for the exigencies of the Cuban War. Formed with the involvement of some of the wealthiest men in Spain, the bank was by the late summer of 1876 to provide the funds needed for the prosecution of the war, but with a shocking rate of interest and onerous financial conditions involved.[14] Before these funds became available, however, Jovellar's incompetence in the Cuban arena had become apparent and the government was, as a consequence, to replace him in the military sphere with General Martínez Campos on October 19, 1876.[15] It began thereby the move to a successful armistice but one accompanied by a heavy political price.

Meanwhile, the government of the United States continued to demand Spanish action to end the conflict in Cuba. There was strong sympathy for the revolutionists and support from Cuban exiles in New York City. President Ulysses Grant posed a diplomatic problem for the European states and for Spain with a proposal for mediation.[16] There were continuing incidents involving American citizens, some of them holding dubious claims to that designation.[17] Caleb Cushing continued to deal softly in presenting American demands, to enter half protests at the instructions of his own Department of State,[18] and to be impressed with the arguments of Cánovas and his colleagues that the insurrectionists were now largely fighting a racial struggle and that Spain's triumph "would be at the same time the triumph of right and of civilization."[19] But the more realistic German representative reported that the black and mulatto insurrectionists were still secure in their forest fastnesses and that Spain still faced a serious problem in her efforts to establish peace in Cuba.[20]

Germany, too, entered the Restoration with a ship controversy with Spain. On December 11, 1874, the German freighter *Gustave* had been caught in a storm off the northern coast of Spain near the Carlist-held port of Zarauz. Instead of providing succor the Carlists had fired upon the vessel, seized it, and robbed it of its cargo.[21] The Germans in response dispatched three warships to the area and one of the military commanders landed forces in Zarauz early in January 1875.[22] Meanwhile, the new regime hastened to assure the German government that it would guarantee an indemnity for damages and take action against the Carlists in the area involved in the incident. German suggestions of cooperation were rebuffed. The German government, anxious to join with other monarchist regimes in supporting Alfonso XII, agreed to defer to the Spanish insistence on sovereignty even in an area held by insurgents.[23] The occupation of Zarauz was labeled "unexpected and undesired" by the home government and restraint was exercised over naval action, two of the three warships being withdrawn, the other remaining to observe the Spanish action and later to receive a formal salute of apology.[24] Agreement for reparations was concluded late in January 1875.[25]

Germany and Spain also encountered some mutual irritation in respect to events in the Sulu Islands lying between the Philippines and Borneo. These islands were peopled by warlike tribes some of whom displayed considerable admixture of Arab blood from an earlier period of conquest and were predominantly Moslem in religion. They were also a continuing source of piracy and privateering. Spain had had settlements and a fort on the chief island of Joló, but had dismantled it in 1646 and left local control to a native sultan under Spanish vassalage. From that point on Spain had contented herself with occasional expeditions to retard piracy and gain renewed acknowledgment of her suzerainty.[26] Now in the early years of the Restoration she began to discover German and English commercial intrusion into what she still considered her private sphere of interest.

Although she had abandoned direct occupation of the Sulu Islands, she considered that her sovereignty there remained unimpaired. Ships trading with the Sulus were supposed to stop in the Philippines at Manila, Sual, Ilo-Ilo, or Zamboanga before proceeding to the archipelago to the south. Although this did not constitute a significant diversion for traders, it would, of course, carry with it the process of dealing with the often difficult and sometimes corrupt Spanish customs officials and paying duties. Neither German nor English merchants saw any rationale in Spanish regulations and their governments insisted that if customs were to be collected, there must be customs officials in the Sulus themselves.

Early in 1876 the Spanish government dispatched an expedition to the Sulus "to arrest the spread of piracy" and accompanied this with an embargo on commerce which resulted in the seizure of a number of English and German vessels.[27] Both countries reacted with protests in April 1876, and Spain responded that the naval action was concluded and that instructions had been given to facilitate all foreign commerce with the Sulus. Evidently Spanish authorities in the Philippines either had not received or not heeded their instructions because seizure of British and German ships continued and the protests of the two powers increased in vigor with Germany now beginning to join with England in questioning Spain's claims to sovereignty. Threats of naval action were to be raised before a final protocol was signed in March 1877.[28]

By this protocol Spain agreed that all foreign commerce with the Sulus was to be absolutely free and unimpeded without the necessity of stopping at any intermediary ports or paying imposts of any sort except in areas directly occupied by Spain. Although this accord represented a virtual surrender by Spain of her previous position, it did leave her with a tenuous claim to sovereignty. Attacks in the Cortes ignored the very strong positions taken by both English and Germans and the obvious stupidity of a potential war or even quasi war over a group of islands of little economic importance infested by pirates and hostile natives.[29] The diplomatic dispatches emphasize Spain's great concern that Germany should not be pushed into greater cooperation with the British because of her concerns in this area.

Germany also found an attitude of conciliation on the part of Spain in respect to the treatment of German property in Cuba. Spanish concessions in respect to the war taxes imposed there were so favorable that the German ambassador in Madrid reported them with surprise and shock.[30]

In all of these negotiations there was a clear pattern—the Spanish government was anxious to conciliate the dominant state on the continent, a state which shared Spain's suspicions of the French. France's real or suspected support of the Carlists at the outset of the Restoration and her sheltering of Spanish republican exiles thereafter was a source of continuing Spanish concern. Germany was the most obvious Spanish recourse for aid in the event a French government gave more than passive support to Spain's internal opposition. Perhaps the thought of an alliance lurked in Cánovas's mind from the outset. The formal suggestion was not made until 1877.

The Spanish bid for a German alliance came as a diplomatic shock of the first order. There had been little preparation for the approach. Relations with Count von Hatzfeldt had been cordial but not extremely close. There was little evidence of the close friendship with the king to be displayed by his successor Count Klaus zu Solms-Sonnenwalde. Hatzfeldt on his part had spoken frequently of reservations about the Cánovas government. He had joined with the English in protesting violations of religious toleration in Spain. He had presented the *Gustave* claims with vigor. He had followed the Sulu matter diligently. There had, therefore, been no special groundwork for the startling conference which took place on October 31, 1877.[31]

The conference was requested by Cánovas himself. He was, he said, unwilling to leave the matter in the hands of his minister of foreign affairs. He began by speaking frankly of his concern for the course of events in France. Like Germany he could see no advantage for Spain in France moving either to a monarchy or an imperial government. He implied that Germany preferred a republic and indicated that this would not trouble Spain. But he then expressed fear that a dangerous, radical form of republicanism might develop in France. In view of the strength of republicanism and what he called "internationalism" in Catalonia (probably referring both to anarchism and the activities of the First International), a French government sympathetic to these concepts would be a serious threat to Spain. The same kind of sympathies which had led to French support of Carlism in Spain would then be carried across to the other side of the political spectrum. In such a case there would be a very real menace to Spanish integrity and a German guarantee of Spain would be extremely helpful. Such a guarantee would also, he added, be of value to Germany—in normal times Spain could place an army of 200,000 on the French frontier and in case of emergency this number could be doubled.

The tone of the conversation clearly suggested an alliance proposal, although Hatzfeldt at the outset was not willing to characterize it as such. Cánovas indicated his desire to bring Spain out of her existing isolation. Spain was, he said, no longer willing to "keep her hands folded in her lap." "Her task consisted rather in the effort, without an overestimation of her strength and with a continuing reconstruction of her internal organization, to use all means to free herself from the disgraceful isolation into which she had been thrust, partly voluntarily and partly through unfortunate circumstances and to enter again into the great European movement." This, said Cánovas, was "the most important objective of his country," but one which it could only fulfill in consonance with the country "which today stands at the peak of civilization" and exercised a dominant influence on the determination of European politics—the German Reich, for which

Spain had sought in every way possible to express its friendship and desire for conciliation. There was, continued Cánovas, no difference of any sort separating the two states; and Spain, although it disposed of much smaller resources than Germany, could be useful to Germany in many ways.

When Hatzfeldt pressed for further definition, Cánovas again stressed the value of a German guarantee, "without which there would be little advantage for Spain," and added three other items —the suggestion of a visit of the German crown prince to Spain, the union of the royal houses by marriage, and the raising of the status of the legations in Madrid and Berlin to that of embassies.

Hatzfeldt concluded his startling report with his belief that it was in the interest of Germany to help Spain to a better position in Europe. He felt that this action would be of advantage to Germany not only in respect to France but also in respect to clerical questions (apparently thinking of mutual influence in the approaching papal election). He warned that a cool or reserved reception would injure Cánovas's feelings and probably hamper Germany's actions for a long time to come.

The Spanish approach failed to awaken any real enthusiasm on the part of Bismarck. He was at this time much engaged in the supervision of the first of the two estates he was to acquire and his response was, therefore, to come from Varzin. He was obviously much upset that this significant matter had been raised in Madrid rather than in Berlin. This procedure imposed upon Germany the necessity of providing written responses to oral suggestions and placed the German ambassador in Madrid under the obligation of presenting and defending Spanish interests. Hatzfeldt, he suggested, should have stopped Cánovas and corrected this procedure.[32] When the kaiser dissented from this, Bismarck responded that it simply revealed he did not know the technical details of diplomacy since he had never been a minister or a diplomat.[33]

Nor did Bismarck find any great value attached to a potential Spanish alliance. With the uncertainty of Spanish politics little reliance could be placed on Spain. Moreover, Germany had fought Spain's war in 1870, but not one Spaniard came to Germany's aid. On the other hand, he added, the value of an understanding would not be exactly zero, so the response should be polite, not at all cool, show good will, but at the same time make no particular commitments.

Germany would, Bismarck emphasized, always support the Spanish position in Paris. Germany had, he noted, a strong interest in the strengthening of the Spanish monarchy "especially in its present moderate form" and in a defense of its independence. But he had no desire to make a commitment for an uncertain war. A power able to defend itself, he noted, always has friends.

Nor could Bismarck offer much consolation in respect to Spain's secondary objectives. A journey to Spain by the crown prince would not be possible with the disturbed conditions existing in France—there would be far too much danger of fire bombs or other forms of assassination attempts. As for a potential marriage arrangement this was a question not even at the disposal of the kaiser himself, but rather in the hands of the head of the Hohenzollern family, through whom the approach must be made. This was not a state matter but a private one.

The project of a marriage between the princess of Asturias and Friedrich of Hohenzollern had already been broached by Spain on several different occasions. The Infanta Isabella's first husband, Count Frederick Girgenti, had been subject to epilepsy and had committed suicide three years after their marriage. She was at this time twenty-six; the suggested groom was already forty-nine. The German response that this was a family matter had already been duly conveyed. The obstacle here, of course, was that Isabella, already the source of many difficulties in respect to the king's own marriage proposals, would have to initiate the negotiations. Nor was it so extremely unusual that preparatory steps might be initiated through diplomatic circles. The strong German reserve in respect to the matter reflected the doubt that there would be a favorable reception of the idea on the part of the intended groom—"the thought of such a Spanish marriage," said the kaiser, "was about as unpleasant as that of a Spanish fly."[34] At a later point he also suggested that Friedrich* was not likely to win the heart of a young princess and that he was not likely to be interested in another marriage after three previous ones had turned out so badly.[35] Negotiations were initiated with the Hohenzollern family head, Prince Anton,† and dragged on until Spain received the advice in April 1878 that the matter should not be pursued further.[36] Other efforts to find a suitor for Isabella's hand were unavailing. She remained a widow, surviving long beyond most of her Bourbon relatives until the fall of the dynasty in 1931.

This was the last of a series of discouraging events. Bismarck continued to note his reservations in the face of "the stormy approach" of Spain and to instruct his representatives to try to conciliate Spain without granting any formal treaty.[37] The shifting of negotiations to Berlin had already put a strain upon the Spanish effort since the Spanish government did not intend to keep its representative in Berlin, Francisco Merry y Colón later the count of Benomar, in that position if the legation became an embassy.[38] The Spanish would have much preferred to work through Hatzfeldt. Repeatedly Bismarck rejected any move to a formal alliance. When Hatzfeldt tried to suggest the advantages of a Spanish army on the French frontier and mentioned how helpful this would have been in 1870, Bismarck added the marginal comment, "Certainly, but they weren't there."[39] The only really tangible concession that could be offered, along with the continued protestations of friendship and support, was the promise of raising the corresponding legations to embassy status and of continuing the exchange of visits of leading personalities.[40]

*Meant here is Friedrich Karl (1828–85), descended from a younger son of Friedrich Wilhelm III. He had had a distinguished military career in the Prussian wars with Denmark, Austria, and France—was described as a "cold" commander, slow in making decisions, but tough and persistent. He was still at the time of the marriage proposal the inspector general of the Prussian cavalry forces.
†The Prussian rulers had recognized the head of the Swabian branch of the Hohenzollerns as head of the family, giving him primary decision in respect to family matters, but not, of course, significant political influence.

The Spanish government accepted the small sop it received with gratitude, although even this was to be long delayed by the financial obligations confronting both states in the establishment of embassies.[41] By the time this agreement in respect to ambassadorial arrangements had been concluded early in 1878, the French were cognizant of the "secret" negotiations between Spain and Germany. Their request for clarification was answered in conciliatory fashion by the Spanish government with German approval.[42] By this time, indeed, it had become clear to Spain that a formal alliance was not going to be made. Spain began on her own part some approaches for better relations with France. But the disappointment attached to the outcome of these efforts for alliance with Germany must have been considerable.[43]

The episode awakens many speculations. Although the initiative lay with Cánovas and his foreign minister, Manuel Silvela, the king indicated also his desire "to go with Germany."[44] Throughout the period which followed the Spanish monarch continued to be enthralled by German uniforms and to look forward to the visit he planned to Germany, delayed by the death of Mercedes and domestic problems until 1883. There were German suspicions that Spain might have ambitions in respect to Portugal or that she might make use of an alliance arrangement for military action against France on the excuse of intrusions into Catalonia. In retrospect these suspicions seem quite dubious.

Everything foundered, of course, on Bismarck's very low appraisal of the value of a Spanish alliance and upon his desire not to create new French antagonism. Had he followed up on Cánovas's suggestion, his famous alliance system would have begun with Spain. And one could conceive that a careful nurturing of mutual military relationships might well have confronted France with a two-front conflict in World War I.

Such an alliance would, of course, have been a dramatic victory for Cánovas and might well have strengthened his hand at home. For he was by this time beginning to confront really serious opposition and approaching the first real crisis of the Restoration.

Meanwhile, Spanish relationships with France, although never fully cordial and trusting, improved somewhat.[45] The early part of the Restoration had been a troubled period for both countries. Spain had considered France the headquarters of an international Carlist conspiracy which found the opponents of Alfonso receiving contributions and sympathy long after Sagunto. French newspapers often displayed open favor to the Carlist cause and only slightly veiled contempt for Alfonso and his ministers. Money and arms were alleged to be crossing the frontier. Even before the end of the conflict the French mood began to change, as Marshal MacMahon exercised some control over newspapers and local government officials. There were aftermaths of the conflict—French indignation at Spanish extradition efforts in respect to Alfonso de Borbón y Austria de Este, the younger brother of the pretender, who was supposed to have been responsible for atrocities in Catalonia. But the focus tended to change and Spanish concern now centered on the harboring of exiled Spanish republicans, in particular Manuel Ruiz Zorrilla. In June 1877 Spanish diplomatic pressure finally brought the expulsion of Ruiz Zorrilla from France to Switzerland, but the absence was relatively brief and by 1880 he was again using France as a base for organizing opposition to the Alfonsist monarchy. France was also considered to be the breeding ground of socialist and anarchist sentiments and Spanish ministers continued to be wary of their northern neighbor in spite of French protestations of good faith and the conclusion of a commercial treaty apparently satisfactory to both states.

England had been the major critic of the government's conservative religious policy throughout the early period of the Restoration. Sir Austen Henry Layard, the British ambassador, was so much a defender of the Serrano government as to display a scarcely veiled hostility to the Restoration and was during the early years persona non grata with the regime. In June 1878 he was replaced by Lionel Sackville-West, whose official correspondence paid little attention to the course of Spanish domestic politics. A constant flow of complaints in respect to Spanish customs regulations and their implementation occupied the British representatives in Spain. In spite of Cánovas's claim that the

Restoration derived inspiration from the British system of government, little warmth of feeling was displayed by either government.[46]

With the exception of the approach to Germany, therefore, Cánovas's foreign policy had been cautious, circumspect, and undramatic. Nothing occurred which served to bolster his position at home. On the other hand, he had gained the respect of most foreign powers and a recognition of the permanence of the Alfonsist monarchy. His conduct of domestic policy, however, was less circumspect and less successful.

5

The King
and the Parties

HE FIRST TWO YEARS of the Restoration had been marked by the dominance of Cánovas over the whole process of government and constitution making. There had been slight hints of royal intervention at some points—in respect to the permission for the duke of la Torre to return to Spain and in respect to the return of Cánovas after the interim government of General Jovellar. But the king, already showing signs of his physical weakness, remained very much in the background. It was Cánovas who seemed to his opponents "indispensable to the majority . . . because he is not only its chief, but its soul, its life, its conscience, its faith, its hope, and almost its benevolence (*caridad*)."[1] Cánovas's increasingly reactionary position during the latter part of 1876 and the early part of 1877 brought the first major appeals by the opposition for the king to use his royal prerogatives to free Spain from an untenable political situation.

The controversy centered around the composition of the upper house of the Cortes, the Senate. The elections of January 1876 had been held with universal suffrage allowed for both houses. Romero Robledo's management was underscored in the results. Two archbishops, fifty-one members of the nobility, twenty-six generals, seventeen ministers or ex-ministers, and fifty-eight ex-senators or ex-deputies became senators. Only thirty-nine senators were newcomers.[2]

The Constitution of 1876, adopted after this election, provided for three classes of senators—elected senators, senators by right of property or position, and life senators to be named by the crown. The number of elected senators was set at 180 and the combined number of those holding office by right of property or position and life senators named by the crown was not to exceed 180. Those holding office by right of property or position included high church officials, army leaders, counselors and attorneys of the realm, and grandees who had an annual assured income from real estate of seventy thousand pesetas. Those eligible for election (when the existing Cortes was dissolved) or being named to that position by the king were subject to a lengthy set of conditions again favoring church officials, nobility, military officers, former governmental officials, and a relatively small group of academicians and intellectuals.[3] In February 1877 a royal decree spelled out the details of future election arrangements for senators with controls strongly in the hands of the provincial deputations and municipal representatives who were, of course, dominated by Cánovas's Liberal Conservative party.[4]

And in April 1877 the king exercised his royal prerogative, naming a lengthy list of life senators. It was obviously Cánovas's list. And the results were in the eyes of the Constitutionalists catastrophic. They emerged with a total of only thirty senators. Cánovas's supposed opposition on the right, the Moderados, were much better treated. They exercised more than eighty votes in the Senate.[5] The consequence was that a legislative body by its very nature conservative became so strongly reactionary that any prospect of a change of its control to the opposing party seemed excluded. This meant that all of Cánovas's promises for a peaceful exchange of power, the *turno pacífico*, were meaningless. In the eyes of the Constitutionalists Cánovas was welching on his commitments, undercutting the parliamentary system he had established. They adopted, therefore, the only weapons available—impassioned pleas to the king in their newspapers[6] and abstention from participation in legislative procedures until some concessions came their way.[7] A further threat was involved—abstention from all political activity would leave Cánovas's system without His Majesty's Loyal Opposition. This in turn would wreck even the pretense of parliamentary procedures.

Alonso Martínez's group had joined in criticism of Cánovas's Senate.[8] Now employing the term "Centralists," they regarded Cánovas as dissident from his own policies and themselves as the genuine advocates of the Constitution of 1876.[9] They did not, however, abstain from the Cortes debates and for the first time gained a representative on the secretariat of that body.[10]

The mood of opposition groups as the Cortes opened was bleak and gray. It seemed to them that "Señor Cánovas is everything; Señor Cánovas has triumphed over all the world . . . and conservative politics may consider that it has won a true triumph, because Señor Cánovas, its chief, is irremovable, immovable, invincible, powerful among the powerful and master among the masters."[11] The situation was one "without an exit" —Cánovas was "condemned to be powerful."[12] Changes in government, charged the opposition, were being effected behind the scenes and without public explanation. Thus Manuel Silvela, no longer a Constitutionalist dissident but now a full member of the Liberal Conservatives, moved into the cabinet as minister of foreign affairs to join another former dissident, Martín de Herrera, now minister of overseas territories and Moderado Calderón Collantes, now minister of grace and justice.[13] José Elduayen, civil governor of Madrid, was suddenly relieved from his post with rumors suggesting he had refused to promote an unqualified employee in spite of Cánovas's order. (Later rumors were to say that he had been fired at the king's order because he had expelled from Madrid an actress mistress of the monarch.)[14] And periodicals continued to be denounced with a regularity which indicated that the government was not relaxing its vigilance.[15]

The opposition parties were in serious disorder. The Consti-

tutionalists, as has been noted, had decided on virtual abstention. The Moderado press was engaged in theological disputes
which heralded the later controversies within that party and required the intervention of the cardinal archbishop of Toledo,
Moreno, to restore quiet.[16] The Centralists were again disappointed by the actions of their chosen leader José Posada Herrera. They had continued to hope that he would lend his personal prestige and wide political acquaintance to their cause.
Each year they had waited patiently for him to emerge from his
tent to take the proffered role of leadership. There were rumors
of letters from his home at Llanes and rumors that the great
man had at last ended his inactivity. But his expectant followers
were disappointed. The Liberal Conservatives managed each
year to get his agreement to serve as the president of the Congress of Deputies and the Centralists were left with ineffective
leadership. Again on this occasion strong rumors of his retire-
ment proved false and Posada Herrera once again chaired the
lower house of the Cortes.[17]

In his speech of April 26 accepting the presidency, Posada
Herrera at least half hinted at criticism of those who had elected
him. He deplored "recent attitudes" which he could not help but
observe with sorrow but hoped would be overcome by "the patriotism of all." Two indispensable forces must, he warned, be
found in all assemblies—"the indisputable authority and sovereignty of the majorities and the rights, also respectable, of the
opposition." "But," he continued, "neither can the authority of
the majorities be respected if it is not exercised with prudence
and justice, nor can the rights of the opposition command respect unless they are exercised within the limits of national
experience and interests."[18]

The abstention of the Constitutionalists from parliamentary
debate thrust the leadership of the opposition into the hands of
the Centralists, now openly in the lists against Cánovas. The
three major speakers were Germán Gamazo, the marquis of la
Vega de Armijo, and Alonso Martínez. The debate strikingly
underscored the parliamentary weakness of the Centralists—
only Alonso Martínez handled himself well. Although Gamazo

spoke against the injustice done in the elections to "one of the parties, our brother," his major attack rested on the treaty signed with England and Germany in respect to the island of Joló, where he maintained Spain had surrendered its sovereignty.[19]

Gamazo's speech occasioned a hail of government responses. Although the weight of reason seems to lie with the government speeches in respect to the Joló matter and Gamazo was shown to be poorly prepared on this issue, the virulence of government speakers revealed their anger and contempt for the Centralists. Calderón Collantes bitingly labeled them "the little group of the clock," referring to their position beneath the clock in the hall of the Congress.[20]

The marquis of la Vega de Armijo confined himself largely to the issue of the Senate and its domination by the Liberal Conservatives. Stressing the affinities of the Centralists with the abstaining Constitutionalists, he charged the government with an open policy of "isolation," ending its effort for conciliation and turning to reaction and repression.[21] Again the reaction of Romero Robledo showed the sensibilities of the Liberal Conservatives to these charges. Denying that he had manipulated elections or that *caciquismo* was new with this government, Romero Robledo criticized the Centralists for talking of affinities with the left and working with the right.[22]

Alonso Martínez spoke with dignity and effect. He expressed the great reluctance he felt in now taking up the role of opposition. He believed that the Constitution of 1876 had been viable and just at the outset, but considered it a major error that the government forces had not left sufficient vacancies in the Senate to give the Constitutionalists an assurance that they could eventually take over the government. It was, he felt, the duty and obligation of the government to assist in the organization and advancement of the opposition parties. Only by giving political outlets to opposition could revolutions be avoided. But the government, he charged, embarrassed and harassed its opponents. Among other things he charged that the entry of Manuel Silvela and Cristobal Martín de Herrera into the cabinet had been meant to embarrass the Centralists.[23]

Both Silvela and Martín de Herrera responded that their loyalties now lay with the majority. The Centralists, said Martín de Herrera, had not yet developed a platform, a set of principles upon which a party must be based.[24] At this point Cánovas arose to deny any obligation of the majority to help its opponents and to advise the Centralists to return to the folds of the Constitutionalists.[25] It was obvious that neither Cánovas nor his supporters had any sympathy with the concept of center parties. Cánovas's model for parliamentary government was England and references to the role of center parties in other parliaments had no impact.

Nevertheless, the center group did number at the high point of its fortunes thirty-one deputies in the Congress.[26] Their debates against the fiscal policies of the government were rudely interrupted by the sudden proroguing of the Cortes on July 11. Several days later, following the removal of Saturnino Álvarez Bugallal, the attorney general, came the report that a parliamentary commission had discovered mismanagement of the floating debt with some embezzlements of considerable funds.[27] Obviously the government preferred to deal with this problem quietly rather than allowing it to become the subject of a parliamentary interpellation. Álvarez Bugallal, who retained considerable respect on the part of liberal observers, was replaced by Ricardo Alzugaray, and a little later the director general of the treasury resigned "because of ill health."[28]

The Center party was still hoping to be joined in opposition to Cánovas by Posada Herrera, but were, as usual, disappointed. Letters from Llanes and supposed interviews with Posada Herrera were the subject of a bitter newspaper controversy.[29] One Constitutionalist organ, *Los Debates*, suggested a reconsideration of fusion between Centralists and Constitutionalists but found opposition from *La Iberia* and *La Mañana* and skepticism from *El Constitutional*.[30] Reports indicated that personal differences between Sagasta and Alonso Martínez were still too strong and on August 7 the Centralist organ *El Parlamento* wrote finis to the concept of fusion and proclaimed the continuance of Posada Herrera as party chief, although the "chief" made no response to the suggestion.[31] Late in August one of the Center party deputies, Alejandro Groizard, met with Sagasta to discuss fusion once again, but found the price to be complete abdication of any independent position—the old party must be restored exactly as it had been.[32]

And despite anticipations all during the fall of 1877 that Posada Herrera might at long last move to take an active role, the man from Llanes once again accepted candidacy for the presidency of the Congress for the coming Cortes sessions![33] His candidacy was, however, short-lived. By the end of January 1878 Posada Herrera changed his mind and announced his intention to retire, withdrawing his candidacy for the presidency of the Congress but giving no indication of his future role.[34] On February 13, 1878, the Center party grouping met again for an inconclusive session. Gen. Juan de Zabala y de la Fuente, who had served as one of the prime ministers under Serrano, was suggested as a possible replacement for Posada Herrera, but final choice was left to the party's directorate.[35] But Zabala at seventy-four would have been too old to lend much fire to the work of the party.

Meanwhile, the monarch and his plans had become for the first time the subject of political controversy. In February 1877, having recovered from one of the early incidences of illness and still looking somewhat pale and wan, Alfonso had visited Albacete, Valencia, Barcelona, and Gerona before boarding a vessel of the Spanish fleet at Las Rosas. Unfavorable receptions in these traditional strongholds of Carlism and republicanism led Cánovas to change governors there, but the king's reception in rural areas was more favorable. With the fleet Alfonso sailed southward to Málaga and Cádiz, showing better seamanship than some of Spain's high naval personnel! Affairs were better arranged in the South where Cánovas attired in gala blue trimmed with gold and a hat bearing the arms of Spain met the monarch.[36]

Even before he set out on this rather lengthy journey, the monarch's marriage plans had become the subject of widely broadcast rumors and discussion. During the days of his exile he had met and fallen in love with the third daughter of the duke of Montpensier, María de las Mercedes. The circumstances of the marriage of Isabella's sister Luisa to Montpensier, his involvement in the Revolution of 1868, and his course of conduct thereafter have already been noted. When the king, therefore, indicated his intention to marry his seventeen-year-old cousin, the plan became the source of bitter controversy. Both Cánovas himself and Manuel Silvela, his foreign minister, had been opposed to the project at the outset but allowed themselves to be persuaded to support the king. English and German reactions to the proposal were lukewarm. The French, of course, favored it.[37]

Most hostile of all was Isabella, who had once accepted the project while in exile, but was now adamantly opposed. The son and the mother engaged in acrid disputes with the queen coming from Seville to the Escorial to make her opposition known not only to the family but to foreign representatives as well and threatening to leave Spain. The controversy continued throughout the fall months of 1877 with the king evidently critical of his mother's life-style and her liaison with the current favorite, Ramiro de la Puente.[38] Before the end of the year Isabella had returned to Paris[39] to cause new scandal there by entertaining the pretender Carlos and his wife Margarita in the Basilewsky Palace. Newspaper stories had the guests being received by Isabella's servants with the title of "majesty" and other high honors.[40] The queen wrote to the Paris satirical newspaper *Figaro* disclaiming any motives other than family friendship, but the letter did not relieve the situation much.[41] One malevolent but not entirely unconvincing explanation of the visit was that Isabella feared she might be brought back to Spain and committed to a sanatorium and wanted sanity witnesses![42] More probably, she was simply venting her spite against her son.

Behind the scenes it was also clear that Cánovas and some of his ministers had opposed the king's marriage plans but had been forced to accept the king's will. The Liberal Conservatives supported the project in the Cortes although with somewhat less than accustomed fervor.[43] Obviously Cánovas would have preferred more of a marriage of state and was to have the opportunity to arrange one long before he anticipated.

The association of the bride's parents with the liberal cause in the earlier period made it difficult for the Moderados to accept the marriage project, particularly so because of their continued emotional attachment to the queen mother, who so publicly opposed the union. After debating the issue throughout the late fall of 1877, the central committee of the party approved the marriage arrangements, but with three negative votes, including that of the party's leader, Claudio Moyano, who indicated his intention of opposing the marriage in the Cortes debates.[44] The actions of Isabella in entertaining Carlos and Margarita added to the party's difficulties. Dealing with these issues brought renewed government action against Moderado newspapers—denounced repeatedly, *La Paz* found no peace and *El Mundo Político* received some justified penalties for a scurrilous letter in verse, "a mi amigo el conde de."[45] One of its jibes pictured Cánovas planning to build a "palace" near that of Adelardo López de Ayala in the elegant new borough of Salamanca. When this was done, suggested the newspaper, the avenue concerned, then called the street of the "pajaritos" ("little birds") should be renamed that of the "pajarracos" ("big, ugly birds"—also "sharp fellows").[46] Again it paid for its wit with a suspension.

Claudio Moyano carried out his threat to oppose the marriage project in the Cortes. He softened his opposition by explaining that it related only to the history of the Montpensier family—their role in the revolutionary period, their opposition to Isabella II, and their advocacy of freedom of religion. His criticism, he said, had nothing to do with Mercedes herself—one doesn't even speak of angels! In the end Moyano was joined by 3 other opposing votes in the Cortes against 311 votes approving.[47]

The proper notifications were made and the royal marriage consummated in state on January 23, 1877. "Mamá" did not attend but the grandmother, María Cristina, and Francisco de Asís did, shrinking, "a little wizened figure, in the depths of a mighty, swaying tortoise shell coach." The wedding was a popular one, gaining for the king the first real signs of genuine enthusiasm—he had married for love "like the poor people do."[48] In spite of her French father there was also some feeling that the bride was really a Spanish princess. The king's sister-in-law had emphasized this when she wrote of María: "She was a real beauty. Her large dark eyes, shadowed by sweeping lashes, her hair of the true Andalusian black, her mouth and delicate complexion made her a real prototype of lovely Spanish womanhood, so delicate and distinguished."[49]

Manuel María de Santa Ana, the founder and director of *La Correspondencia de España*, collected presents for the queen and his newspaper "palace" became a popular place of exposition. The streets of Madrid were filled and all available rooms taken—it was estimated that 80,000 people had come to see the wedding. There were free theaters and three bull-fights with thirty bulls being killed. A great hippodrome (racetrack) was being built, but was not ready for the wedding. Nevertheless, all was gala and gladness.[50]

But the cold wind of the Guadarrama blew through the city during the days of the wedding ceremonies, chilling the bones of the spectators. Perhaps it was an omen. The marriage for love was destined to last only one hundred fifty-four days. Before it ended, the newspapers had followed the last days of the unfortunate Mercedes as her life slowly seeped from her in suffering and anguish.[51] Typhus fever was to be the diagnosis in retrospect, but poor care on the part of her physicians contributed to its fatality.[52] Rumors that the queen had been poisoned were too terrible for the American ambassador to report but not to prevent their appearance in scurrilous republican journals.[53] The second bride of Alfonso would bring from Austria her own physician.

At the time of Mercedes's death she was eighteen, the king twenty. Perhaps for the first time in several centuries there was something of a real popular identification with the monarch in his sorrow. The couplets of a song which became popular then are still well known:

Where do you go, Alfonso XII?
Where do you go in your sadness?
I go in search of Mercedes
Whom I haven't seen since last night.
You, Mercedes, have already died,
You are dead, as I have seen.
Four dukes bore her body
Through the streets of Madrid.
Her face was that of the virgin,
Her little hands were of marble
And the veil which covered her
Was a bright red crimson.[54]

Something of the Spanish passion for tragedy and death now clothed the figure of the young king. The tragic figure of the young monarch sadly roaming the cold halls of the palace at Riofrío became part of the folklore of modern Spain.[55]

During the time of Moderado criticism the government's religious policies had swung a little to the left. In the town of Ignatorf in the province of Jaén, the mayor and two Catholic clerics forced the Catholic baptism of the newborn baby of a Protestant family. After government investigation a royal decree condemned the mayor's action and ordered him not to engage in such measures in the future.[56] Apparently, however, no punitive action was taken.

Another incident occurred in Alcoy in Valencia early in 1878. On this occasion the mother of a Protestant family as she approached death became the pawn in a struggle between the parish priest and the Protestant pastor. When she supposedly consented to take the last rites, her body was taken by the priest and the mayor to the town mortuary. The family, however, remained with the Protestant pastor and he later helped them to recover the body and, with great effort, to obtain a permit allowing the woman to be buried in a Catholic cemetery. But the Protestant pastor was jailed for having disobeyed the mayor when he took the body from him. Although Catholic newspapers reported that the pastor, a Reverend George Simeon Benoliel of the American Baptist Union, had been released the following day, he came to trial late in the year "for impeding the free exercise of the Catholic worship," and was fined sixty pounds and costs. An appeal to the superior court at Valencia obtained a reversal. However, for "insult to the authorities" Benoliel was condemned to two months imprisonment and half the costs.[57] Complaints in respect to his treatment brought the intervention of the British ambassador and a royal pardon.[58] Even the British ambassador, however, considered that the Protestants were seeking to create incidents to embarrass the government.[59]

After Alcoy, religious controversy centered most largely around the plans and policies of Fernando Calderón Collantes. Cánovas had shifted him from the post of foreign minister to that of grace and justice early in 1877.[60] He was probably hoping that this would reduce foreign and domestic criticism of the government's religious policy. But throughout the latter part of 1877 and early part of 1878 Calderón Collantes stirred up an enormous ruckus with a reform of the penal code designed to strengthen and make more rigid the penalties against Protestant religious manifestations. *El Imparcial* carried its criticisms to extremes of vituperation, declaring that Cánovas could not follow Calderón Collantes in this matter without surrendering to the Ultramontanes and calling on the minister of grace and justice to resign. Ministerial newspapers divided on the issue and apparently the code was modified before being adopted.[61] But in spite of all criticism Calderón Collantes retained his post and even received the Order of Castille early in the following year.[62]

Meanwhile, the Constitutionalists, promised thirty senatorships, agreed to end their abstention.[63] Shortly thereafter came the first positive cooperation of the Constitutionalists and Centralists with both groups agreeing to cooperate in votes for the organization of the Congress of Deputies, joining to vote for Sagasta as president and a Centralist candidate for vice-president.[64] But the majority Liberal Conservatives still dominated the Cortes and the poet Adelardo López de Ayala replaced Posada Herrera as president.

The debates in the Cortes during this year of 1878 were dull and uninspiring. The Centralist deputies were less active than they had been during the absence of the Constitutionalists. Alonso Martínez was very much in the background. Alejandro Groizard provided the Center's answer to the speech from the throne, stressing the continuance of dictatorial government.[65] The vitriolic Calderón Collantes responded with new references to the "group of the clock" adding that the term referred to the Centralist position under the clock in the Hall of the Congress, not to any idea that their time had come. He also charged that the group was "perturbadora"—disturbing on the political scene because they left the majority without giving force to the opposition. He compared them, in ill-chosen fashion in view of the political background of his party leader, to the Liberal Union of an earlier day, which he intimated had also been useless.[66]

The Constitutionalists leveled their strongest criticism at budget arrangements with Venancio González denouncing the continued government deficits in his reply to the speech from the throne.[67] A little later the Centralist deputy Javier María Los Arcos provided one of the few devastating exposés of the period as he analyzed government expenditures to build a huge hippodrome (race track) in Madrid. Some funds for the project derived from those assigned in the budget to port improvement, some from those set aside for improvements in livestock breeding, and some from university and educational funds.[68] The minister of development, the count of Toreno, seemed little disturbed by these revelations, suggesting that the expenditure of funds for fiestas (including horse-racing) was perfectly legitimate, that horse-racing tended to improve livestock, and that he had not spent all of the funds allotted to him in any case![69]

Francisco de Paula Candau, also a Center party deputy, made one of the most effective presentations during this Cortes session, challenging Romero Robledo on the prevalence of banditry, on continued removals of municipal officials of opposing political persuasion (most notably in the municipalities of Chiclana, Santander, and Rivadavia), and on the crisis conditions in the treasury and budget arrangements. In the interpellation dealing with the financial problems, he gave one of the most dramatic pictures presented during this relatively quiescent period of the pressures of inflation and the resultant discontent in the cities of Spain.[70]

Romero Robledo, like Calderón Collantes, handled the Center party quite roughly in his responses, on one occasion calling Alonso Martínez into a debate from which he was quite evidently abstaining. Later in the year the minister of the interior went out of his way to deny any positive role to the Center party —Alonso Martínez and his group, he stressed, had never belonged to the majority.[71]

This relatively mild and high-minded political grouping was being buffeted from all sides during this period. *El Imparcial*, in spite of its liberal sympathies, labeled the Center party "a useless wheel."[72] *El Tiempo* criticized the conflicting roles of Alonso Martínez as Moderado, Liberal Unionist, Amadeist, and republican.[73] The putative leader of the Center party also suffered an ironical attack from the government organ, *El Globo*, which traced his varied political history, accused him of hunger for ministerial power, and predicted that he would never be a top leader in any political organization and would be forced to recognize the authority of Sagasta.[74] This was too much for *El Imparcial*, which now defended him from these unjust criticisms, asserting "the rectitude of his intentions and honesty of his motives" as well as his ability as jurisconsult, statesman, orator, and publicist.[75]

Throughout this period the one holdover in the Cortes from republican groups was Emilio Castelar, who had directed Spain's destinies during the conservative stage of the republic. Castelar's orations were always the occasion for filled galleries in the hall of the Congress, as his moving oratory ranged over all of history and all of the European scene to end in denunciation of Cánovas and his ways. James Russell Lowell, the American minister to Spain, provided a picturesque description of Castelar's oratory. Although he found Castelar more eloquent than Cánovas, he reported that Castelar's speeches obscure his subject with a rainbow tinted mist, through which the most familiar objects look strangely unreal. His principles of action (I might almost call them principles of diction) have always, like the goddess of Homer, a convenient cloud into which they withdraw at need from mortal apprehension. But if the use of speech be to move men rather than to persuade them, he is, I am ready to believe, the greatest of contemporary orators and comparable with the greatest of any period.[76]

Lowell's comments underscore Castelar's minimal role in the Restoration period. His artistic performances served to enhance the aura of artificiality in the Cortes, to emphasize that this body functioned more for theater than for authentic parliamentary government.

In this period when it might seem to have been appropriate to have loosened the reins of governmental controls, the Cánovas regime continued and even increased repressive measures. Press denunciations multiplied and discussions began of a very reactionary press law.[77] In spite of long-continued and bitter opposition in the Cortes and in the press, the law became effective on January 7, 1879.[78] It required previous authorization for the founding of a periodical and the founder had to be Spanish, have had two years of residence in the area where the periodical would be published, and pay either 250 pesetas in territorial taxes or 500 in industrial ones. Control over the editor, including deposit of the periodical each day before publication, was, however, absent from the law.

Similarly long discussion over electoral laws finally ended with the publication of a law requiring voters to be contributors to state taxes, either in the form of agricultural taxes of 25 pesetas or industrial ones of 50 pesetas. Freed from this regulation were members of the royal academies and of ecclesiastical councils, government officials receiving at least 2,000 pesetas per year, retired government officials, general officers of the army and navy not in active service, retired military men, sculptors and painters who had won national prizes, professors and masters of all government schools and of primary or secondary schools if officially so designated, notaries, secretaries, and so forth, of courts. Obviously along with the monetary qualification went ability to read and write, but the government had not been willing to accept the latter as the sole requirement.[79]

The government's position in Barcelona during this period was made difficult by its support of an exceedingly high-handed official, Mayor Cástor Ibáñez de Aldecoa. Encountering tremendous resistance to the imposition of high taxes on the consumption of gas, Aldecoa took extreme measures against press criticism, prohibiting the sale of hostile newspapers on the street. A strike of gas workers lasted more than seventy-two days.[80] As opposition continued, trials of those brought in for opposition went before military rather than civil courts.[81] Eventually the government made some concessions, but the impression of dictatorship had been enhanced in one of the most democratic and republican areas of Spain.

Government penal arrangements also carried with them the possibility of preventive arrest of persons considered dangerous to public order.[82] This act may well have had varied objectives. Although the government treatment of the Basque provinces in the wake of the Carlist War had sought a compromise between their former complete autonomy and deprivation of all their special privileges, they were far from being reconciled to defeat.[83] They were already the seat of new industries making them more advantaged than the rest of Spain and resentful of a position in which they seemed to be subsidizing more backward sections of the country. The Carlist Tradition continued strong. The pretender boasted during his trip across Europe in this period that he could still raise an army of 30,000 men if he chose.[84] And the Carlists were not above joining with republicans if it carried the possibility of the destruction of a hated Restoration system.[85]

Catalonia was still the major home of Spanish republicanism. But the Restoration government trampled less harshly on Catalan sensibilities than those of the Basques. And the development and expansion of the cotton industry there tended to tie Catalonia into the national state—the cries for protection of "our poor and feeble industry" could only be satisfied on a national scale and had already begun to win support on the part of both major parties.[86] Nevertheless, republicanism carried with it the lure of greater autonomy and its strength in Barcelona was a continuing cause of governmental concern. Very probably the government often identified republicanism and radicalism with the manifestations of despair on the part of an oppressed working class which was not likely to find either in Catalan nationalism or republicanism any real hope for better treatment.[87]

As has been noted, anarchism had some strength in Catalonia but found its strongest support in the agricultural South. Under severe repression even before the Restoration, the anarchist movement lost some strength in the early years of Alfonso's reign, but did survive. Its continued strength was to become manifest when Cánovas gave way to Sagasta. The Spanish government was not alone in fearing the movement and in regarding it as an offshoot of the First International. The harsh measures employed by Cánovas were similar to those taken by many other European governments. The government also sought, unsuccessfully, to combat the banditry endemic in many parts of Spain. Stagecoach travelers were often in danger and, on occasion, passengers on trains.[89]

Although this was a period of economic expansion, the great masses of rural poor continued to skirt the margins of existence and the growing urban populations found little relief from the misery that came from inflationary pressures on the cost of living.[90] Governmental agencies did little. The only significant thrust for social reform came from a remarkable individual working with government toleration but little support. This was the dramatic advocate of penal reform, the most remarkable woman of Spain during this period, Concepción Arenal. After years of personal effort to alleviate the hardships of prisoners and their families, she did have the opportunity to bring her cause before the king in July 1876 and February 1877. The king was sympathetic and a Committee for Prison Reform was established in

March 1877. But the famous "Model Prison" completed in Madrid at this time was not really a reform and Concepción Arenal spent the latter part of her life seeking to further penitentiary changes and defending the rights of women without "an hysterical feminism." This, too, had little success. Spanish women continued to be the "victims of the egotism of their milieu and of the egotism of men."[91]

Meanwhile, politics was a game played by the more fortunate classes with very limited views of social welfare. The restiveness of the common people contributed to the sense of malaise that existed by the end of the year 1878. Anger and frustration were the consequences of "the dead sea of politics," as Cánovas's opponents characterized his regime.[92]

But the opposition was in considerable disarray. Constitutionalists and Centralists had still found no real meeting of their minds. The Constitutionalists were firmly behind the leadership of Sagasta, but the Center party had not been able to agree upon a leader. Although Alonso Martínez seemed worthy of this designation by his role in the Cortes, his colleagues were not willing to acknowledge his leadership. The Moderados, on their part, were also divided with a considerable portion of its leadership and some of its press revolting against the continued emphasis on religious unity on the part of Miguel Moyano and the extremist newspaper *El Pabellón Nacional*.[93]

But the Liberal Conservative party was not a solid unit either. Francisco Silvela, elected vice-president of the Congress of Deputies by the majority, had in the meetings of that body taken exception to the government sponsored budget, opposing the continued amortization of existing debts by contracting new ones.[94] The sudden firing of officials and rotation of ministers provided grounds for the charges of the liberal press that their opponents were troubled by internal dissension.

But the most serious division among the Liberal Conservatives lay concealed in official communications between the government at home and General Martínez Campos, who had given the government the long-sought victory in Cuba but followed this accomplishment with an increasingly rancorous argument over the administration of Spain's most prized overseas possession. This argument was to bring to Cánovas the most serious crisis he had yet confronted. It also brought to Spain the first call for greatness which had sounded in centuries, a call to which she was not to respond with vigor and energy.

6

Martínez Campos
Versus Cánovas

T HE DULLNESS of the Cánovas regime cast a shadow across the throne as well as across Cánovas himself. Alfonso was considered to be the puppet of the prime minister, sealed off from other influences. Although the drama of the king's romantic loss and his days of sadness at Riofrío gained some popular sympathy, they did not abate the concern over hard times and the continued lure of republicanism. Cánovas himself remarked to the German chargé that he felt the king should "move into the foreground" and the German envoy, Solms, stressed the need for the monarch to be identified with more than a single party. The British ambassador, Sackville-West, was even more forthright: "Although His Majesty has displayed great aptitude in public affairs and is indefatigable in attending to the business of each Department in the Monarchy, still there is wanting that prestige in the Monarchy, as at present constituted, which is necessary to inspire confidence and to obtain support in moments of difficulty." [1]

On October 25, 1878, the king narrowly escaped death from the double-barreled pistol of one Juan Oliva y Moncasi, a barrelmaker from Labra in the province of Tarragona in Catalonia. [2] Although Cánovas immediately labeled the would-be assassin a socialist and internationalist, the event emphasized the necessity of a second marriage of the monarch and of an indisputable succession to the throne. A miscarriage had indicated the likelihood that the first marriage would have been childless even if Mercedes had survived.[3] A male heir to the throne was desperately needed. Alfonso's own health was poor and another female inheritance would kindle the waning fires of Carlism. There was also the fear that the death of Alfonso could bring a controversy over the possible return of Isabella, who continued to be suspected of all sorts of intrigues. Manuel Silvela, talking of her actions with the British ambassador, said frankly she was "not right in her mind."[4]

The king's sadness had apparently found rather early surcease from the presence in Madrid of one of the king's earlier *amantes*, the Viennese contralto Elena Sanz, who was to bear him an illegitimate son early in 1878. Although her claim for this and a second natural son born later caused the state some financial embarrassment at a later date, the existence of these sons augered well for the prospects of an heir.[5] There was, however, always to be concern that the king's gallantry in Madrid, accompanied by vices of drink and tobacco, may have contributed to the rapid progress of the virulent tuberculosis that was to bring him to an early grave.[6]

The king himself looked forward to remarriage with little enthusiasm. This time he was quite willing to accept the demands of state. The choice of an Austrian princess was deemed most appropriate. Since she would be Catholic, there would be no religious problem and a hearkening back to Hapsburg antecedents in Spain might be helpful. Chosen for the delicate negotiations involved was Augusto Conte, a diplomat of long and varied experience not identified with any of the political groupings in Spain. He was, however, quite aware that the government wanted his negotiations in Austria to be successful so that there would be no return to the idea of Alfonso marrying the sister of Mercedes. The king in his interview with Conte suggested that the lady chosen be "discreet, of lady-like bearing, and agreeable even if she didn't possess great beauty."[7]

The lady upon whom fell the choice of the Spanish negotiators was to bear her own shadow of tragedy. Comparing the photographs of the first and second wives gives little if any edge to the first. Far from being a "German amazon" as Alfonso had feared, the Austrian Archduchess María Cristina was by no means an unattractive figure.[8] The description of her by the American minister James Russell Lowell had some of the poetic qualities with which its writer was so richly endowed:

> The new queen attracts sympathy by the gracious cordiality of her manners, her youth, and the dignity of her bearing. She is good looking without being beautiful. She has the projecting chin of her race, though softened in her by feminine delicacy of feature. One seems to see in her a certain resemblance to Marie Antoinette, and she mounts a throne that certainly appears less firm than that of France when her Kinswoman arrived in Paris to share what all believed would be the prosperous fortunes of its heir apparent. Such associations lent a kind of pathos to the unaffected happiness which lighted the face of Maria Cristina.[9]

There had, of course, been for the monarch some temporary zest in the process of choosing a second consort. The death of his grandmother, another María Cristina, in August 1878, and of his favorite sister the Infanta Pilar in April 1879 had slowed the process of courtship. The official meetings of the monarch and his intended took place in August 1879 and they were married in December 1879. It was again a marriage of state attended by all the elaborate trappings of royalty and this time "mamá" attended, but it didn't attract the same popular enthusiasm as the first one. It appears that for María Cristina the marriage was one of love as well as of state. Unfortunately the feeling was not strongly reciprocated. The new queen lacked the passion of the first—"stiff necked" and short-sighted so that she had to wear eyeglasses, she was too much a contrast with María de las Mercedes.[10]

By the time of the marriage the political situation in Spain had greatly altered. The reference of James Russell Lowell to the insecurity of the throne was not without justification. Two months before the assassination attempt of Oliva there had been an effort for a military uprising. The background is unclear. Cristino Martos, who had previously served with Ruiz Zorrilla, persuaded General Serrano to meet with the exiled republican leader in Biarritz. Although the temperaments and backgrounds of the two men were radically different, it appears that Serrano agreed to some cooperation. It is doubtful, however, that Serrano thought in terms either of republicanism or armed revolt. But republican leaders such as Salmerón and liberal generals such as Lagunero and Gándara were set for revolution. Like later risings under Alfonso, this one misfired. On August 8, 1878, one Maj. Isidro Vallarino del Villar raised the cry for the republic and down with taxes in the little village of Navalmoral de la Mata in Cáceres. Some thirty or forty armed men in republican uniforms responded. After moving through several small towns of the region, twenty-four mutineers were arrested; the rest escaped to Portugal.[11]

Although the incident was a minor one, it weighed heavily on the mind of the monarch. In December 1878 the king had one of the first of what was to be a lengthy series of extremely frank and forthright personal conversations with the new German envoy, Klaus Eberhard Theodor, Graf zu Solms-Sonnenwalde.[12] The personality of the monarch is more strongly revealed in these conversations than in any of the biographical sketches which have appeared. Clearly he combined a high degree of political acumen and realism with a certain cynicism, which must have been a saving grace in the midst of the political wonderland of personalism, self-esteem, and hypocrisy which characterized Spain during that period.

The king admitted that he had not been able to establish a completely secure base within the Spanish military. Although he felt that the lower ranks were fairly secure, he was still much concerned about the loyalty of many of those in the overextended group of general officers. Many, he related to Solms, had received promotions when they took part in the revolution against his mother. Many more, including some of those in the first group, had received promotions at the time of his return.

And there were still many who would gladly see another revolution if thereby they received still another promotion. The problem of military loyalty remained a continuing concern throughout the reign of Alfonso XII. During the year which followed it was to assume new and more threatening dimensions due to the replacement of the civilian prime minister Cánovas with his archrival General Martínez Campos.

The end of the year 1878 marked the completion of four years of unremitting pressure and challenge for Cánovas. Although his critics doubted the sincerity of his protestations of weariness, they carry some conviction. Clearly the architect of the Constitution of 1876 was a little troubled by the fact that the Cortes still in existence was that which had been both a constitutional Cortes and an ordinary one.[13] No new elections had followed the promulgation of the constitution. The unremitting pressure of the Constitutionalists for ministerial change also had its effect. Although their embittered references to the Constitution of 1869 had declined and their reservations about the Bourbon restoration had been replaced by impassioned appeals to the monarch to alter the political leadership,[14] Cánovas continued to shy away from an outright transfer of power. The delicate balance he had established between the religious fanaticism of some of the Moderados as well as former Carlists and the liberal quest for religious toleration, the still precarious financial position of the state, the evidence of continuing republicanism in some sections of the country, and the failure of opposition groups to rally around one authoritative leader, as he envisaged the proper role of an opposition, left Cánovas still concerned that a transfer of power to the Constitutionalists might result in a precipitate erosion of stability.

On the other hand there was evidence of problems within the Liberal Conservative regime itself.[15] Romero Robledo controlled the party's political machine. In that area he was without peer, but his qualifications for parliamentary leadership were minimal. Political patronage of an extensive character underlay the internal workings of the system. There were on some occasions public reflections of administrative abuses. Given the nature of the regime, such abuses and any efforts for their rectification were ordinarily hidden from public view. But it may be surmised that at times these became significant enough to result in some of the sudden and seldom explained shiftings of personnel which occurred. How these were determined and by whom is uncertain. The personalism of the Cánovas system transformed government business into a complex pattern of friendships and influence. Not that this was so different from the status of matters in earlier or later Spanish history. But censorship, *caciquismo*, and other aspects of the Cánovas dictatorship drew a heavier veil than ever over the governmental machinery. Nevertheless, there were signs by the end of 1878 that personal rivalries and disgruntlements were appearing within the supposed Cánovas monolith.

More serious than these jostlings at home was the problem of governmental policy in Cuba. Before the arguments over the issue ended, the personalities of Cánovas and his associates and the workings of the Cánovas system had been more clearly revealed than was the case during the whole previous four years of its operation. That which began as a little rumble within the Cánovas machinery became a *cause célèbre*, a governmental crisis of major proportions which underscored the weakness of the Cánovas system, drew opposition groups together in a temporary alliance, and brought the first basic change in governmental orientation since the Restoration. In the course of these peninsular events the Cuban problem found no satisfactory solutions. The second-class status of Cuban citizenship was dramatically underscored and it became obvious that only the independence of the island offered its inhabitants a chance for economic stability.

As has been seen, Cánovas's major rival, Gen. Arsenio Martínez Campos, hero of Sagunto, of La Seo de Urgel, and of the valley of the Baztán, had been sent to Cuba on October 19, 1876. It was hoped that he would be able to succeed where so many had failed. The war on the island had been taking an enormous toll both in Spain and in Cuba itself. Before it was concluded 200,000 lives had been lost and 700 million pesos spent. The weight of these expenses placed on the backs of the Cubans amounted to a public debt of 159 million dollars by 1878, a load of 100 pesos on every Cuban taxpayer.[16]

The Spanish government, thought American minister Caleb Cushing, was looking for more bravery and "dash" when they sent Martínez Campos. Cushing believed in the possibility of success—"he [the general] has the desire, and the genius, to win, and he generally does it." Like everyone in Madrid Cushing was also aware of the general's ambition.[17] One can only speculate whether Cánovas in sending Martínez Campos to Cuba expected him to lose some of his glamor, or whether the prime minister was simply happy to have his rival 3,000 miles away from home base.

But there had been another aspect of Martínez Campos's accomplishments in Spain—the ability to negotiate with and conciliate his enemies, an ability which had greatly facilitated his success in Catalonia.[18] And, as in Catalonia, Martínez Campos began his duties in Cuba with an open policy of "attraction," of offering amnesties and indulgences to the insurrectionists.[19] The military situation had improved: 24,000 reinforcements preceded him and an additional 14,000 accompanied him. He had, therefore, some 70,000 effective troops which he distributed among the eight commands he created.[20]

The methods used by the general were effective counter-guerrilla warfare. The island was divided into "general commands" and each of these subdivided into brigades. A central depository was provided in each zone for food, supplies, and medical treatment. Troops were no longer sent out with heavy equipment and cannon useless in view of the bad roads. Rather they went only lightly encumbered so that the element of surprise was no longer solely on the side of the insurgents. As pacification proceeded in any area, the size of the ranging bands was reduced, first to companies and then to bands of fifteen, spreading out in all directions to seek out those in hiding. For those who surrendered, treatment was generous—the stubbornness of their resistance was attested by their virtually naked and starved condition.[21]

The insurgents were clearly wearied by the long struggle in

which they had engaged and undoubtedly Martínez Campos's proclamations and his reputation for humanitarianism produced an effect. It is also clear that Martínez Campos had been authorized to negotiate directly with the revolutionary leaders, although the extent of the concessions he was entitled to offer remains uncertain.[22] Quite clearly the funds provided by the loan from the Hispanic-Colonial Bank were employed for more than normal military purposes.[23] Then, too, the disposition of the United States to avoid war and the reduced emphasis on annexation must have been known to the revolutionaries.[24]

On February 10, 1878, Martínez Campos's dual policy of decisive military action and direct conciliatory negotiation with the insurrectionary leaders had eventuated in the debatable Peace of Zanjón. Although gratefully received both in Spain and Cuba, there were also critics. General Manuel Salamanca y Negrete, later to be Martínez Campos's most bitter critic in the Cortes, was to call it "an accursed peace," claiming it had been purchased, not won.[25] Its provisions were vague and ambiguous. The first article promised Cubans "the same political conditions, organically and administratively," which were enjoyed in Puerto Rico. This was followed by an amnesty of political offenders since 1868 under the aegis of "a forgetting of the past." Other terms provided for freedom to Asiatic colonists and to slaves who had served in the insurrectionary forces, a moratorium on compulsory military service until peace was fully established, and the promise that the government would facilitate the departure of those who wished to leave the island.[26]

The peace was accepted in the name of the Cuban revolutionaries by Gen. Máximo Gómez and applied everywhere except in those areas where the mulatto insurrectionist Antonio Maceo continued his tenacious resistance. But he, too, came to realize the hopelessness of the situation and, on May 9, surrendered to Martínez Campos and was allowed to leave for Jamaica.[27] There were those among Martínez Campos's critics who believed that there must have been secret clauses beyond the published terms of the peace treaty, but Martínez Campos repeatedly denied this.[28] It must, however, have become obvious to those who negotiated with the general and his agent, Gen. Luis Prendergast, that Martínez Campos envisaged extensive reforms in Cuban affairs during the period to follow.

Until Zanjón administrative responsibilities in Cuba had been exercised by Gen. Joaquín Jovellar. With the conclusion of the peace Martínez Campos replaced Jovellar as governor general of the island and began the series of reports and personal letters which set forth far reaching projects of reform, confronting Cánovas with a new Sagunto—a new crisis in which the general refused to heed the warnings of the civilian leader.[29]

Martínez Campos identified himself strongly with Cuban complaints and Cuban interests. The Peace of Zanjón, he said, must not be "a momentary peace" but "the beginning of a bond of common interest between Spain and her Cuban provinces." The Cubans must not be treated as second-class citizens, "but put on an equality with other Spaniards in everything not inconsistent with their present conditions." He bitterly criticized the evils of prior Spanish administration—"the unfulfilled promises made to the Antilles during various periods," "the evils employed, the poor administration of justice," "the abuses of every sort, the failure to devote anything to the branch of economic development, the exclusion of the natives from every area of the administration," and "the belief of the governments that there was no other means available to them than terror." He also expressed his respect for the revolutionary leaders, including Antonio Maceo, "a mulatto who was once a mule driver and is today a general, who has immense ambition, much valor, and much prestige, and who hides under his rude courtesy a natural talent."

The general emphasized that peace could be preserved only by reforms. A full study of the conditions of property, of slavery, of the penal code, of the Cuban support payments to Spain was in order and efforts must be made to advance public works and promote education. The most pressing need was that of tax reductions. He emphasized "the ill estate of public affairs, the misery in two departments, the poor and bad harvests of the Vuelta Abajo (which almost destroyed the tobacco for two years)" and warned that these conditions aided the maneuvers of some émigrés abroad and intensified "the fear and alarm of the conservative classes." This situation led him to suggest the reduction of the territorial contribution to 10 percent in the rural areas. He recognized that this would bring financial problems but counted it unavoidable.

The heart of his reform proposals, however, was tariff reduction. He regarded Cuba's commercial situation as completely untenable—of its 66 million pesos of products 50 million went to the United States, which was now imposing high tariffs as a reprisal for those of Spain. The only solution Martínez Campos saw was to reduce barriers between Cuba and the home country until the relationship was "almost that of the coastal trade (*casi a cabotaje*)." Spain, he stressed, must get its sugar, tobacco, and coffee from Cuba, not from France, Virginia, and Brazil. His advocacy of these measures was insistent. When letters from Cánovas indicated opposition, Martínez Campos's reply was vehement:

> What advantages does Spain obtain by placing burdens on the products from here? . . . What reasons are there that a province, a part of the whole, rests under a restriction, a burden like this? If it were because Spain produced sugar, coffee, and tobacco for its own consumption, it would be reasonable; but when these articles come from other countries because between the taxes they suffer here and the surcharges imposed upon them there they can't circulate within the home country, absurd, absurd, and absurd.

Martínez Campos indicated that if he could not be assured of the acceptance of his reform proposals by the home government, he was prepared to resign. Alternatively, he suggested that he give up the position of governor general, retaining that of captain general of the island, while Cánovas assumed the role of minister of overseas territories and came to Cuba with a commission charged to investigate the needs of the island and provide for their remedy.

Meanwhile, within the limitations of his authority Martínez Campos initiated a fairly comprehensive series of reforms in

Cuba. The first political assemblies since the time of Ferdinand VII were held and political parties began organization and preparation for the election of representatives to the Cortes. Lands confiscated from former insurrectionists were returned and those who volunteered on the side of Spain also received land. Railroad construction was increased; taxes on cattle, horses, and mules for agricultural production were reduced; aid was given to retrograde mountain areas; and there was also some beginning in the reform of financial administration.[30] Although the content of the letters he sent back to Spain was not made public at this time, the thrust of the general for reform was clear and his popularity in Cuba was great.[31]

The strength and vigor of Martínez Campos's reform proposals shocked the Cánovas government. Not only was the general advocating tax reductions which would occasion enormous difficulties for the home country even if pursued on a temporary basis, he was also implying that permanent concessions would be necessary for taxation and trade. In the light of the enormous expense associated with the Carlist War at home and the Ten Years War in Cuba, Cánovas could not conceive how devastating deficits could be avoided. He was also acutely aware that Martínez Campos's suggestions for commercial reform would run counter to the interests of powerful and influential economic groups at home.

Under these circumstances Martínez Campos's advocacy of fundamental reforms in Cuban-Spanish relationships confronted Cánovas with a real dilemma. Could he allow Spain's most prestigious general to bombard the government at home with unfulfilled pleas for reform, so that a new insurrection, if it came, would discredit the civilian regime and underscore the prescience of the military? Could he bring Martínez Campos into his own government as minister of war, as the general suggested in his correspondence, without creating enormous dissension within the cabinet and weakening his own prestige?[32]

Cánovas found a third and more devious expedient. Late in January 1879 Martínez Campos was recalled from Cuba still expecting to enter Cánovas's cabinet as minister of war. He arrived in Madrid on February 28 and by March 8, after a swirl of political consultations, found himself president of a cabinet with a strong Cánovist tone. Cánovas had exerted his personal influence to bring two of his closest political followers to accept membership in the cabinet—the marquis of Orovio as treasury minister and the count of Toreno as minister of development.[33] Also Cánovas's choice was the minister of overseas affairs, Salvador Albacete, previously a subsecretary in that ministry. A former Moderado who had accompanied Queen Isabella II during the first stage of her exile, Albacete was a man of courtly manners and cultured background, but had no great ambitions and lacked sufficient enthusiasm and preparation for the great task he was undertaking.[34] In retrospect the whole process of cabinet formation indicated Cánovas's intention to give Martínez Campos apparent responsibility for the conduct of government, including the effectuation of Cuban reforms, while effectively restraining him from carrying out the ambitious program he had projected in his correspondence. The general's political inexperience was strongly reflected in his assumption that Cánovas now intended to support his reform program.

Martínez Campos's own political stance was undefined. Many observers counted him close to the Moderados—there had been talk that he resented Cánovas's somewhat cavalier treatment of the former queen—and the Moderados looked to better relations with him than with Cánovas.[35] On the other hand, Martínez Campos's record both in Catalonia and Cuba had been a liberal one. Six months earlier the prestigious liberal newspaper *El Imparcial* had pointed to his liberalism in Cuba shown "not in words but in deeds, not in promises, but in realities. There [in Cuba] no periodicals are denounced, nor is there suspicion in respect to the democrats, or special judgments and preferences in respect to this or that opposition group." The general, said *El Imparcial*, was "more liberal, more sympathetic to democratic tendencies" than Cánovas.[36]

Some of the liberal thrust was reflected in the early days of the new government. The new minister of the interior was Francisco Silvela, an able Madrid lawyer, whose brother had been minister of foreign affairs under Cánovas. Silvela was one of the few political leaders of the era who preserved a reputation of impeccable integrity.[37] He quickly aroused the ire of Romero Robledo with changes of personnel in the ministry and the transfer of a "Special Treasury of Beneficences" from the Ministry of the Interior to the Treasury.[38] The advent of the new government had been accompanied with the dissolution of the Cortes and preparations for new elections. Although Silvela stressed the continuity between the Cánovas cabinet and that of Martínez Campos in his circular to the civil governors, his electoral instructions accorded freedom of action to all citizens without a mention of legal or illegal parties.[39] After five years of silence the Progressive Democratic party led by Cristino Martos met in Madrid, extended greetings to the exiled republican Manuel Ruiz Zorrilla, and, with some dissension, agreed to take part in the new elections.[40] Denunciations of newspapers continued, but they were less numerous and indulgences freeing those suspended increased.[41]

The stance of the Martínez Campos government, therefore, appeared somewhat more liberal than that of Cánovas, but there was no real atmosphere of political change. The meeting of the party on May 31, 1879, prior to the opening of the Cortes, breathed an atmosphere of sweetness and light, with Martínez Campos paying tribute to the previous ministry and using the term "Conservative Liberal" in respect to the party to emphasize his separation from its critics.[42] Cánovas, in turn, proclaimed that he would be "the first, the most loyal, the most subordinate, and the most firm" of the government's supporters.[43] But there were clouds on the horizon—over 100 deputies in the newly elected Congress of Deputies were unqualified supporters of Romero Robledo increasingly hostile to Silvela;[44] most personal friends of Martínez Campos who had campaigned for seats in the Cortes had been defeated;[45] and both Centralists and Constitutionalists regarded the government as nothing but an interim expedient devised by Cánovas.[46]

The first session of the Cortes ran from June 1 to July 26, 1879. Subjects other than Cuba predominated, although the abolition of slavery received some attention. The most significant action passed by with little notice. A royal decree of July 11 lowered the direct taxes on nonsugar plantations to 16 percent and those on sugar plantations to 2 percent. In the controversies of the following year it was revealed that this was the beginning of Cánovas's realization that his experiment with the Martínez Campos government was dangerous.[47] But the press paid more attention to General Salamanca's virulent attacks on the Peace of Zanjón[48] and to the antics of Romero Robledo's supporters, "the Hussars of Antequera," who displayed considerable hostility to Silvela.[49] Discussion of the abolition of slavery began with Martínez Campos stressing the promises implied in the Peace of Zanjón and the deputy for Cuba Rafael María de Labra providing emotional support.[50] Cánovas gave every indication of keeping his promise of strong support and the session ended with charges that the ministry was a "protectorate" of the party leader.[51]

Under the surface it was clear to observers that there were serious divisions among the members of the majority and the vacation period between the Cortes sessions gave evidence that the course of Cuban reforms would be a troubled one. Romero Robledo, already involved in a tiff with Silvela in the Cortes, was alleged to be strongly opposed to the abolition of slavery on the island.[52] His friendships and personal relationships with the owners of large sugar plantations were well known and the vacation period saw him receiving a tumultuous reception in Catalonia.[53] Cánovas was reputed to favor the abolition of slavery in Cuba but to be hostile to major commercial reform. His vacation period also took him to Catalonia, where he was received by his industrialist friend Manuel Girona and by Senator Fernando Puig y Givert, also an ardent defender of the cause of Catalan manufacturers. Under the auspices of his friends Cánovas visited factories and made inquiries into the causes of the industrial crisis then existing in Catalonia.[54] Widespread rumors also circulated of the strong dissidence of Treasury Minister Orovio and of the less pronounced opposition of the count of Toreno.[55]

Moreover, some of the strength of the government position

was sapped by a new outbreak of revolution in Cuba, the so-called "Guerra Chiquita" or "Little War."[56] Although this was of very limited scope and government forces in Cuba took rapid and effective action, the appearance of the names of some of the insurrectionists who had been involved in the negotiations for the Peace of Zanjón undercut the government's demand for a loyal observation of its provisions and the fulfillment of its spirit.[57]

On November 3 the Cortes resumed its sessions. This time the Cuban issue highlighted the sessions. General Salamanca renewed his bludgeoning of the Peace of Zanjón.[58] The economic proposals of the government, looking to the end of tariffs on products from Spain by 1883 and the reduction of Cuban tariffs on the import of foodstuffs became known.[59] Martínez Campos sought to separate his program from any relationship to the Peace of Zanjón—his program, he said, derived not from the treaty but from the necessities of Cuba.[60] Behind the scenes there were arduous negotiations among party members. On November 16 Cánovas let it be understood that all party problems had been solved.[61] Presumably the Senate project for abolition would contain some modifications making it more palatable to Romero Robledo. It was, therefore, something of a shock when Martínez Campos raised new objections on November 20—later events suggest that the principal issue was that of combining economic reforms with the abolition project.[62] By the report of friends, Cánovas and Romero Robledo now considered themselves free to act in opposition and the fall of the cabinet seemed inevitable.[63]

The crisis was, however, temporarily postponed due to the approaching second marriage of the monarch. Although Martínez Campos was disposed to resign, he made known his anger at the party magnates who had been aware of his position when he assumed the ministry and his feeling that their actions had compromised his personal dignity.[64] Nevertheless, he met with Cánovas on the night of November 27 and apparently achieved some reconciliation on the question of the abolition of slavery but struck strong objections to his proposals for economic reforms and his desire to present them to the Cortes along with the abolition project in a sort of "package deal."[65]

The breach between Cánovas and Martínez Campos was now irreconcilable. On the night of December 7 came the fall of the cabinet on the issue of the Cuban budget prepared by Albacete. Orovio led the opposition with the charge that the budget was *indotado*, not covered by sufficient tax support to avoid a deficit. Toreno agreed and Martínez Campos confronted also the unexpected defection of Silvela, who told him the projects had no chance of getting through the Cortes and that he would not be willing to captain new elections.[66]

The resignation of Martínez Campos came at a time when the twenty-nine deputies and senators from Cuba and Puerto Rico were unanimously behind him and when Gen. Ramón Blanco y Erenas had telegraphed news of progress in the suppression of the new insurrection in Cuba.[67] It also came in spite of hints by the king that he might support an alternate ministry headed by Martínez Campos. Obviously without a strong leader for new elections, this would be useless.[68] An effort by the king to form an alternate ministry under the enigmatic quasi Centralist José Posada Herrera met failure, and on December 9, 1879, Cánovas returned with a cabinet similar to that of the previous March.[69] The able but controversial José de Elduayen as minister of overseas territories would now assume the task of resolving the sticky question of Cuban reform.

The new cabinet confronted a campaign of virulent recriminations surrounding the fall of the Martínez Campos government. In the Senate the fallen general did not hesitate to express his anger at the course of events.[70] Debates in the Congress of Deputies were delayed by a ludicrous incident in which Cánovas, who had promised to meet opposition debate in the Senate, rudely left the lower house, "putting on his hat" and departing precipitately without, as the opposition deputies felt, showing proper respect for the house.[71] For over a month, as a consequence, they abstained from attendance until Cánovas made a halfway acceptable explanation of the incident.[72] The height of the debate over Cuban reforms, therefore, stretched from the middle of January 1880 to the end of June of that year, carrying with it acrimonious personalities as much as a real discussion of issues and resulting in a major alteration of political alignments on the left of Cánovas's Liberal Conservative party.

It should be noted that the forensic encounters involved were of real significance in the Spanish political scene. Although the Cortes was the product of a "made election" (the one captained by Francisco Silvela somewhat less rigidly than the previous one by Romero Robledo, but still tilted drastically to the advantage of the Liberal Conservatives), the encounters on the floor of the Congress of Deputies and the Senate provided the only really free opportunity for the statement of opposition viewpoints. At times there was almost as much interest in the proceedings as there was in the action in the bull ring in Madrid. There was also something of a similarity in the conduct of affairs. The orators were to state their points with words of grace and beauty. The charge of the opposition against the administration *toreros* was to be met with verbal *faenzas*, *pasos natural*, and *pasos de peche*. The *olé*'s of the bull ring were replaced by the more polite *muy bien*'s of one's friends. But buried in all the rhetoric there was a considerable amount of factual material. [73]

On the side of personalities Martínez Campos and Cánovas exchanged fire over a field of issues ranging from the significance of the Pronunciamiento of Sagunto to the circumstances surrounding the creation and fall of the Martínez Campos government. [74] In these debates Martínez Campos revealed a remarkable development in oratorical style, meeting Cánovas, who was respected by both friends and foes for his mastery of the forensic game, on a basis of equality. [75]

The basic issues in respect to Cuban reform came through somewhat less clearly than the personalities! The law for the abolition of slavery which Martínez Campos had agreed to was adopted by the Cánovas government and carried through with little apparent change. [76] The freed slaves were placed under a "patronage" system amounting to police surveillance of ill-paid labor. Contrary to the expectation of the government, five Cuban senators opposed the project, explaining that the government had promised to submit its project of economic reforms at the same time.[77] In the final vote in the Senate only 148 members participated, less than half of those admitted to membership, a debatable quorum.[78] Clearly the law involved considerable internal opposition within the majority party. There were still fears on the part of the sugar plantation owners of a loss of cheap labor without an assurance of a betterment of tax and market conditions.[79] A serious question raised by liberal Cuban leaders and Cristino Martos of the Spanish Progressive Democratic party was the charge that the law endangered the status of thirty to forty thousand free Negroes, who might be included under the patronage system and even become subject to corporal punishment.[80]

The debate over the economic reforms was much more complex and much more rancorous than that concerned with slavery. It made it clear that the Martínez Campos government had fallen over the issue of a draft budget not yet placed into final form. Albacete stated in the course of the debates that he had proposed the continuation of the reduction in direct taxes on plantations which had been set forth in the royal decree of July 11, 1879, along with the gradual reduction of tariff duties over a five-year period. Rates on peninsular wheat imported into Cuba were also to be reduced from the existing 35 percent *ad valorem* duty to free entry in five years time. Nothing in his program, he stressed, was actually anti-Catalan. His budget, he stated, had preserved the export taxes on sugar and he maintained that with economies in the military side of the budget and a renegotiation of the loan involving the Hispanic-Colonial Bank, there would have been not a deficit but a surplus.[81]

The most significant issue in Albacete's program was that of tariff reduction. Martínez Campos read into the record the vehement letters he had addressed to the home government from Cuba. The heart of his reform proposals had been the reduction of tariff barriers "*casi a cabotaje*," almost to the level of the coastal trade, and Albacete's budget was clearly headed in that direction. In the discussions of Albacete's budget and in the later Cortes debates the *casi* dropped from the scene and *cabotaje* became an emotional platform, a *bandera* for its supporters and the target of its opponents. Since both Silvela and Martínez Campos had suggested the possibility of compromise on specific budget terms, it is clear that Orovio and Toreno, speaking in behalf of Cánovas, Elduayen, and other party leaders, were opposed to any suggestion of a possible adoption of the principle of *cabotaje*.[82] Undoubtedly the potential damage to the interests of Spanish sugar growers and Catalan manufacturers and shippers, with the consequent loss of their political support, weighed heavily in the decision of party leaders.

The issue of the Hispanic-Colonial Bank was a complex one. It had provided the earlier Cánovas government with the last loan obtained in 1876 under very severe conditions—it was to be repaid in five years at an interest of 12 percent and the bank was given first claim over all tariff duties collected in Cuba over twenty-two and a half million pesos and was to be indemnified if the tariff were reduced. Harsh as these conditions were, critics recognized the poor state of government finances at the time as some justification and acknowledged the assistance provided by the loan in bringing the war to a close. But one well informed critic raised the question whether the returns from the loan had come to the state in the form of hard money or, as he had heard, in the form of depreciated treasury notes! If the latter case were true, then enormous profits had accrued to those involved with the bank.[83]

The debate over the fall of the Martínez Campos government merged without a real break into the debate on the Cuban governmental budget presented by the Cánovas ministry. The author of this new budget was José de Elduayen and he began the debate on it, but moved shortly afterward to the Ministry of Foreign Affairs, being replaced in the Ministry of Overseas Territories by Cayetano Sánchez Bustillo.

Elduayen's budget was portrayed as setting forth the Cánovas reform program for Cuba.[84] In analysis it did contain some notable concessions. The basic budget set forth rates for direct taxes of 16 percent for urban or industrial wealth, 10 percent for agricultural. Export taxes on sugar coming to the peninsula were canceled and those on other products reduced 10 percent. There was also a 25 percent reduction on import charges on primary foodstuffs. These concessions were, however, offset in part by surcharges to cover debt services and there was a lengthy section of the *dictamen*, or justification of the budget, which repudiated all concepts of *cabotaje* and defended the interests of peninsular sugar growers.[85]

Elduayen did succeed, probably by compromise concessions, in getting three Cuban members of the Cortes commission to sign the budget proposal, although they took little part in the debates.[86] He also received some grudging admission from opponents that there were concessions, although these same opponents found his budget as *indotado*, subject to deficits, as that of Albacete. Lacking in the budget or its support statement, however, was any tone of real concern for Cuban interests—rather it told the Cubans that they were really better off in many respects than peninsular Spaniards.[87]

One notable feature was the canceling of the loan contract with the Hispanic-Colonial Bank, an action which Elduayen had earlier proposed. How the special clauses of the loan contract giving particular guarantees to the bank were handled was not disclosed—very probably some additional payment was made.[88] The government did also promise (and carried out the promise) to initiate commercial negotiations with the United States for the reduction of import duties on wheat coming to Cuba (set at 12.5 percent) in return for a reciprocal reduction in United States' sugar tariffs. These negotiations were, however, to drag on into 1884 without bearing fruit.[89]

Absent, of course, were any government proclamations of projects for reforming the Cuban administration, for a reduction of the dead weight of state bureaucracy there, for using Cubans in administrative posts, for cutting down on the salary differential between Cuban and Spanish administrative positions, for working for a conciliation of the races, for bringing to the Cubans a real sense of identification with the homeland, a genuine feeling that Cuba was a province of Spain, and that Cubans had whatever rights and privileges this entailed. The small insurrection virtually extinguished by the time of these debates was used as an excuse for the continuation of emergency laws and sterile arguments were set forth as to why the Constitution of 1876 did or did not apply in full to the island.

Basically, of course, the cause of Cuban reform was dead before the beginning of this momentous debate. But the might-have-beens were strongly underscored. First and foremost was the fervent support given Martínez Campos by the Cuban deputies. One deputy dramatically portrayed the general's charismatic appeal as he proclaimed in the lower house: "It should not be said that he had no program. General Martínez Campos did not need to write and distribute programs; he was his own program; he was the personality most prominent in that situation, and he was nothing other than the [personification of the] reforms." [90]

Secondly, the virtually unanimous support of the Spanish generals for Martínez Campos underscored their disillusionment with the struggle in Cuba. The list of the general's "friends" included Gen. José Gutiérrez de la Concha, entitled the marquis of la Habana for long and significant service there beginning in 1850; Gen. Blas de Villate y la Hera, count of Valmaseda, who had entered service in Cuba even earlier than Concha and left the ranks of the Moderados to support Martínez Campos; Gen. Joaquín Jovellar, who had preceded Martínez Campos in his second term as governor general; Gen. Manuel Cassola; Gen. José Luis Riquelme; even the stiff and autocratic Gen. José Laureano Sanz y Posse, who knew well the problems of Cuba from long experience in Puerto Rico; and, of course, Generals Luis Prendergast y Gordon and Luis Dabán, who had served with Martínez Campos in Cuba. Gen. José López Domínguez gave early support for the sake of liberalism; his uncle, Gen. Francisco Serrano, duke of la Torre, had been an early advocate of Cuban reform and later gave Martínez Campos his personal support. The duke of Tetuan and Adm. Francisco de Paula Pavía y Pavía had been loyal cabinet members under Martínez Campos. [91]

Obviously, the Constitutionalists and other anti-Cánovas

groups joined in the attacks on the Cánovas ministry although their real zeal for Cuban reforms may be doubted. The existence of this large group of prestigious leaders hostile to the Cánovas regime provided the motive power for a fundamental alteration of the Spanish political scene. Largely under the inspiration and mediatory action of Manuel Alonso Martínez, a movement for the fusion of all opposition groups got underway and resulted in a temporarily successful combination of forces including Martínez Campos and his friends, the Centralists, the Constitutionalists, and two deserters from the ranks of the right-wing Moderados, the count of Valmaseda and the count of Xiquena.[92] Democratic representatives such as Martos had supported Martínez Campos's reforms but did not join the Fusionist grouping.[93]

Throughout the remainder of the year 1880 and into 1881 the turmoil awakened by the new Fusionist grouping continued. Although the "Guerra Chiquita" in Cuba was ended on June 29, 1880, it was obvious that Cuban problems had not been solved. Cánovas presided over a Congress on Morocco in Madrid in May–June 1880 but could not claim a diplomatic victory from the outcome.[94] Romero Robledo still controlled the provincial elections taking place in the summer of 1880 except in the Basque provinces, where the continuance of Carlist sentiment was revealed. And Alejandro Pidal y Mon began the move which would later take many of his fellow Moderados into the Cánovas camp.[95]

The opening of the Cortes late in December saw the speech from the throne, written of course by Cánovas, met with strong denunciation by Sagasta and his fellow Fusionists, with the king shortly thereafter displaying special cordiality to Sagasta and Alonso Martínez.[96] On February 7, 1881, the monarch for the first time since the Restoration exercised his royal prerogative to withdraw confidence from Cánovas and call Sagasta to head the government. Although Spanish historians have often portrayed this move as masterminded by Cánovas, there is strong evidence that the king made the change on his own initiative.

The story of this first major independent action of the monarch is strikingly revealed in the diplomatic dispatches of the

British and German representatives. At the outset the king had been irked by Martínez Campos's political role. He told the German envoy that he was going to make every effort to remove the general from the Cortes because he thought it all-important to get the army out of politics. A few months later the British ambassador was reporting that the king was completely in the hands of Cánovas's supporters and excluded from "all influences which might tend to any initiative on his part." Both British and German representatives expressed their concern for the separation of the king and the military. The kaiser was aghast at the situation and conveyed personal orders to his envoy that he was to see the king and stress the importance of a close relationship with the military. Solms tried, but did not find the monarch at that time very enthusiastic about military affairs. Nevertheless, when Cánovas's fall did come, Solms was assured on what he considered reliable information that it was not a planned affair and that the king acted on his own initiative, with concern for the position of the military being the decisive factor.[97]

Sympathy for the liberal cause also played a role. Although the king was supposed on this occasion to have said, "The liberals are like the measles; one must suffer through them at least once in one's lifetime,"[98] the monarch's statements in the years that followed reflected a genuine desire to adopt a liberal position.

But the change to liberal leadership was not to aid the cause of Cuban reform. Although there was renewed lip-service to *cabotaje*, the implementation was niggardly and unsuccessful, and Martínez Campos, serving in successive cabinets and other political posts, did not return to Cuba until after the outbreak of the ultimate revolt in 1895.[99] Long before then the charisma of the general had faded and the disillusion of the Cubans set them on the path to independence.

The cause of Cuban reform had foundered on the shoals of internal Spanish politics. Cánovas, who was in so many ways a realistic statesman seeking to shake Spain loose from the dead ties of the past, fell far short of the mark of a statesman on this issue. There were, of course, valid reasons for his shortcomings.

First of all, the personal issue was significant. Cánovas considered his own prestige vital for the maintenance of the Restoration monarchy and Martínez Campos was a clear threat to that prestige. Secondly, Cánovas regarded the reduction of military influence as a prerequisite for stable government. His deep fear of military coups is evident throughout the early years of the Restoration. Martínez Campos had evaded his wishes at Sagunto. If he now became the savior of Spain in Cuba, the country might well begin another era of military caudillos. Thirdly, significant economic interests stood strongly opposed to change —the financial interests profiting on government loans; the wheat growers who feared the loss of the Cuban market to the United States; shippers who profited from Spain's differential flag duties by carrying the products of the United States to Spain where they were "nationalized" and carried back to Cuba under the Spanish flag for a cheaper entry than if they had come directly from the United States;[100] sugar interests which wished to develop peninsular production and peninsular refineries;[101] and Catalan industrialists who exploited the protected Cuban market rather than seeking to meet competition from abroad. And these interests had strong ties to formidable leaders of Cánovas's party —the cost of acceptance of Martínez Campos's program would have been the division of the Liberal Conservative party, which Cánovas had formed as the cornerstone of the new system, one of the two great parties he visualized as alternating in Spain as occurred in England.

Cánovas sought for compromise, but wearied when success was almost obtained. He kept close control over the king, although the young monarch became increasingly concerned and finally did intervene. And, most serious of all, the exasperation of dealing with the powerful opposition led to a tone in the debates which could not help but wound Cuban sensibilities. Romero Robledo once told Labra in the Cortes that Cubans should be glad to have from Spain her "name, language, banner, traditions, and the means to belong to a cultured and civilized country."[102] But the weakness of Spain's civilized impulses, the selfishness of her economic interests, and the lack of vision of her political leaders had been strikingly underscored in these events. Had Cánovas followed Martínez Campos's suggestion of heading a mission to Cuba for on-the-spot investigation of reforms, had he possessed the will and courage to make a real trial of Martínez Campos's *cabotaje*, had he had the vision and the self-abnegation to join his own charisma with that of Martínez Campos in fundamental economic reforms within Spain as well as in Cuba, both would have been enormously strengthened in the period that followed and the partnership might have endured. One of Cánovas's biographers summarized this tragic period when he wrote: "The Peace of Zanjón offered us the one occasion which contemporary history presented to leave America with glory and honor, but the directing classes and public opinion turned their backs on it because of ignorance, indolence, and bad faith, committing the gravest and most transcendental error of the nineteenth century." [103]

7

Liberal Interlude: The Trial of "Fusionism"

HE FIRST REAL CHANGE in government under the Restoration had come with the personal intervention of the monarch. Observers believed that the king's action had been triggered most largely by the fear of a new military pronunciamiento. He was later quoted as having said that if he maintained Cánovas in power, "he should sooner or later have been forced to put himself at the head of the troops in order to dominate the popular movement." And the British Ambassador, Lionel Sackville-West, feared that the crisis had resulted in "the successful reassertion of the military element as the source of political power in this country." But he also reported that the king's "promptitude and decision" had won him increased personal prestige, confirming his freedom from "the reactionary influence of his sister, the Infanta Isabella" and from court intrigue.[1]

As will be seen, it was not the military but the monarch who was from this point on the only potential source of a cabinet

change if it involved the alternation of parties. He was the ultimate arbiter of Spanish politics. But Alfonso XII was to prove
himself cautious in the use of these powers. He never forgot
that he was a constitutional monarch, that he was supposed to
remain in the background of politics and allow the responsible
ministers to carry out their governmental obligations. There
were to be times when he had some regrets in respect to this
position, but caution and moderation led him to intervene only
when he was convinced that the stability of the state and the
welfare of the country required it.

The fall of Cánovas concluded over six years during which
"the architect of the Restoration" had dominated affairs in Spain.
He had established the new government, provided it with a
constitutional framework, freed it from the civil war in Spain
and in Cuba, and defended it against all potential dangers. All
in all his regime had been mild with respect to most of its enemies, but the aura of dictatorship had never been absent. The
promise of a pacific exchange of authority had been long delayed
and the existence of "administrative irregularities," which elsewhere would have been labeled corruption, was universally
known—even within the royal palace.

There was, therefore, a sense of relief and an anticipation of
better times with the advent of change. Even the king found the
release from "papa" Cánovas's tutelage welcome. But disappointment was quick to follow. Politics in Spain fulfilled the French
adage, "le plus ça change, plus c'est la même chose," "the more
the change, the more things are the same." The Liberal coalition
was short-lived. With division came an excessive lightening of
controls. And just less than three years later Cánovas was to
return to restore stability and guide the state during the king's
last troubled days of rule.

Sagasta, who led the new government, had been in politics
for twenty years before the Restoration. Whatever inclination he
may once have had for engineering pursuits had long since disappeared. Unlike Cánovas he had no real interests secondary to
his preoccupation with politics. And like most Spanish politi-
cians of the period his sense of self-esteem was highly inflated—

a comparison with Cánovas leaves little if any advantage to the Liberal leader. Dark and rough in appearance, reflecting a peasantlike shrewdness and never looking as though he would feel at home in a monarchical parliament, Sagasta exuded much more the atmosphere of a professional politician than did his rival.[2]

Sagasta's first cabinet reflected the coalition character of the Fusionist grouping which had brought Cánovas's downfall. Martínez Campos as minister of war and Rear Admiral Francisco de Paula Pavía y Pavía as minister of the navy represented the dissident military groups and tended to provide a guarantee against dangers to the dynasty.[3] Alonso Martínez's legal talents as well as his position in the Center party were recognized in his post as minister of grace and justice. Another Centralist but a close friend of Sagasta and firmly in his camp from this point on was Antonio de Aguilar y Correa, marquis of la Vega de Armijo, a liberal grandee capable of providing splendid hospitality for the king, who became foreign minister. Sagasta's replacement for Romero Robledo, to be the "Great Elector" for the Liberals, was Venancio González, a lawyer with long political experience. Returning to the Treasury Ministry, which he had held under a previous Sagasta cabinet, was Juan Francisco Camacho, to prove one of the ablest but also the most controversial of the new cabinet members. The well known publisher, editor of the *Revista de España*, José Luis Albareda, became minister of development and the distinguished Constitutionalist deputy Fernando de Léon y Castillo became the minister of overseas territories.[4] Not represented in the cabinet and apparently ignored in its formation was the duke of la Torre, Marshal Serrano.[5] The repercussions from this neglect were not to be long delayed.

The first weeks of the new government had all the bliss of a honeymoon. The government promised amnesty to political émigrés and opened the way for political meetings and banquets of the republican parties. The suspension of newspapers condemned for press offenses was lifted and charges pending against others were retired. Those university professors who had been dismissed during the days of the marquis of Orovio's period as minister of development were reinstated and academic freedom promised—subject, however, to a prohibition against injury or calumny.[6]

Sagasta also won favor with the royal family by several of his early actions. The recognition of the Princess María de las Mercedes as princess of Asturias, which Cánovas had postponed in hope of a male heir, made clear the succession to the throne.[7] From this point on it was well known that María Cristina preferred the Liberal statesman to his Conservative predecessor. Isabella II was also permitted to return to Spain and wrote appreciatively of her happiness at seeing Sagasta "at the side of my son."[8] Sagasta's first speech in the Cortes emphasized his firm adherence to the throne. Behind the scenes it was also to be clear that the young monarch gained a much greater degree of personal freedom than he had enjoyed under Cánovas and took a much more active role in the affairs of state. The king hoped that the change to the Liberals might also be accompanied by a reduction of the corruption which had been attached to the Cánovas regime, although he was to be disappointed in this respect.[9]

It could not really have been anticipated that Sagasta and his party could avoid the pent-up quest for office within party ranks. *Empleomania*, the mad pursuit of government employment, affected the Liberals as much as it had the Conservatives. The press for new jobs was so great that Sagasta had to leave his own home during one night. Within two weeks all subsecretaries of the ministries and state council, seven directors in the Ministry of the Interior, forty-seven civil governors, the chief justice of the press court, the chief justice of the supreme court, the four director generals in the Ministry of War, three captain generals, and most of the directors in the Ministries of the Navy, of Overseas Territories, of Finance, and of Development had resigned, either voluntarily or under pressure.[10]

This rapid vacating of municipal, regional, and national offices created a large class of out-of-office bureaucrats, the *cesantes*, waiting anxiously for the opportunity to get back "in" and, if possible, recoup the financial loss they had suffered. The wisdom of the king's opposition to the wholesale change of officials was amply demonstrated in the years which followed.

Meanwhile, Venancio González as minister of the interior displayed all of the astuteness and disregard of fair play in election management that had marked his predecessor, Romero Robledo. Government candidates won by a margin of almost seven to one in the municipal elections of May 3, 1881. The Cortes elections held on August 20 and September 2 also provided the Liberals with a more than secure control of parliamentary affairs so long as they cooperated. But the practice of leaving the opposition with an effective representation to present their views in the public forum continued. And the opposition raised the same cry against unfair and illegal election practices which they themselves had confronted in previous years.[11]

However, the "Fusion" of varying forces which had brought the fall of the Cánovas regime was by no means a solid union. *La Epoca*, the leading opposition paper, maliciously called it "a union of antipathies, intolerances, passions, and hatreds."[12] Perhaps this was extreme, but the gestures of the regime toward lightening political restraints and liquidating the Cánovas dictatorship unleashed a variety of forces which created political confusion, social unrest, and later open rebellion against the government. Events seemed to confirm the thesis that a Liberal government could not be trusted to preserve peace and order.

One of the earliest consequences of the change of government was a renewed activity of the so-called "democratic" forces both inside and outside Spain. Those who used this term were in a quandary as to whether "democracy" could be sought under monarchical aegis or could exist only under a republic. The Cánovas regime had, of course, considered illegal any political grouping which did not accept the established institutions of the state—the monarchy and the church. The Liberals removed the distinction between legal and illegal parties and a series of meetings and banquets began in Biarritz in France and then within Spain. By July 2 the Democratic-Progressive party was officially organized in Madrid in the house of Cristino Martos, including a number of leaders from the days of the republic and still uncertain whether to take part in the approaching Cortes elections. The choice between campaigning, which would seem to accept the existing institutions, or abstaining was left to the separate districts. On July 22 the party chose as its president Laureano Figuerola, who had been professor of economics at the University of Madrid, along with two other professors, Gumersindo de Azcárate and Eugenio Montero Ríos. Their acknowledgment of the inspiration of Ruiz Zorrilla, who rebuffed government efforts for reconciliation and remained in exile in Paris, indicated that the party was far from dropping its republican sympathies.[13]

On the other hand, Emilio Castelar, who had also been a president during the republican era but had served in the Cortes all through the Cánovas regime, seemed to present a different approach. In a letter to a well known French journalist, Emilio Girardin, Castelar paid tribute to the accomplishments of the Cánovas government, the stabilization of the country, and the end of the civil wars in Cuba and in Spain, but suggested that the Sagasta government now presented the possibility of crowning these accomplishments with the laurel wreath of liberty.[14] In this letter and in the events that followed Castelar became associated with the word *posibilista*, implying the "possibility" of obtaining the advantages of a republic under the aegis of the monarchy. For Castelar and a small group of associates the word *republican* contained a romantic sentiment they could not desert although they worked within the existing government. Critics designated him a *Republicano embolado*, comparing him to the bulls in a Portuguese bullfight who had been rendered harmless by wooden balls placed over their horns.[15]

One group of democrats adopted a firm support of the dynasty. This group, which called itself the Democratic-Dynastic party, had a much larger and more practical support than the others. Fernando Colom y Beneito, a lawyer with frequent access to the pages of the prestigious newspaper *La Correspondencia de España*, was its president and its membership included such distinguished names as those of Segismundo Moret y Prendergast, professor of economics at the University of Madrid who had served as colonial and treasury minister during the revolutionary period; Victor Beranger, poet and eloquent Catalan deputy; and the able deputy the marquis of Sardoal. Sardoal set the tone of this group by proclaiming Alfonso XII more "a democratic than a Bourbon" monarch.[16]

Further confusing the political scene was the existence of a Centro Militar, which belied its professional position when it elected as president the liberal General López Domínguez.[17]

These groups operating outside the political sphere of Sagasta's Fusionists weakened the force of the coalition and placed a pressure on its most numerous members, the Constitutionalists, to show their "liberal" character. The effects of this pressure were to be significant during the following year, as will be seen.

From the conservative side the government confronted not only the protests against the wholesale expulsion of officeholders but the charge that the educational reforms of the Minister of Development Albareda threatened the stability of the religious establishment. The opposition asserted that the professors who were returned to their posts were "libre cultistas"—for religious freedom—and that the reform program undercut the constitutional guarantees of the church.[18] The bishops had protested these actions and the archbishop of Toledo, Cardinal Moreno, went a step further in July when he issued a pastoral letter complaining about the treatment of the Pope in Rome and calling upon the Spanish ministers, deputies, and newspapers to protest the continued mistreatment of Christ's vicar. There had been some efforts on the part of Spain and Austria to heal the breach between the Papacy and the Italian state, but feelings had been too strong to accomplish anything, especially since the Italian state had allowed an insulting demonstration to take place during the passage through Rome of the funeral procession of Pius IX, whose body was being moved to a burial place outside the Vatican city.[19]

For the Fusionist government (and the same would undoubtedly have been true if Cánovas had been in office) good relations with Italy were too important to be threatened by brash pronouncements of church officials. Martínez Campos, who was acting as prime minister while Sagasta was on vacation, called Cardinal Moreno in and accused him of hostility both to the government and the king. When the cardinal raised the question of conscience, the general roughly suggested that the prelate's conscience might well take a different turn if the government locked him up or punished him for his actions.[20] *La Epoca*, long a spokesman for Cánovas, condemned the letter but so softly that it began to signal Cánovas's move to rapprochement with the Moderados.[21] In the end the government took no action.

Meanwhile, the government confronted other problems. It was an open secret under Cánovas that the gaming houses in Madrid continued to operate although they were illegal. For this privilege each gambling house had paid a fee of 35,000 pesetas monthly to the governor of Madrid, the marquis of Heredia Spínola. This sum was supposed to be used for charitable purposes, but no formal accounting was kept. Under Sagasta the new governor of Madrid, the count of Xiquena, closed the gambling houses except for a brief period during the festival for the bicentennial observance of the death of Calderón de la Barca. Apparently the representatives of the gambling interests of the day launched a terrorist campaign against this action, constructing paper bombs and exploding them to cause fear and disorder. On June 20 one such bomb exploded near a group of children and seriously injured a number of them. The police were able to apprehend about nineteen of the bomb makers diligently working in one of the gambling houses.[22]

During the following year Xiquena and Romero Robledo were to be joined in a Cortes debate on the issue during which Xiquena charged that Romero Robledo had himself profited from the gambling houses, a charge which he could have proved, believed the German ambassador, but had to retract when Cánovas threatened the walkout of his party with the attendant disruption of the parliamentary system.[23]

The coming of the Sagasta government had provided the young king with a much more meaningful role in affairs. Lengthy cabinet meetings prior to the elections had suggested

[133]

the monarch's concern about the housecleaning of government offices. He had early reservations in respect to Albareda's program, fearing it might go so far as to allow professors to preach republicanism in the classroom.[24] On the other hand, he openly proclaimed his liberalism and sponsored an invitation to Russian émigré Jews to come to Spain. He and the cabinet pointed out that there was no legal impediment to Jewish residence in Spain, but the German ambassador believed that if, as was unlikely, many came, they would find as much hostility and danger as ever in the northern provinces and Catalonia.[25]

The summer of 1881 found the monarch on a ceremonial visit to the northeast with elements of comedy mixed with the pageantry. Even with allowances for the exaggerations of official reporting, the king's reception in this journey through the northern provinces was enthusiastic. The German ambassador noted that he had a good speaking ability, "which is so important in Spain," and suggested he ought to travel more. In Ferrol he presided over honors for Adm. Victoriano Sánchez Barcáiztegui, who had been killed on a brave but probably rash expedition during the Carlist period. He visited La Coruña, Pontevedra, and Vigo, examining the naval installations and ships there. The king could scarcely have been well impressed by what he saw. When the ships in the fleet fired off salvos in the seas off Vigo, a cannon on the corvette *Tornado* came loose from its moorings, killing one of its attendants and injuring seven others. A little later when the fleet put out to sea at his orders (Rear Admiral Pavía had wanted to stay in port), it ran into a storm and practically all the naval personnel were seasick, while the king, the queen, and the queen's Viennese physician were unaffected. Pavía himself fell coming out of his cabin suffering serious injuries and the ships of the fleet encountered considerable difficulty in weathering the storm. Clearly the Spanish fleet was not of a character to strike fear into her adversaries.[26]

The king had also begun the preparation of army reforms, the details of which he carefully worked out himself. He was to find, however, serious obstacles to the implementation of his plans and the issue was a continuing one throughout the Liberal period.

On September 20 the monarch opened the newly elected Cortes with the traditional speech from the throne. The speech spoke of reforms but emphasized the value of peace and the achievement of progress by the "ordered exercise of constitutional liberties." The army was described as "the ornament and bulwark of the country."[27] Sagasta in the meeting of the Fusionists preparatory to the opening of the Cortes had paid strong tribute to the monarch's liberalism—Spain's ruler had no lessons to learn from the other liberal monarchs of Europe. And in florid terms he promised that the Liberals would act so as to leave Alfonso's name in letters of gold on the pages of history.[28] Unfortunately Sagasta and the president of the Senate both stressed the need for unity within the government majority, but failed to stress the nature of a Fusionist party—with appropriate references to the non-Constitutionalists.[29] Posada Herrera, who had so often accepted the presidency of the Congress of Deputies under the Conservatives, now did the same for the Liberals. His candidacy had found some opposition from the left wing of the majority, which had favored Antonio Romero Ortiz, a grand master of the Masonic Order, but efforts in this direction were halted by the opposition of Serrano.[30]

It was, of course, already widely rumored that the duke of la Torre had been irritated by Sagasta's failure to consult with him on the cabinet formation or the governmental program, but at this point he was maintaining a stance of full support as well as emphasizing his absolute loyalty to the monarch. The king welcomed this declaration and regarded it as a sign of the permanence of the new government.[31] But Serrano's adherence to Sagasta was less than lukewarm, as the events of the following year were to demonstrate.

The Sagasta government presented the Cortes with several programs praiseworthy in character but arousing much controversy. In addition to the educational reform begun before the opening of the parliament, Alonso Martínez as minister of grace and justice and Camacho as treasury minister presented far-reaching reforms in the judicial and budgetary spheres. The re-establishment of oral and public judgments in criminal cases was carried through and an indication given that a law for trial by jury would be proposed shortly. Tribunals were reorganized to clarify judicial procedures.[32]

The most striking aspect of the Sagasta program was financial reform. Camacho began in December 1881 and completed late in May 1882 a conversion of the public debt, by which older bonds, railroad bonds, and more recent bonds were all converted into new obligations at varying rates of discount negotiated with the bondholders. This was accompanied by a new budget which replaced two years of heavy deficit expenditures with a surplus of 300,000 pesetas. This was accomplished by a drastic tax reform. The hated tax on salt was eliminated as were also road and bridge tolls and port duties. Taxes on real estate, agricultural products, and cattle raising were reduced. Postal rates were also cut. But there were increased taxes on industrial property and a new licensing tax on shops. The government dispositions for these were complex and they did create real hardship for many small businessmen. Camacho also indicated that the government had begun negotiations for a commercial treaty with France designed to be only the first in a series of such reciprocal trade treaties.[33]

The rationale of Camacho's program is unclear. The changes cleared away or reduced some highly unpopular taxes. But the new ones were arbitrary and poorly conceived. Although Liberal support would be enhanced by the reductions, the industrial taxes would undercut Liberal strength and aid the Liberal Conservatives. And the proposed tariff reduction created an uproar in Catalonia where the more liberal elements of Sagasta's Fusionist coalition had great strength. There is no evidence that the tax changes were sponsored by or aided specific privileged groups—in the final outcome, although Camacho's debt conversion was a progressive step and fairly well stabilized government finances until the close of the century, his tax reforms weakened the government coalition.

Camacho's proposals aroused virulent debate in the Cortes and organized protest outside accompanied by demonstrations and violence. The original center of disturbance was in Madrid, where street mobs denounced the new taxes and industrial organizations threatened resistance to payment. Romero Robledo was blamed for stirring up the Madrid merchants and took the lead in the Cortes in criticizing the government's economic policies and their consequences in Madrid. In the heat of the debate his opponents charged that he was irked by the closing of the gambling houses and was defending the cause of those who were responsible for paper bomb outrages.[34]

Much more severe were the reactions in Barcelona, where the National Association for the Support of Manufactures led the demonstrations. Businesses were closed, leading to desperate conditions for unemployed workers. Arson, window-breaking, the seizure of tramways, and the tearing up of streetcar tracks accompanied the protests. Very probably republican and other radical groups took advantage of the situation to aggravate the government's problems.[35]

In Barcelona the proposed Franco-Spanish Commercial Treaty was a more serious cause of disturbance than taxes. The treaty negotiations had coincided with the strong move toward Catalan nationalism initiated by Valentí Almirall with his book *España tal cual es* in 1881 and his formation of the Centre Català in 1882. The cause of Catalan nationalism mingled with hostility to the treaty and anger at Camacho's taxes in such battle cries as "Catalonia and fueros and down with the treaty of commerce" and declarations of war "against these used up and wasteful men . . . with their free trade and new taxes." Although the treaty was ratified by a strong majority in the Cortes, the debate had taken its toll of government support. Even Liberal Catalan deputies such as Victor Balaguer found it necessary to oppose government free-trade policies. Cánovas was not yet an avowed protectionist, but here as earlier in respect to Martínez Campos's proposal of *cabotaje* with Cuba, did defend existing tariffs. He pointed out that the major trend of tariff policies was toward protectionism—even on the part of the liberal United States.[36]

Likewise a subject of controversy, only partly revealed in the Cortes debates, was the project for military reform. The young king told the German envoy that he had himself worked out the reforms being proposed.[37] The monarch had intended to leave the term of service of the cavalry, artillery, and engineers at three years, but to reduce that of the infantry to two and a quarter years in order to create a larger reserve. The minister of war, Martínez Campos, was moving in his attachment to his (the king's) person, added the monarch, and he would not allow the Liberal government to bring a change in that position. If necessary to prevent such action, he would dissolve the Cortes rather than allow the army to be disorganized. Unfortunately, he added, if it came to that, he could not claim credit for decisiveness, since he would only be copying "your excellency, Prince Bismarck."

Martínez Campos, continued the monarch, was guarantor of the security of the army, keeping "undependable elements" under control. But, said the king ruefully, Martínez Campos was frightfully incapable of defending his army reforms—he doubted that the general understood them himself. Every time that the marshal reported that he had spoken in the Cortes or before the commission dealing with the reforms, the king suffered a mild shock anticipating that the general had again committed some great blunder. In the commission the king had run into immovable opposition on the part of the generals to the reduction of the term of infantry service. The generals had complained that this would pose a great injustice for their men and asserted that they could not accept the reduction unless the king gave them a direct order to do so. This, reported Alfonso, he was unwilling to do, and he had had to accept the three years service term, although it added 30,000 men to the infantry. The Spanish army, he noted, was in its present organization "absolutely unusable." But the military reforms were to be long delayed and the monarch continued to be worried. One cause of concern was French action in North Africa—the king fearing that some French dictator might use difficulties in that area as an excuse for the invasion of Spain.

Spain had been shocked by the news of the French seizure of Tunis in 1881. The French anticipated some countermove in Morocco on the part of Spain. During the last troubled year of his term in office Cánovas had convened a conference in Madrid meeting in May 1880 to deal with Moroccan affairs. Although the conference gave Cánovas and Spain some public exposure, Spain gained little and France emerged with her rights there unimpaired. The French felt that Cánovas had earlier missed his best opportunity to expand Spanish holdings in Morocco and that the Madrid conference had been a mistake. Now in 1882 the French anticipated that the Sagasta government might be more active in Morocco, perhaps extending its control between Ceuta and Melilla. Perhaps it was the king's caution which restrained his Liberal ministers. Spain did send an expedition to prevent the sultan from undercutting the Spanish position in Santa Cruz de Mar Pequeña, but took no other dramatic action in Morocco.[38] The real cause of concern, however, was closer home, as the events of 1883 were to show. The unreliability of the Spanish army in respect to domestic politics continued to be a grave cause of concern throughout the Liberal period.

Spain also confronted problems from the right wing of politics. The Carlists were disorganized with serious dissension in their ranks. The Moderado newspapers *El Siglo Futuro* and *La Fé* were in a running controversy of great bitterness. Cándido Nocedal, the publisher of the former paper, was the titular civilian leader of the Carlists, but his authority was disputed, with Nocedal probably commanding only a minority of the Traditionalists. The pretender himself, after a disquieting pilgrimage about the courts of Europe, had settled down in the Venetian palace of Loredán, the gift of Archduchess Beatrice of Este. In January 1882 Nocedal began the organization of a pilgrimage to Rome set for April of that year. The government was worried about these plans, not only because they smacked of a Carlist demonstration in Spain but also because they might lead to fanatical incidents in Rome and bad relations with Italy. Some members of the Spanish episcopate opposed the project from the beginning and the papal nuncio said at the outset that the pope had approved the pilgrimage only under the condition that it be led by the bishops, not the laity. But the nuncio's explanation was soon contradicted by the publication in *El Imparcial* of a papal circular placing the pilgrimage under the leadership of Nocedal and his son Ramón and directing the bishops to cooperate. The nuncio in a conversation with Solms expressed anger at the revelation of the circular but did not deny its accuracy. He explained that for the bishops to take control of the organization would bring confusion, an explanation that failed to satisfy the German diplomat. This arrangement clearly left the pilgrimage under Carlist control.[39]

The government was, of course, tremendously disturbed by these events. Solms saw the marquis of la Vega de Armijo emerge from an interview with the nuncio furiously angry. He would, he asserted, request a statement from the pope. If the Spanish ambassador's reports from the Vatican were inaccurate, he would be recalled; if not, he would insist on the recall of the nuncio. The nuncio had tried to assure him the Carlists planned no revolution, but had failed to convince the foreign minister. The government's position was strengthened by internal opposition to the nature of the pilgrimage—the archbishop of Santiago had denounced the idea of a pilgrimage led exclusively by a political party.

Before the end of the controversy the pretender's unwise and extremist support of Nocedal had awakened an organized protest of some 250 Traditionalists and efforts to persuade the pretender that his counselors, as often before, were unwise. As for the pilgrimage, the pope under obvious pressure directed the archbishop of Toledo to secure the withdrawal of Nocedal from its leadership and the dissolution of the committees he had formed. The pilgrimage was to be exclusively religious and arrangements placed in the hands of the bishops. The papal nuncio became a cardinal but withdrew from Spain shortly thereafter.[40]

The reaction of the political leaders was interesting—Cánovas saying it was too bad the Spanish bishops had been divided for the first time since the Council of Trent, thus signaling the move to the right he was to make a year later. But the marquis of la Vega de Armijo found it a propitious sign that for the first time Spanish bishops had stood up against Rome in behalf of the interests of their dynasty.[41]

In the midst of these difficulties there were constant reports of opposition within the government ranks to the more conservative cabinet ministers—Alonso Martínez, Martínez Campos, and Camacho. Difficulties derived both from the budgetary dispositions and the reorganization of the courts. Only the position of Martínez Campos seemed impregnable, with the king adamantly behind him and the potential alternative, López Domínguez, suspected of having earlier been involved in an unsuccessful military coup.[42]

The pressure on the government increased with the duke of la Torre, General Serrano, back on the scene—in his customary equivocal position. Still professing loyalty to the dynasty and support for Sagasta, the general criticized the Fusionist grouping, which he said had not worked, and advocated the return to the principles of the Constitution of 1869, which he declared much more democratically drawn up than that of 1876. During the months of September and October, Serrano engaged in a series of puzzling maneuvers including negotiations with Cánovas. By October, Sagasta was bitterly aware that Serrano was creating an alternative party, although Serrano still denied hostility to the prime minister, claiming he was simply seeking new adherents to the monarchy. The directive committee of the so-called Dynastic Left formed on November 24, 1882, including under Serrano as president, Victor Balaguer, Admiral José Beranger y Ruiz de Apodaca, Manuel Becerra, Generals Fernández de Córdova and Ros de Olano, Eduardo Gasset y Artime, publisher of *El Imparcial*, Montero Ríos, and Moret. Neither Serrano's first speech in the Cortes in behalf of his new party nor Sagasta's passionate response made the best impression on their auditors.[43]

Critics attributed the formation of the new party to maneuvers engineered by Cánovas to embarrass the Sagasta government. There were, of course, also renewed rumors of the ambitious machinations of the duchess. On his own part Cánovas brought into his party formation most of the former Moderados, completing a shift to the right of his party, which now began to discard the word "Liberal" in its title.[44]

In the midst of these developments the king continued behind the scenes to give strong support to the Sagasta government, although he told Moret and the marquis of Sardoal that he would have no opposition to their holding governmental posts.[45] On the other hand he made it clear to potential opponents that he would have any general or officer taking up arms against him shot.[46] Serrano's days of glory came quickly to an end shortly after the formation of his party due to a private scandal—a marriage arrangement for his son who was impotent, which resulted in a nullification of the marriage but not in the return of the handsome dowry which had accompanied the bride.[47]

Having survived the challenge of the Dynastic Left the government moved to a ministerial crisis occasioned by a strictly internal dispute. Treasury Minister Camacho, although able, was brusque and stubborn, unwilling to follow Sagasta's lead in giving in to "little justified political exigencies." The crisis which followed was apparently arranged. The Minister of Development Albareda had already been critical of Camacho for his parsimonious treatment of his ministry. Now, early in 1883, came a virulent dispute over Camacho's proposal to balance the budget by the sale of all the public lands! No compromise was reached and by January 9, 1883, Sagasta had reformed his ministry, dropping the controversial members. The marquis of la Vega de Armijo remained as minister of foreign affairs and, at the king's insistence, Martínez Campos continued as minister of war. The lawyer and life senator Justo Pelayo Cuesta replaced Camacho as treasury minister. Vicente Romero Girón, a friend of Ruiz Zorrilla, replaced Alonso Martínez as minister of grace and justice —strongly emphasizing the leftward orientation of the changes. Rodríguez Arias became minister of the navy; Gaspar Nuñez de Arce, the poet, became minister of overseas territories, and Germán Gamazo was named minister of development. Venancio González, who had left the Ministry of the Interior to be replaced by Pío Gullón, a newspaper publisher, had done so for personal business reasons.[48] All in all, although the cabinet still retained a Fusionist character, it had lost greatly in quality. Camacho was perhaps the most able treasury minister Spain had during the Restoration period.

The first period of Liberal government, therefore, had closed on a less than inspiring note and the year 1883 was to see the harvesting of the consequences of indecisive and incompleted reforms and to demonstrate the extreme difficulty confronted by a Liberal government in Spain in trying to draw a line between liberalism and radicalism.

8

Liberal Interlude:

Crisis and Dissolution

 HE YEAR 1883 provided more excitement on the Spanish political scene than had existed at any time since the Restoration. For Alfonso XII it was a year of mixed triumph and disillusion. For Spain it brought a variety of internal disturbances suggesting that the Restoration stability was not secure without strong measures of control. And once again liberalism, as it had during the revolutionary period from 1868 to 1874, split into rival factions motivated as much by personal differences as by attachment to ideals.

The year began with a lurid incident in the little town of el Agarrobillo, near Jérez de la Frontera, where the body of a field worker, Bartolomé Gayo, known as "el Blanco de Benaocaz," was discovered. The dead man had been murdered some two months earlier and the death was blamed on a "popular tribunal" of what authorities labeled a Black Hand organization.[1]

There was to be then and later those who believed the government had invented the organization. This has proved to be false. Throughout the Cánovas period several anarchist groups, one of them known as the Black Hand, operated clandestinely in Andalusia. Intolerable conditions existed in the Spanish South. Poverty, misery, and depression were intensified by a cost of living much higher than in other parts of Spain. Hunger had brought desperation during the late seventies and found no relief from the Sagasta government. Anarchist newspapers, pamphlets, and pronouncements continued in spite of police controls. Threats to and mishandlings of public officials in the area took place. But the Andalusian anarchists were *sui generis*, bound neither to international organizations nor to the larger workers' movements in Madrid and Barcelona. The quest for bread and blind anger at their exploiters undergirded the Andalusian anarchists and they found little sympathy with or from the workers' movements elsewhere.[2]

During the Serrano period the earlier Sagasta regime had been in large measure responsible for the repression of workers' movements. But the Constitutionalists had castigated Cánovas for distinguishing between legal and illegal parties and movements and when Sagasta assumed power, workers' organizations began to hold public meetings. A *Federación Regional Española* (Spanish Regional Federation [of workers]) had operated secretly under Cánovas but now met in congress in Barcelona on September 24, 1881, and reorganized as the *Federación de Trabajadores de la Región Española* (Federation of the Workers of the Spanish Region). By the time of its second congress in Seville it had 663 sections, 218 local federations, and counted 57,000 members, with its greatest strength in Andalusia. But the congress in Seville saw serious differences of opinion within the federation in respect to the value of strikes, the means to be employed to achieve workers' objectives, and the relationship of the Spanish movement to those outside of Spain. The congress brought a fundamental split between the workers of Andalusia and those in other parts of Spain. Those of Andalusia reverted to their clandestine organizations. Those elsewhere began to fear the effects of the activities of their counterparts in the South and to denounce their "criminal" activities.[3]

At the same time a socialist movement having a history going back to 1871 began to take on new significance. This began with an *Asociación del Arte de Imprimir* (Association of the Printing Art) which had originally been opposed by Pablo Iglesias but came under his leadership by 1874. The association accumulated a strike treasury and Iglesias, at twenty-four, began his long career as the dominant figure in Spanish socialism until a few years before his death in 1925. In 1879 he joined with Victoriano Calderón, Alejandro Oncina, Gonzalo Zubiaurre, and Jaime Vera in establishing the Socialist Workers' party of Spain and providing it with a program supposed to have been revised by Marx and Engels. The Socialists were fewer in numbers than the anarchists but gained much public notice in 1882 with a strike of the typesetters in Madrid. Some 1,000 of the 1,400 typesetters in Madrid were affiliates of the association. By June they had won victories in forty-six printing houses and lost in fourteen. The socialist movement added to government concerns in this period, but did not reach full effectiveness until the publication of its journal *El Socialista* began in 1886.[4]

Anarchist violence and socialist strikes provided an excuse for stern governmental action. Although the police investigations of the death of "el Blanco de Benaocaz" brought to light detailed descriptions of the plans and organization of the Black Hand in the province of Cádiz, the trial of those responsible revealed private motives more than ideological ones. Sixteen persons were tried; seven were condemned to death, eight to over seventeen years imprisonment in chains, and one freed. But the government had already engaged in massive arrests of those associated with the Black Hand. During the months of February and March 1883 the Guardia Civil arrested more than 5,300 persons in Jérez and Cádiz. They were reported to have used torture to prove guilt. Many of these were tried by military courts without a reasonable chance to defend themselves.[5]

In April 1883 Pablo Iglesias and other members of the typesetters' strike committee were also arrested and tried. They fared far better than the anarchists. Ably defended by federalist republican Pi y Margall, they drew five months prison terms.[6]

All in all the Liberals showed themselves to be still very conservative in respect to social reform. They were, of course, affected by the prevailing fear of anarchism and the International which haunted most of the courts of Europe. Government action against social revolutionaries was much more effective than its action against republican political and military movements.

In the midst of these domestic difficulties the king's mind was more on personal affairs than on the problems of state. Early in 1883 plans for the marriage of the Infanta María de la Paz to Prince Louis Ferdinand of Bavaria, which had been stymied two years earlier, were suddenly completed.[7] The king was delighted —the marriage plans brought to the fore all of his predilections for Germany and Austria. Throughout his reign the combination of his school experiences and his tremendous admiration for the accomplishments of Bismarck and the kaiser engendered a romantic attachment to the concept of a Spanish-German alliance. Now with this new marriage attachment the king's desire to revisit Austria and Germany became a consuming passion. Already close and often excessively frank with the German envoy, Count Solms-Sonnenwalde, the king was to make him a frequent confidant and friend during the remainder of his brief life.

In April as part of the wedding ceremonies the king wore a Bavarian uniform and called in Solms to see the "handsome uniform." The young monarch's only regret was that it made him an infantry officer as had also a similar gift by the Austrian emperor. Things to come were presaged by his comment that he should like to have been a cavalry officer. Solms used the occasion to seek the king's aid in furthering the negotiations for a commercial treaty between Spain and Germany which seemed to be breaking down on the opposition of the treasury minister, Pelayo Cuesta. The monarch promised that he would do all he could to further the negotiations. And he added,

> I am completely convinced that the only real support I have lies in Germany and that only from there can come an effective assistance. Who can know whether or not in France sooner or later a Red Gambetta may come to control who will consider it necessary to seek activity outside France in order to create new self-confidence in its army and to make republican propaganda. They would not take on Germany or even Italy, but would fall on the weakest prey. In a year I shall have brought it about that I can call up 400,000 men

and the French would have no easy game this time, but they would still be stronger than I am. The goal of my wishes would be that if it came again to a fight between Germany and France, I would fight with Germany against France. I can lead 300,000 men abroad and that could be valuable to you because we Spaniards are better soldiers than the French and we would tie up a considerable number of their troops. You could rely upon my cooperation in the next occasion under any kind of circumstances.[8]

Solms continued in the period that followed to press for the conclusion of the negotiations on the German-Spanish Commercial Treaty, suggesting some connection between it and the visit the king planned in Germany. By June 14 he learned that Sagasta and Martínez Campos had been able to overcome the treasury minister's feeling that the treaty was not advantageous enough for Spain and on July 5 Solms received authorization to sign the copy in Madrid.[9] By July 27 the Cortes ratified the treaty by which Germany reduced from 30 percent to 10 percent the duties on cork, Spanish fruits, fresh grapes, and olive oil, while Spain limited her duties on spirits, iron, steel wire, and rails.[10]

But the government found little joy in the events of the spring and summer of 1883. There was criticism of the foreign minister and minister of overseas territories for the handling of relations with France in Africa. Massacres of Spanish subjects and burning of their properties by the Arabs in Algeria in 1881 had led to lengthy negotiations resulting in a promise of indemnity, which was delayed in the French parliament until late in 1882. The Spanish government still found opposition to providing the corresponding indemnity which had been promised to French citizens who had suffered loss during the Carlist wars.[11] At the same time Martínez Campos was disposed to resign over pending cuts in the military budget and Minister of Grace and Justice Romero Girón had become responsible for a much criticized release of a young man convicted of murder.[12]

With rumors of a possible move to the left the king showed his willingness and ability to win adherence even on the part of such confirmed democrats as Cristino Martos.[13] This engendered a counterattack on the part of extremist democrats, who began to circulate the story that relations between the king and queen had become more than cool after the queen surprised her consort in the midst of one of his romantic adventures. Efforts to recount the story in democratic newspapers resulted in the government's use of press censorship in the matter as well as an almost duel between military friends of the monarch and the editor of the newspaper *El Liberal*. When the newspaper came off free in the press courts, threats of violence against the paper and renewed threats of resignation on the part of Martínez Campos ensued. A little later the story surfaced again in the Paris newspapers.[14]

Later events were indeed to suggest that the king did indulge his taste for romantic pastimes during the Sagasta period and that nightly escapades hastened the onset of his fatal illness. But María Cristina bore her cross patiently, although she did have her most serious rival, Elena Sanz, expelled from Madrid. Her very genuine attachment to her husband continued. Apparently she accepted his shortcomings as not so unusual among monarchs.[15]

The king's strong Germanophilism continued. In May 1883 Solms brought to him the kaiser's gift of membership in the House Order of the Hohenzollerns. Alfonso again raised the question of his attendance at both the Austrian and Prussian maneuvers in the fall. His strongest wish, he said, was to meet the kaiser. Solms answered "with reserve," since he did not yet know what the reaction would be at home.[16]

The Spanish king then went on to unburden himself in respect to Spanish politics. He had had, he said, two great ambitions when he came to the throne. One was to exclude the army from politics. This he believed he had accomplished—successful pronunciamientos were now impossible. His other great ambition had been to bring morality to Spanish public office. But in this he had completely failed. Perhaps the number of those who stole had fallen from 85 to 80 percent, but this was all. Sixty-five percent of the deputies were, he said, paid by the officials whom they got into lucrative jobs. And the worst thing about it all was that it was taken as a matter of course—"He who steals millions is a highly respected man; one presses his hand in polite society; I myself have such friends; pleasant and agreeable individuals, whom one ought to have locked up. But he who steals 10 francs will certainly be arrested and punished."

Solms felt that the king's bitterness was related in part to the probable involvement of the minister of grace and justice in scandals surrounding the Alcalde of Madrid. "I belong," said the king, "to a Race which does not steal, and I hate men who do it. I have also expressed my views on internal morality in the cabinet sessions." But he added that the situation was not new— there had been complaints under Cánovas, not against Cánovas himself but because he was too lenient with his friends. "I have charged Cánovas himself with this problem in a cabinet meeting. Thereupon he answered me: 'Yes, if we want to have reliable officials, we must bring in Germans and Englishmen; as long as we have Spaniards as officials, they will always steal. And in the long run it's all the same to me.' What shall I do with a man who has no understanding of morality?"

And the monarch concluded his frank disquisition on Spanish politics with an odd proposal—"I am, of course, constitutional and liberal in my views, but regardless of this I must recognize that there is only one way of bringing the country into order; it consists in throwing out the whole parliament, all of the con- stitutional and parliamentary system, chasing all the officials out, to punish ruthlessly those who steal, to exercise strict jus- tice, and after twenty years to go before the country and say: 'This is what I have done and if you are not content with it, hang me!'"

Meanwhile, the Austrians were very anxious that the king make his planned trip in the fall.[17] The Spaniards also proposed a visit to Great Britain, but were told that the queen was too ill to entertain visitors.[18] Count Morphy, the king's former tutor who now served as his private secretary, approached Solms in respect to the king's wish to attend the Prussian maneuvers— fearing the young king had gone ahead making his plans without proper clearance and invitations. Solms responded that he was sure the kaiser's interest in Alfonso would guarantee a welcome, but inquired whether the Spanish ambassador in Berlin had been given instructions.[19] A little later the French military attaché in Madrid, the viscount de la Cornillère, asked if it were true that the king was going to Germany. If so, he added, he would need to visit other courts also. But the Spanish minister of foreign affairs, the marquis of la Vega de Armijo, related that he had approached the French about the king attending *their* maneuvers, but had been strongly discouraged. If the Spanish king attended, the republican officials noted, all the generals and high officers would have to be presented to him and it would become the maneuvers of the king of Spain rather than of the French. The monarchist impulse would be unavoidable. Solms, of course, told the viscount that all he knew of the whole affair was what he read in the newspapers.[20]

Back home in Germany Alfonso's plans did occasion a good deal of discussion. The kaiser himself made the decision that the visit should be to a place outside Berlin—Bad Homburg to be the choice. The kaiser directed that a copy of the program of the maneuvers be sent to Alfonso and suggested again the propriety of the location at Bad Homburg.[21] By early July another obstacle had been cleared from the path with the final conclusion of the hard-fought negotiations over the Spanish-German Commercial Treaty.[22] During July the king firmed up his plans for visiting Germany, once again telling Solms of his tremendous admiration for the kaiser. In accordance with the kaiser's wishes, he planned to be in Bad Homburg on September 21 after a stop-over, incognito, in Frankfurt. The king expressed his wish to see Solms in Bad Homburg and it appears this may have occurred although Solms left no personal account of the visit. Final arrangements had been made on August 4, one day before a whole series of fateful events.[23]

Spanish politics had been in even more disorder than usual throughout the spring and summer of 1883. Serrano's Dynastic Left continued to talk of making monarchy and democracy brothers, but to criticize the government.[24] The German envoy heard that his party had received funds from French capitalists and industrialists.[25] The democrats also attacked the government with such vigor that Sagasta imitated the conservative stance of Cánovas in reproving his opponents.[26] But while he was taking this strong position in defense of the monarchy, Sagasta confronted a disturbing incident behind the scenes. His minister of grace and justice, Romero Girón, accompanied the king to a festival at the estate of the duke of Sesto. There, evidently with his consent, he was tossed in the air in a blanket by the young aristocrats present—an action which Sagasta resented not only as an insult to the minister himself but to the entire cabinet.[27]

The government's problems led Spanish republicans at home and abroad to believe that they had arrived at a propitious time for change. A "Republican Military Association" had been created with 1,200 affiliates by 1883. Supposedly directed by Ruiz Zorrilla from Paris and supported by former republican leaders Estanislao Figueras and Nicolas Salmerón, it looked to the establishment of a republic by military conspiracy. Zorrilla was reported to have provided funds for an extensive uprising. The charges were prepared, but the resultant explosions had all the force of penny firecrackers.[28]

Events began on August 5 with the rising of a fair number of troops in the fortress town of Badajoz on the Portuguese frontier. The regiment of infantry of Covadonga, that of cavalry of Santiago, an artillery company, and a number of other units took over the garrison, removed all civil and military officials, and proclaimed the republic. On the same day Minister of War Martínez Campos, who was acting as prime minister while Sagasta was on vacation, dispatched General Blanco with a regiment of troops toward Badajoz and by the morning of the next day sent two more regiments toward the city. Before they arrived, the brave insurrectionists, although supplied with 30,000 rifles and some artillery, decided that discretion was the better part of valor and crossed the frontier into Portugal![29]

Two days after the rising at Badajoz came another small explosion in Santo Domingo de la Calzada in the province of Logroño. A cavalry lieutenant led an abortive rising here with a considerable number of troops following him until a loyal colonel with a few men sounded his bugles and the lieutenant's following dissolved behind white flags of surrender. Only the lieutenant continued his resistance and died in a ludicrous skirmish.[30]

More serious was the third rising which took place at the fortified city of La Seo de Urgel on the French frontier. Here a lieutenant colonel and several captains with a considerable number of troops rose but were thwarted by the opposition of the artillery commandant of the place, who marched with his men to the nearby village of Puigcerda, where he and the governor of the place announced their loyalty to the government and organized resistance. On the same day the more important insurrectionists took refuge in the Republic of Andorra.[31]

Nevertheless, the risings did stir a ruckus in government circles. Apparently the greatest source of insurrection lay with the sergeants in the Spanish army who confronted a situation in which there were already too many officers and hence no hope of advancement. Since most men subject to the draft could get out of service with a fairly moderate payment, the soldiers were uneducated and felt a strong sense of attachment to their sergeants. All that was needed was money to awaken their interest in revolt and they were willing to try it. And the indications again were that Ruiz Zorrilla, ever the government's chief enemy, had found funds to bribe them.

All in all, with an army of 80,000 men having 18,000 officers and 600 generals, the Spanish military establishment just did not make sense, said Solms. In his view the only solution was to institute universal military service to obtain better soldiers, reduce the number of officers, and introduce examinations to certify the ability of the officers. On the other hand, he, as well as other observers, pointed out that the real lesson of the risings was that they accomplished so little. They obtained no real public following and the nature of their failure made them more ludicrous than threatening.[32]

But the king was irritated beyond measure. Just on the eve of his long desired journey to Austria and Germany came these events. He would be riding with the kaiser on maneuvers when he would suddenly receive a telegram and have to say, "Excuse me, I must go out to look for a couple of regiments I've lost."[33] He had thought to join the Concert of Europe, he said, but it appeared he might have to join the Concert of Africa![34] He was afraid he'd be criticized in Germany for his "miserable army," but Solms assured him that it was not the custom in Germany to criticize the kaiser's guests and that the energy of his actions under the circumstances undercut all criticism.[35]

There was, however, some criticism among the king's advisers and even on the part of Solms. Once again the necessity of the monarch's maintaining a military pose was underscored. Perhaps the strongest caution came to the monarch from Manuel Silvela, who spoke to him as "an old man and faithful servant." When the bad news came from Badajoz, the king, Silvela told him, should have returned to Madrid in uniform and on horseback, not with a straw hat and a jacket! "Your majesty," said Silvela, "must in such moments put on your uniform and, if possible, go on horseback to the battle scene." "Didn't I tell you that?" asked the queen, who was present at the time. And Silvela went on to advise the king that he must follow the example of the northern kings such as the king of Belgium, who always wore uniform, looked as if they were enjoying troop reviews, entertained generals and officers at dinner after reviews, and distributed cigars to the sergeants. When the king objected that he would not hesitate to put himself at the head of his troops in case of need, Silvela said that no one doubted the king's courage, but he must exercise his kingly office twenty-four hours a day, 365 days of the year. He would like, he said to Solms, to have commented on the king's private life, but did not want to do so in the presence of the queen. He and Cánovas had not been strong enough in their controls over the king and the present ministers were even more disinclined to say anything which would displease the monarch. And Solms agreed that the rumors of the king's private adventures had injured his public image.[36]

In his conversation with Solms, Silvela emphasized that the events concerned must not lead the king to change his plans to visit Germany. The example of the kaiser would be beneficial and Spain could not rely upon France—indeed, there was suspi-

cion that the risings might have been arranged to discourage the
visit.

Solms's own views coincided closely with those of Silvela. He
felt that the king should be his own minister of war, always
wear uniform, and obtain more prestige for the generals, who
in spite of long service and experience often had less social standing than young grandees.[37] He was pleased to see the king apparently following Silvela's advice with the queen entertaining
the sergeants of troops who participated in a parade in Madrid
and the king visiting Valencia, Barcelona, Zaragossa, Vitoria,
and Burgos—appearing in uniform and inviting the generals and
high officers to dinner. Whether these visits were all "triumphal
processions" as one report said or somewhat less successful as
others suggested is debatable. But Solms was convinced that
corruption was a greater cancer in Spain than military indisci-
pline and that the king was the only one who had a possibility
of dealing with it. When the monarch returned from his visit
to Valencia, his face bore "a suffering expression" which presaged the onset of fatal illness, but the German did not then
realize its full significance.[38]

Strict military discipline and court martials were also consequences of the uprisings. Gen. Ramón Blanco y Erenas, counted
the ablest officer in the Spanish army after Martínez Campos,
took over a thoroughgoing reorganization of the infantry and the
purification of the officer corps from insecure and revolutionary
elements after the king's return from his journey.[39]

Inside Spain there was considerable opposition to the king's
projected journey to Austria and Germany. A fair amount of it
derived from the apparent approach to Germany,[40] some of it
from the fear of more uprisings. There was also concern for the
itinerary—should the king go through France or sail by ship to
Genoa (as Bismarck suggested).[41] Germany was unwilling to
join with Spain in requests that France expel Ruiz Zorrilla or
in protests against republican propaganda.[42] But the king was
adamant in respect to his plans and overcame all opposition.

On September 1 the king lifted the brief suspension of constitutional liberties which had followed the uprisings and on the

same day the king and queen arrived at La Coruña, where they visited the garrisons, leaving two days later for San Sebastian and reviewing troops there on the fifth. On the same day they departed for Hendaye, from which María Cristina returned to La Granja. By September 12, after an unofficial journey through France and a visit with his sister in Munich, the king arrived in Vienna, plunging with joy into the brilliant receptions of the court and admiring the charges of the famous Austrian lancers and "the Wagnerian spirit" of the artillery.[43] The Austrian emperor was tremendously impressed with his royal visitor, who rode well and kept up with him on the maneuvers—an unusual accomplishment. The king was obviously happy and, wrote the German ambassador there, "makes a very extraordinarily pleasing and appealing impression on me as on all who had the honor to speak with him."[44]

While Alfonso was in Austria the kaiser and Bismarck carried on something of a debate in respect to honors for their intended guest. The kaiser asked Bismarck whether he ought to give Alfonso a regiment—as he pointed out, the Serbian king would be there at the same time and Alfonso already had the Prussian Order of the Black Eagle while the Serbian monarch did not. Perhaps he might be given the chain of the Hohenzollern Order. Bismarck's response was negative to both suggestions. Alfonso was too young to be given a regiment and the chain of the Hohenzollern Order had never been given to foreigners. It would be better, felt Bismarck, simply to promise to bring Spain into the council of European states. And Bismarck added a prescient warning—"Outward manifestations of German origin will make more difficult his relationship with France."[45]

On September 20 Alfonso left Vienna, going through Frankfurt-on-the-Main, where he remained several days before he traveled on to Bad Homburg. The German maneuvers were indeed everything Alfonso had anticipated. Along with Alfonso as guests were Albert Frederick of Saxony, Milan I of Servia, the Prince of Wales (later Edward VII of England), the duke of Braganza (later Charles I of Portugal), and the three sons of Crown Princess Victoria, who also attended and took part in the inaugural processions adorned with the uniform of the Hussars like "an elegant Amazon." A total of 30,000 troops took part, including 25,000 infantry, 3,000 cavalry, and 100 artillery pieces.[46]

In the midst of this brilliant company Alfonso with graceful manners and perfect German won the strong approval of the kaiser. All of Bismarck's advice about the regiment vanished and the kaiser made Alfonso not only a colonel of a regiment, but of the regiment of Uhlans No. 15, which had distinguished itself in the Franco-Prussian War and was then stationed in Strassburg. Alfonso had no thought of refusing the offer—he was finally a cavalry officer. On the twenty-third he appeared in his new uniform, adding to the concern of France with a half-concealed toast during the banquet of the kaiser that he would support Germany in the event of a new war.[47] The press in Vienna and Berlin began to talk of a Spanish approach to the Triple Alliance, but Paris newspapers joined in wrathful denunciations of the Spanish monarch.[48]

Alfonso left for Brussels on September 27 to be received courteously by Leopold II, with the king's coterie, the marquis of la Vega de Armijo and the duke of Sesto, talking of the king's return by sea but Alfonso opposing the idea as undignified. He would go to Paris "even if it cost him his life." On September 29 he arrived in Paris to be greeted by a crude crowd with whistles and jeers and cries of "Down with the Uhlan!" and "Death to the Prussian!"[49] After this reception, which Spaniards considered arranged rather than spontaneous, the king almost left without going to formal receptions, but was prevailed upon to stay and accept a reasonably profound apology by President Grévy.[50]

But diplomatic echoes reverberated for some time and the monarch's reception in Spain reflected a strongly awakened nationalism accompanied by impressive demonstrations of respect for the Germans and the Uhlans as well as for their insulted monarch.[51] Only Bismarck seems to have kept his head and restrained German demonstrations of support for Spain's protests in Paris.[52] But the kaiser once again overrode Bismarck to convey his respects for Alfonso's courage.[53] Eventually Bismarck himself relented in part and paid tribute to Alfonso in his conversations with the Spanish envoy in Berlin, Count Benomar, although he still secretly expressed his doubts that Germany could really rely on Spain in event of war.[54]

Similarly, Alfonso also restrained the extremism of cabinet members such as the marquis of la Vega de Armijo, who was saying, "There is no way to deal with these Frenchmen except to show your teeth." The king declared it impossible with an army of 400,000 to consider war with a country which could mobilize a million men.[55] The change of ambassador in Paris and foreign minister at home, which followed shortly, bore a direct relationship to the diplomatic difficulties with France.[56]

The effects of the king's journey, the army revolts of the late summer, and the continued criticism of the government by the Dynastic Left finally brought the overthrow of the Sagasta government on October 11, 1883. The cabinet crisis was initiated by the resignation of Martínez Campos, who had been the object of much criticism earlier and was labeled "unpopular" with the troops. In the light of later events it may also be guessed that the king, more determined than ever to carry through his proposed army reforms, was not convinced that Martínez Campos could effectuate them. Then, too, the monarch was strongly moving to a liberal position in this period and anxious to conciliate forces as far left as possible. Although he offered to maintain Sagasta in office with a reconstituted cabinet, it may be hazarded that he anticipated a cabinet with more representation from the Dynastic Left than Sagasta was willing to head.[57]

As a consequence, the cabinet which replaced that of Sagasta on October 13, 1883, was headed by the enigmatic chief of the Dynastic Left, José Posada Herrera, whose strange career during the Cánovas period has already been noted. As will be recalled, Posada Herrera had been the titular head of the ill-fated Center party but again and again accepted the presidency of the Congress of Deputies with Liberal Conservative votes. Sidelined by the Sagasta regime, he had become identified with Serrano's Dynastic Left and, with the duke of la Torre's position still somewhat shaded by the litigation over the marriage of his son, became the logical alternative to Sagasta. The brief period of his prime ministry suggests that he was already too old to effect dynamic leadership and that he accepted a completely untenable position in heading a cabinet without majority following and with the king unwilling to grant a decree of dissolution to allow new elections. Posada Herrera proclaimed a policy of "concilia-tion" and perhaps there was some element of reason in bringing into governmental positions some of the more radical liberals either to strengthen their ties to the monarchy or to underscore their ineptness. But the brief period from October 1883 to Janu-ary 1884 was one of the strangest in the bizarre history of Span-ish politics. The jealousy and intractable character of the Liberal leaders undercut all possible reform movements.[58] Most to blame was Sagasta himself, who sabotaged Posada Herrera's efforts for compromise—the British ambassador found him guilty of "deliberate treachery."[59]

The minister of the interior Segismundo Moret began a proj-ect to centralize the administration of the forty-nine provinces of Spain into fifteen regional organizations as well as to improve the administration of the police and of penal and charitable institu-tions. He created a Commission of Social Reforms strangely headed by the former prime minister Cánovas del Castillo. Gen-eral López Domínguez, Serrano's nephew, became minister of war and began an energetic prosecution of the king's army re-forms, including the institution of universal military conscrip-tion. The marquis of Sardoal as minister of development turned his hand to educational reforms and Aureliano Linares Rivas, the minister of grace and justice, began to work for reforms in the law codes. Treasury Minister José Gallostra planned tax reduc-tions and Estanislao Suárez Inclán as minister of overseas terri-tories proposed the abolition of the pillory and shackles which as used in Cuba still made the patronage system little more humane than slavery.[60]

But the major thrust of the new government was toward the establishment of universal suffrage, which all the Liberals had once favored so strongly. Strangely enough Sagasta joined with his erstwhile opponent Cánovas in strongly opposing the move. The project failed of passage in the Cortes and brought the fall of the Posada Herrera ministry on January 18, 1884.[61]

During the Posada Herrera ministry the German Crown Prince Frederick William paid a gala return visit to Spain. Arriving at Valencia on November 22, 1883, he was received in Madrid the following day. At a sumptuous ball the king again wore his Uhlan uniform, then went hunting with the crown prince at the Pardo, and visited military maneuvers with his guest before accompanying him on a visit to Seville, Tarragona, and Barcelona. The crown prince was agreeably impressed with the hospitality and carried back to Germany one improvement for the German armies—the use of Spanish shoes and leggings. Although there were reports in German newspapers of strong statements by Alfonso ("my people are chained for eternity to the German people"), he actually took special care that the visit should not add to existing French hostility.[62]

The German reaction to the period of the Posada Herrera ministry was largely negative. Not that Solms was badly impressed with the foreign minister, Servando Ruiz Gómez, who had gone to school and lived in Germany for some time, although his language usage was rusty.[63] But Serrano now became Spanish ambassador to France and German concerns for his liberal leanings led to rumors that he was in close touch with Ruiz Zorrilla. Serrano's position, incidentally, was a lucrative one. The embassy provided free living and with his pay as ambassador, the funds for official duties, his pay as a marshal, his pension for the Order of San Fernando, his pay as Senate president, and secret funds from the foreign ministry, Serrano collected, according to Solms, the princely sum of 440,000 francs a year.[64]

By the early part of 1884 the Germans were also much concerned with the position of López Domínguez, mistrusted by almost everyone but his own party and "remarkably" the king. They noted that the general was placing untrustworthy regiments close to Madrid, "where they can be watched," said the king, but with Solms's reaction that he would prefer to keep dynamite at a distance rather than in his own bedroom.[65] Rumor also had it that if new elections were held under the existing minister of the interior the results were likely to go republican and the German ambassador in France began to receive a series of letters from "a person in his confidence" (obviously strongly Cánovist in political complexion) who reflected fears that the king was responsible for the untenable situation: "But the king leans to the Left, because this [party] lets him lead his private life as he wishes, that is as a young Southerner with hot blood wishes, while the Conservatives and especially Cánovas prescribe for him reserve, royal worthiness, and dignity, particularly in reference to the tragic irregularitries of the government of Isabella II." Everything, said the correspondent, was endangered, "and the king bears a great part of the responsibility for this, by his frivolity, manifold excesses, and search for popularity with the masses."[66]

Bismarckian marginalia conveyed interest in and horror at Spanish developments. When Solms wrote that it was a strange parliamentary monarchy where only the *Machtspruch* (fiat) of the king could decide issues and regulate affairs, Bismarck replaced the word "strange" by "proper" (*regelrechte*) and added the comment, "every parliament goes astray if it has no royal leadership" and the question, "Who else then?" in respect to the king's decision on all questions. On the comment that the king had worn his uniform ever since the summer revolts, he noted "good," but when he read that the minister of the interior could not guarantee that elections would not go republican, he added the sharp note, "When a king keeps such ministers, there is little hope that he can keep himself." On rumors of a possible pronunciamiento by López Domínguez came the note, "His Majesty should preempt the play and make a pronunciamiento against Lopez!" And, finally, on the note that the king leaned to the left, "Then he can not be helped."[67]

Eventually it was decided to convey to Solms the sense of Bismarck's comments, at first with the instruction to carry them to the king when the opportunity arose, but shortly thereafter as the situation worsened, with the urgent note to *find* an opportunity to talk to the king. Although Bismarck felt that universal suffrage might possibly help the monarchy as it had in Germany, he warned that a ministry which carried the threat of republican elections should not be kept one day longer, that a minister who brought a danger of revolt should be arrested and shot, and that an ambassador like Serrano should not be kept where French gold was available to support republican sentiments.[68]

On January 15, 1884, Castelar made in the Cortes a bitterly anti-German speech in which he claimed that the kaiser had not honored Spain by wearing his decoration of the Order of the Golden Fleece and was using Alfonso to provoke France against Spain. The marquis of la Vega de Armijo responded that the kaiser had not only worn his Order of the Golden Fleece but also the Order of San Fernando, that at the royal banquet in Germany Alfonso had sat between the kaiser and the kaiserin, that the gift of a regiment was not an unusual action, and that Castelar himself had been pro-German until France became a republic.[69]

But the fall of the Posada Herrera government on January 18, 1884, apparently came without the benefit of German advice. It was only after the king had already called upon Cánovas to form a new ministry that Solms was able to convey to him Bismarck's sentiments. He still found the young king professing his own leanings as liberal, "yes, in fact, advanced liberal," and still convinced that López Domínguez had greatly furthered the cause of army reform. But from one of Cánovas's ministers Solms learned that at the end the king *had* developed some suspicions of the liberal general when he found excisions from a police history of questionable officers.[70]

However, the real cause for the fall of the Posada Herrera ministry lay in the scruples of its members. Although it was assumed at the time that the king had been unwilling to grant the government a decree of dissolution of the Cortes, this was not so. When he made the offer, the minister of the interior, Segismundo Moret, indicated that his party was too young and uncertain to guarantee results without the use of "controlled elections" and he was opposed to these. When the king proposed that Posada Herrera take over as minister of the interior to run the elections, he, too, was unwilling to do so. With a budget deficit looming for the coming year and the only way to cover it action by a clear majority in the Cortes, the only two alternatives were to call back Sagasta or go to Cánovas.[71] The king yielded to Posada Herrera's argument that Sagasta had been the major cause of discord among the liberals and followed his advice of appointing Cánovas—without even consulting with Sagasta.[72]

The liberal experiment had ended in fiasco. But the monarch's thrust for liberalism had not been soured. He fully anticipated a return to the Liberals after a period with the Conservatives, but was wise enough to see that the existing mixture of liberal parties had made that course untenable. Fate was to determine that the final period of his reign would find him once again under the sometimes irksome but more stable tutelage of "Papa Cánovas."

9

Cánovas —

Last Minister of

Alfonso XII

 N JANUARY 18, 1884, the king had reverted to the Conservative leadership of Cánovas del Castillo. From that date until the king's death on November 25, 1885, the king's first prime minister again directed the course of politics. It was a dark and gloomy period. The word "Liberal" which had originally had a leading place in the designation of Cánovas's Liberal-Conservative party disappeared. A considerable portion of the former Moderados joined its ranks. The stance of the government was almost reactionary—it dealt vigorously with political opponents, quelled small military uprisings ruthlessly, instituted new actions against the opposition press, dealt harshly with protesting students, stopped off liberal reforms, and moved back toward protectionism. Sagasta and his Liberal followers blamed Cánovas for the shipwreck of the previous ministries and the polite tone of previous debates in the Cortes was to be missing during much of this period.[1]

In the midst of this political gloom the king moved unhappily,

beginning the final stages of his bouts with a progressively virulent tuberculosis, resenting the one-man role assumed by Cánovas, and unhappy with some of the ministers and their methods.
Sorrows and difficulties continued within the royal family. And
various natural and unnatural catastrophes enhanced the gloom
—new military revolts and rumors of dangers, talk of the Black
Hand, a disastrous railroad accident, the ravages of Asiatic
cholera, the effects of terrible earthquakes, and some serious
difficulties with the Germany he loved and admired so much.
In the midst of it all the king had no closer confidant or friend
than the German envoy, Solms-Sonnenwalde, whose dispatches
reflect again and again the king's feelings down to the last stages
of his illness, when Solms spent an hour and a half by the king's
bedside while the royal family waited outside. It was in a very
real sense a time of tragedy as one of Spain's most able and
intelligent kings lost the physical vigor which he needed to carry
through the necessary reforms in a political system which was
already proving too sterile to carry through the modernization
and revitalization of the state.

Most of the members of Cánovas's cabinet were already well
known at home and abroad. Romero Robledo returned to his
accustomed post as minister of the interior and Francisco Silvela,
his past and future rival, became minister of grace and justice.
Over the king's protest, supposedly because he had thrown one
of the king's romantic attachments, the Italian singer Adela
Borghi, out of Madrid while he was civil governor, José Elduayen became minister of foreign affairs. But Elduayen's reputation had been challenged for more valid reasons than his treatment of a king's mistress and in spite of his widely acknowledged
financial ability, he was to display serious shortcomings as minister of foreign affairs. Gen. Jenaro de Quesada, known as a strict
disciplinarian, became minister of war and Rear Adm. Juan
Antequera minister of the navy (he had commanded a Spanish
vessel, the *Numancia*, on a journey around the world). Fernando
Cos-Gayón became treasury minister and Manuel Aguirre de
Tejada the minister of overseas territories. New and highly significant in the ministry was Alejandro Pidal y Mon, the leader

of the so-called Unión Católica, who became minister of development. Pidal had taken this position with the express support of the pope, Leo XIII, in a move taking cognizance of the fact that no real "Catholic union" was possible and that it would be better for the church to work within the existing government to defend the place of religion in society. But Pidal y Mon's move found opposition within the ranks of those who had been the Moderados and virulent controversy continued between him and the Carlist-oriented Catholics and their newspaper *El Siglo Futuro*. On the other hand, although Pidal y Mon was an able orator, he enjoyed "needling" his more liberal opponents and contributed strongly to the reactionary aura of the cabinet.[2]

The report on the new cabinet by the American envoy, John W. Foster, was strongly negative. "It is," he stated, "very plainly a Conservative Ministry—how far it will prove a retrograde one will depend mainly upon Señor Cánovas who has so unreservedly the support of his party and is in temperament so decided in his purpose that he can mould the administration to his will. For the present it would seem as if all liberal progress had come to a halt in Spain."[3] Foster went on to note the ultramontane character of Pidal and the reactionary position of Aguirre, who had opposed the abolition of slavery and of the use of the ball and chain, as well as the "ultra-Conservative" character of Quesada.

Among the earliest actions of the new government was a delay of portions of the commercial agreement relating to trade with Cuba which had been reached by the United States and Spain and the beginning of a clear indication through the Council of State that the Spanish-British Commercial Treaty concluded under the preceding government was not likely to be ratified. Elduayen made it clear that he had earlier rejected terms such as those the Liberals had accepted and was not going to accept the present treaty unless Great Britain made better terms.[4]

The government, of course, moved to dissolve the Cortes and to set new elections for deputies for April 27 and for senators for May 8. Romero Robledo proceeded with dispatch to prepare for the requisite government majority. With the example of the procedures used by the Liberal minister of the interior Venancio González to undercut criticism, Romero Robledo pulled out all stops in his orchestration of the political scene. Solms found the situation taking on a "somewhat hateful character" and questioned why the government which could easily control 330 of the 430 electoral districts in Spain should be so concerned about the other 100. When Solms asked Cánovas why this was necessary, the latter responded, without convincing the German envoy, that he could not be sure of his followers.[5]

Most republican groups abstained from taking part in the elections, most notably the Federalist Republicans led by Francisco Pi y Margall, one of the former presidents of the first Spanish republic. The Republican Possibilists also decided to abstain but some members of that group broke party discipline and became candidates. On the other side of the political spectrum Cándido Nocedal, as hostile as ever to Pidal and his Unión Católica followers, conveyed to his Carlist friends the anathema of Carlos VII against any friends of the "Tradition" who took part in the elections.[6]

There was genuine fear that republicans might use the prospect of a reactionary government as the signal for revolt. Ruiz Zorrilla was again supposed to be supplying funds from French sources to aid the cause of revolution. Although the reports of a German police counselor who sought to assess radicalism in Spain emphasized the predominance of the Federalist Republicans and reported that they had been allowed to meet openly and organize in Spain in 1882 and 1883, the Germans assumed that if a successful pronunciamiento occurred, all of the old republican leaders would rally to the cause.[7]

On March 16 the government took preventive action, arresting and imprisoning a General Velarde, Brigadier Villacampa, and fifteen sergeants. A little later two more lieutenant generals, Ferrer and Hidalgo, were arrested. The government accused these officers of conspiracy. In later details it was learned that there had been serious suspicions of all of these under the previous ministry and a warning had been conveyed to Quesada by the former Minister of the Interior Moret, but government action was poorly timed and the government was not to be able to prove its case against them.[8]

Perhaps the alleged plot was meant to provide some justification for the arrest of potential republican voters, since the government opposition charged that large-scale arrests of political opponents had preceded the elections to the Congress of Deputies. The government triumph for the lower house found 295 Conservatives in the majority with 39 Fusionists, 27 Dynastic Leftists, 11 Ultramontanes, 6 Independents, 4 Republican Possibilists (who had broken the party decision for abstention), and 3 Progressive Democrats winning. Critics were to say that the new house was "dishonored before it was born" and a Possibilist to complain that the "Census committee falsified; the electors falsified; the alcalde falsified; and the Board of Elections falsified the results." And a later, by no means liberal historian, noted that in places where the opposition was supposed to be strongest, the Conservatives won huge majorities, and in other places where the voters were considered apathetic, the electoral urns literally vomited votes! But in later debates Romero Robledo noted with equanimity that the Liberals had overturned the governments of 1,600 ayuntamientos before *their* elections![9]

Two days after the election there was a real but minuscule republican revolt in the north, with a small band of men led by the former Captain Hinginio Mangado, who had led one of the risings in 1883, now leading a small band of men back across the border but all of them being killed in an encounter with the civil guard.[10] The government sought to make something more of a rising taking place at the same time in Santa Caloma de Farnés in the province of Gerona, where they arrested two officers, a Major Ramón Ferrándiz and a Captain Manuel Bellés and some fourteen followers.[11] When court martials later failed to assign the death penalty to the two leaders of this rising, the government overrode them and turned a deaf ear to impassioned pleas for clemency from home and abroad. The king was prevented from pardoning those sentenced by threats of cabinet resignation.[12] There was also some effort to suggest that a catastrophic train derailment on the line from Badajoz to Ciudad Real might have political action behind it.[13]

There was also continued talk of Black Hand activity in the South, although neither Solms nor a German police agent who came to study socialist activity in Spain was convinced of its seriousness. They felt it was probably just a continuance of the robber-band activity endemic in that area.[14] And in Gerona there was also a Carlist spark which struck no flames on the part of the Traditionalists.[15]

The opening of the Cortes seemed to turn the clock back to the pre-Liberal period. The message from the throne stressed law and order. There were new debates on the Cánovas conception of legal and illegal parties. Isabella II was at least partially rehabilitated as the only victim of the Revolution of 1868 and the Moderados suggested the possibility of her restoration! Posada Herrera recovered his position as a political butterfly hovering separate from any party designation and Martos also left the Dynastic Left, which now ceased to be a viable political party.[16] And Cánovas's minister of development Pidal found himself in a difficult position between more intransigent Catholics on the right and critical opposition on the left, managing to stir up a ruckus with the Italian government, which found some of his remarks with respect to the position of the pope offensive. Before it was over, Cánovas had to smooth over the situation with a clear declaration that Spain had no intention of clouding her relations with the Italian state and considered the position of the pope in Rome fully secure.[17] But the tone and the mood of the Cortes was strongly reactionary.

Later in the year Elduayen was to greet Solms overjoyed with the news that the pope had sent greetings to the king on his birthday, recognizing him as "the Legitimate and Catholic King of Spain." With this, felt Elduayen, the pope's break with the Carlists was complete. But the difficulties with Italy still continued—Elduayen believed that Castelar as a friend of the Italian ambassador Mancini was stirring him up to protest Pidal's remarks.[18]

In the midst of these events the king was ill and unhappy. Cánovas resumed his schoolmasterly tutelage of the monarch, forbidding him to go in disguise to the great costume ball hosted by the former ambassador to France, the duke of Fernan Nuñez. The king vowed in revenge that he would have his own costume ball the following winter and insist that all the ministers come in costume.[19] A little later the king was to complain that Cánovas "knows everything, decides everything, and interferes in everything, even in military matters of which he knows nothing and that he gives no consideration to the king's views and wishes." As an example he cited Cánovas's intention to use 25 million pesetas to fortify Spain's harbors, for which that sum was completely insufficient. The money, said the monarch, should be used to buy needed matériel for the army, but there was, of course, more graft to be obtained from construction than from buying cannon. In private the monarch also conveyed his criticism of Quesada's leadership in the army reorganization and of Romero Robledo's and Elduayen's election procedures.[20] Solms believed that Cánovas was making a serious error in trying to deal with Alfonso as he had when he was a boy of seventeen, but did suggest that the king had been spoiled by the leniency of the Liberal ministers.[21]

The monarch suffered throughout this period recurring attacks of illness which his doctors labeled "catarrh" but left him pale and weak and beginning to show a soberness which had not previously characterized him. But apparently neither his own disposition nor the advice of ministers could curtail his strenuous activity and lack of caution—the failure to wear an overcoat in the most inclement weather, for example.[22] The king's illness came at a time when his sister, the Princess Ludwig Ferdinand of Bavaria, was also very ill in Madrid and underwent a "terrible operation" as a part of a difficult delivery, with Queen María Cristina holding her in her arms during the operation and tending her night and day until recovery.[23] For the princess did recover and live to a ripe old age of eighty-four although the Queen's Austrian doctor had considered her case hopeless.

But the king's health continued to be a cause of concern, leading him to go to a health resort at Betelú near Tolosa during the summer, although he was still going on the hunt in the midst of heat which the German envoy found exhausting.[24] He returned from Betelú, his face still thin but some of the freshness of spirit and liveliness restored. His reception in the Carlist country had been excellent and he spoke with Solms and the Austrian ambassador with enthusiasm.[25] But from this time on there was a running comment on the king's health in republican journals in Paris, which emphasized the seriousness of his illness, and a continuing effort on the part of the court and the government to deny it.

The king was also somewhat concerned by the government's effort to mend fences with the French. Elduayen explained to Solms on a number of occasions that Spain had no intention of deserting her friendship with Germany, but the Germans noted that the new French ambassador, Baron de Michels, was constantly "hanging on Cánovas's apron strings."[26] The monarch still remained much interested in the change of the respective German and Spanish legations to embassy status and acted on Solms's suggestion of having Spanish officers trained in Germany with what the king considered excellent results.[27]

One action for which the king was given primary credit has a strangely modern note—a royal ordinance on May 8, 1884, which sought to revise the administration of the mountain lands to prevent deforestation and damage to the environment. Again this action was attributed to the king's experience with the forest administration in Germany and Austria.[28]

And the Germans on their part considered the king Spain's last best hope. Perhaps the police agent who investigated radical movements in Spain said it best when he reported:

> Whether the king, Alfonso XII, whose fresh, youthful spirit and optimistic influence make a marked contrast to the demoralizing pessimism which dominates the country in consequence of the shameless party selfishness and apparent impossibility of political reform, will be able to overcome the other opponents of his monarchy . . . and thereby to begin a new era for his country must be answered by future developments. His task is all the more difficult

because the errors and sins of his predecessors have deeply shattered the faith of the Spanish people in a monarchy so that it will take years of effort and a government with extraordinary good fortune to reestablish the moral basis of the monarchy and give it a reawakened popular consciousness that the welfare of Spain is only to be gained from an enlightened prince filled with the love of his country.[29]

But the king's illness dragged on into the fall and Cánovas on his part showed signs of declining verve and energy.[30] The African cholera, called after its supposed Indian origin the "terrible guest from the Ganges," made its inroads into Spain in September 1884, with Romero Robledo adopting extreme measures on the French frontier from which it had arrived.[31] Labeled excessive at this point, Romero Robledo's measures find justification in view of the horrible consequences of the plague during the following year. They did, however, awaken the strong criticism of Manuel Silvela, who had taken over the embassy in Paris and came back to Spain to protest the closing of the French frontier. The failure of the cabinet to listen to his arguments and the government's curt response when he suggested a visit of the monarch to affected places reflected the high-handed tone Cánovas assumed during this ministry and marked the beginning of some disagreement with Cánovas on the part of this respected political leader.[32]

But the king's mood had become more pro-Cánovist. "Sagasta was, of course, much more agreeable for me," he told Solms, "but I feel myself safer with Cánovas." And he suggested that he might keep Cánovas in office five years. Solms, however, was not convinced that Cánovas was doing a good job. He had neither the energy nor the working ability he had shown previously and turned over the decisions and tasks of the various ministries to their cabinet heads. Even old acquaintances complained of his haughtiness. And not much was being accomplished. Although army discipline was being improved, the navy, which should have had small ships to police the Cuban coast, purchased a much larger one at the cost of 20 million pesetas with the rumored commissions for the sale amounting to two million.[33]

Cánovas himself was quite sanguine in respect to the security of the army. When Solms raised the question of a tour of Andalusia by López Domínguez, the prime minister indicated he had no real worries about the general. López Domínguez had not, he told Solms, had a distinguished military career—there were at least thirty generals in his rank of lieutenant general who were more prominent than he was and he had no real possibility of bringing the outstanding marshals of Spain under his leadership, let alone the civilian liberals, who had their own ambitions. Besides he was basically conservative—had been brought up in good society and was only liberal because of his ambition. All in all, he was not of the cast of Espartero, Narvaez, O'Donnell, and Serrano. Besides, he felt the monarchy now had firm roots and although Ruiz Zorrilla might still cause difficulties with paid revolts, there was no real danger to be anticipated.[34]

However, the government's attitude soon changed. Cánovas's remarks came just a week before the beginning of student riots in Madrid. Before order had been restored, the government was professing deep concern over the possibility of a republican revolution. It all began with a formal address on October 1, 1884, by Professor Miguel Morayta, a professor of universal history, on the occasion of the opening of the academic year of 1884–85, a solemn affair under the presidency of Pidal as minister of development. Morayta, labeled a conspicuous Mason and a personal friend of Castelar, spoke on the subject, "Concerning the Origins of Man," setting forth a Darwinist approach.[35]

The reaction to this Spanish precedent for the much later affair of John Thomas Scopes in the United States was understandably extreme. The bishop of Ávila, later to be Cardinal Sancho, archbishop of Toledo, led the protest, directed not only against the professor, who was excommunicated, but Pidal, who had tolerated the delivery of the address with only a very moderate and indirect rebuke to Morayta for the nature of his speech. The students divided with some opposing the speech, but the majority demonstrating in behalf of Morayta, especially because he had also defended the cause of the liberty of science and academic freedom. Discussion and debate ran all through the month of October and well into November with emotions increasing rather than dissipating. Apparently Pidal precipitated the beginning of real difficulties beginning on November 17 as he favored student petitions opposing Morayta's speech. A small demonstration before the editorial offices of the reactionary newspaper *El Siglo Futuro* resulted in some arrests by the Civil Guard. When the students discovered the next morning that those who had been arrested were not released, they were outraged. The high point of the affair took place on November 20, 1884.

Neither the newspaper reports nor the debates which followed in the Cortes clarify the exact nature of the occurrences. Classes continued in the university, but since there were never enough seats in the classrooms to accommodate all of the students who were signed up for courses, there was obviously opportunity for many of them to demonstrate. Very probably there may have been then as in later university demonstrations outside intrusions bolstering the strength of the student groups. The whole affair began with a shouting match at the gates of the university with students indicating their disrespect for the bishop, the minister of development, and the civil governor of Madrid, who had been responsible for the previous day's actions. That worthy had already consulted with the cabinet and obtained permission in the event that there should be renewed difficulty to enter into the university grounds themselves, contrary to the ancient *fueros* or legal rights of the university. Whether the shouting of unpleasant things justified this or not is and was debatable. At any rate one Col. José Oliver, the leader of the Civil Guard at the university gates, burst into the university area brandishing his sword. On the pretext that he and his men had been shot at, they began to make brutal use of their weapons. Blood flowed not only in the halls but also in the classrooms of the university. The government was later to allege that only a ridiculously small number of students had been injured—professors on the scene believed a much larger number had been involved. There had been no effort to distinguish between guilty and innocent—noon classes had just let out and some of those who had been peacefully attending were subject to the actions of the police. When three professors of the Faculty of Medicine tried to mediate, they were rudely treated. Another professor who sought to protect his students was arrested. The rector of the university, Francisco de la Pisa Pajares, a friend of Sagasta, resigned, and an extreme rightist took his place. In the course of the events a large number of students had marched to Madrid's central square, the Puerta del Sol, and authorities later alleged that there had been cries of "Down with the King!" and "Long live the Republic!"[36]

The events set off tremendous and long-lasting repercussions. Pastoral circulars condemned the government for having allowed the speech. Liberal papers both at home and abroad condemned the arbitrary and harsh action of the government against the students and the invasion of the university, which by custom possessed autonomy. Cánovas and Pidal in reply alleged real dangers of insurrection, said the students had not been attacked until they left the university, and asserted that the press was magnifying the incident out of all proportion.[37] But the debate went on well into 1885 and before it reached its end, Manuel Silvela felt it necessary to join with his son Luis, a professor at the university, in protesting the actions of the government even though, in the name of party loyalty, he could not vote against it.[38]

As the German chargé noted, this whole incident was really most unfortunate for the government. Although bad judgment was certainly involved, it had not been planned and represented the "bad luck" of this ministry. That bad luck was intensified on Christmas eve of the same year when Madrid suffered a slight earthquake, which lasted only a few minutes but caused great panic. But much more severe than in Madrid were the tremors in Granada, where the first tremor caused major damage only to be followed by two others, and in Málaga, where there were reports of up to nine separate shock waves. As the telegraph slowly poured its doleful news into the capital, the government became aware that it confronted a natural catastrophe of major proportions. The shock waves had affected the whole south-central part of Spain, all the way from Seville on the west to Almería on the east and from Córdoba in the north down to the Mediterranean coastline on the south. In some places houses were crumpled and in several others deep crevices were opened.[39]

One of the most serious consequences of the earthquakes was that they drove thousands of people from endangered homes to seek refuge from bitterly cold winter weather in the fields, forests, and caves of the regions. Many perished from the cold and many more were later in the year to face even more terrifying consequences of the earthquakes, the onset of a cholera epidemic of major proportions.

The response of the government, the people of Spain, and the king was prompt and generous. A subscription of funds for relief was opened, to which the Papacy, the Spanish consulate, the Bank of Spain, and the king himself contributed funds so that when the monarch set off on January 9, 1885, for the affected regions, he carried with him half a million pesetas to aid those affected. He was accompanied by Romero Robledo, General Quesada, the duke of Sesto, and many of the deputies of the areas concerned. For a king whose health had been so much a source of concern it was a difficult trip. Many places were to be reached only on foot or on horseback. For some days there had been heavy snowfall in the area. And even Elduayen complained that the king did not take care of himself or pay proper heed to wind or weather.[40]

Nevertheless, the king returned from the expedition outwardly appearing "surprisingly strong and blooming." The popularity of his action was denoted by the reception in Madrid, the streets filled with cheering people in spite of pouring rain and a late evening arrival. The misery he had seen had very much affected the king. But part of it was not due to the earthquakes. "The administration in these regions is even worse than the earthquakes," he told an acquaintance, "but I will change that." Solms alleged that some of the opposition to the king's making the trip had derived from Romero Robledo's fear that the king would, as he had, get some glimpses of the poor administration there, adding that the minister of the interior had tolerated the existence of robber bands in that region because they were useful for election purposes. He suggested also that Cánovas was afraid that the king's growing popularity would undercut his own position and prestige. It was the queen's influence based upon urgent advice from Vienna which had led to the king's decision to take the trip, contrary to the advice of his ministers.[41]

Some of Solms's critical notes, here and later, may well have derived from irritation at the foreign policy of the Cánovas government. From the first, as has already been noted, the Conservative ministry had not hesitated to reverse or modify agreements already well underway or even completely negotiated. Along with the modification of the United States-Spanish agreement on Cuban trade and the absolute refusal to ratify the commercial treaty with Great Britain had come renewed difficulties with Germany in respect to unoccupied islands in the Pacific.

As will be recalled, there had been an earlier controversy over the Sulu Islands.[42] This time the controversy concerned the Carolines, a complex grouping of islands which, like the Sulus, bore some geographical relationship to the Philippines and had been touched upon by a number of Spanish explorers in the period of discovery. But the case for Spanish sovereignty in these islands was even less convincing than it had been in respect to the Sulu archipelago.

The major part of the controversy centered around the Yap Island grouping. The Palaus were a lesser part of the confrontation. Both were at a considerable distance from the Philippines and Spain had paid absolutely no attention to them during the past century. A British and German note of March 4, 1875, relating to the protest of the Spanish consul in Hong Kong to an unauthorized visit of a German schooner to the Carolines had set forth the British and German position clearly. Denying Spanish sovereignty in these islands, the note pointed out that there was not a single Spanish employee in the islands. Although the two powers raised no objection to Spain exercising control in these areas, they demanded that until the time Spain established an effective occupation with a government which could guarantee law and order and the security of commerce, she should not seek to extend to these areas the arbitrary commercial regulations which required ships to stop at some remote consular post before taking up trade with the natives.[43]

Spain, on her part, had not really effectively followed up the agreements in respect to the Sulu archipelago which had been the principal focus of controversy in the earlier period. By later reports Cánovas had indicated that his government had no real interest in the Carolines and his foreign minister Calderón Collantes had disavowed the expansionist policy of the then governor of the Philippines José Malcampo y Monge.

When the German government began to emphasize that the Berlin Conference of 1884, in which Spain had participated, carried with it the necessity for effective occupation and international notification in respect to possessions not only in Africa but elsewhere, the Spanish representative in Berlin notified his government of the desirability of prompt and effective occupation not only of the Sulus but of the Carolines.[44]

The warmth of German-Spanish relations had already begun to cool. The rapprochement with Baron de Michels, the French ambassador, continued. In October 1884 the baron had a long conversation with Cánovas in which, at first nervous and excited, the Spanish prime minister charged that France was deserting her alliance with England in participating in the Berlin Conference and moving toward Germany. His warning against negotiations with Bismarck was strongly phrased: "You know Bismarck well; he is the Italian of the North; he wants to *win* in everything; he never concerns himself except for his own affairs; his friends, his allies, in foreign policy as in internal policies, are only his tools; on the day when they have ceased to be useful, he tosses them aside with complete unconcern." Michels, of course, denied France was changing her alliances or her friends.[45]

Early in 1885 the marquis of la Vega de Armijo in a speech in the Cortes claimed that the government had failed to implement the arrangements he had already begun both with respect to Sulu and to the raising of the respective Spanish-German legations to embassy status.[46] Although the German dispatches bear out the validity of Elduayen's response that no real agreement had been reached in respect to Sulu and that the failure of the German Reichstag to provide funds had delayed the embassy project, the Germans were, indeed, very much upset by Cánovas's foreign policy.[47] Even Elduayen's comment about the Reichstag funds had been somewhat misleading—the Germans had all along insisted that the Spanish provision of funds should precede the German and there was considerable indication that the Spanish government hesitated to act for fear that it would have to enter into reciprocal agreements with a large number of other states.

The government was, of course, under considerable attack from the Liberals, who alleged that Spain was looking toward an alliance with Germany and should stay closer with sister Latin states or with freer nations like Great Britain and the United States.[48] But Bismarck began to show irritation with Cánovas's soft responses that Spain was no closer to Germany than to any other state—"his actions awakened the hostility of his excellency," noted a German Foreign Office memorandum. The Germans felt that Cánovas should have taken a stronger stand against rumors of poor German-Spanish relations and Bismarck did not like the assumption that better Spanish relations with France involved a cooler handling of Germany.[49]

The course of events which followed and almost led to war between Spain and Germany centered on the Yap group of the Caroline Islands, to be significant in later history as well as at this time. The German consul in Manila described the situation existing on the major island early in August 1885.[50] On this island there were some 12,000 natives and three foreign nationality groups represented—the German Plantation Society and the German firm Hernsheim and Company, an American named Hokum, and an English citizen named O'Keefe. The natives were energetic and carried on an extensive trade in copra. The land supplied most of their material needs, since they wore only a shift and had swine, fish, chickens, taro, breadfruit, sweet potatoes, yams, and bananas. But they imported tobacco, pipes,

tools, and, most importantly, weapons of all sorts including cannon, since there was chronic warfare among the local chiefs.
The foreign residents would be glad to have a dependable government, but the visit of a Spanish warship a year earlier had
been only for observation, not occupation.

Now, however, the consul conveyed to the German Foreign
Office the news that an expedition was being prepared for in-
stalling a navy lieutenant named Enrique Capriles as governor
of the islands. The expedition consisted of twenty-five native
soldiers from the Philippines with an infantry lieutenant, a European sergeant, and twenty-five penal convicts to serve as construction workers. Four Spanish friars would also take up their
work on the island. The official bulletin, the *Gaceta de Manila*,
had reported the provision of 10,000 pesos for the installation of
a political-military government of the Caroline and Palau Islands.

The consul added that Spanish rule in the Far East had been
disastrous. The regime in Madrid seemed to be fair, but those
whom they sent out acted as though the Philippines were their
own domain and exploited the natives with heavy and arbitrary
taxes, unwarranted seizures of pigs, chickens, and so forth, op-
pressive government monopolies, and harsh action against opposition. A German firm had begun a prosperous and effective
business in the Marianas in 1877, but had been forced to relinquish it when government officials set unfair conditions for its
continuance. As a consequence things had reverted to jungle
there and the same would occur in Yap if the Spanish took over.

The letter from Manila did not arrive in the German Foreign
Office until September 11 and long before that time affairs had
been set in motion for a *German* occupation of Yap. The Foreign
Office had been for some time under pressure from the Hernsheim firm to provide naval support for its activities in the Carolines. Rumors of Spanish plans had preceded the consul's note.
Top secret directives were, accordingly, dispatched to Shanghai
directing Germany's only available warship, the gunboat *Iltis*,
to proceed posthaste to take possession of Yap and other islands
in the Carolines in the name of Germany, but to avoid any conflict with Spanish ships in the area. On August 13 the German

ambassador in Madrid indicated the German intention to occupy the Caroline and Palau Islands. The Spanish replied with a protest and with orders that their expedition, which had been proceeding in its preparation at less than a snail's pace, depart immediately.[51] The consequence was a German-Spanish confrontation at Yap. When the *Iltis* arrived at Yap on August 25, its commanding officer found two Spanish ships, the *San Quintín* and the *Corigedo*, already there. When he went aboard the *San Quintín* to pay a courtesy call and explained the German intention to take possession of the island, the Spaniards protested that it was a Spanish possession. Capriles stated that the Spanish flag had already been raised on the island, but the captain of the *San Quintín* would not back up his story. As a consequence, the captain of the *Iltis* went ahead with his act of possession, but the next day found the Spanish flag raised. Under protest the Spanish officials took down the flag, reloaded provisions which had already been disembarked, and left the scene.[52]

Before these days few Spaniards would have had any idea of the location of Yap or any interest in the Caroline Islands. But from the day of the reception of the first German note in Madrid on, a great public outcry arose against Germany. The Germans at the outset blamed the government for causing it by releasing news of the note and protested against the tone of the press, which they labeled more insulting than the French press had been in 1870.[53] There was a small demonstration in Madrid on August 23 unaccompanied by any menace to the German legation. But news of the Spanish-German confrontation at Yap brought stronger reactions. This time mob action, ineffectually restrained, defaced the German legation and provided a bad reception for Solms, just returning from La Granja.[54]

Although the Germans felt that the Cánovas government was responsible for the initial uproar, the opposition took up the cry with vehemence. Ignoring the great distance of the islands from Manila, over 1,500 miles, and the potential expense for a small return, the opposition forces, supported strongly by the Spanish Society of Africanists and Colonists, took a very bellicose position. Even Generals Martínez Campos and Jovellar joined with

Sagasta in crying for action. There were suggestions that in the event of war Spain would be better off than Germany in view of its position in Manila, ignoring the very obvious fact that Germany in such a case would not confine her action to the Orient. Well might a later historian characterize the mood as one of "madness."[55]

The Germans had on their side the very strong support of the British, who announced their firm maintenance of their position of 1875 that Spain had no sovereignty in the Carolines and their belief that the Germans had priority there, although they added, "yet if the German government deem it advisable to relinquish, in favor of Spain, the right which they may have acquired by prior occupation, Her Majesty's government, of course, cannot object, though for the advantages of trade they would naturally prefer German ownership."[56]

Bismarck had firmly refused at the outset to negotiate until the anti-German notes of the press were quieted. But with the development of increasing excitement in Spain and the accompanying threat of war or the possibility of a republican exploitation of the crisis, the kaiser began to direct moderation. His concern for Alfonso's position was paramount. The Germans wre much worried by the activities of Gen. Manuel Salamanca back in his old position as a political gadfly and also as a republican menace within the military.[57]

Nor could the Germans ignore the very real possibility of military action. They began to collect accurate information on the strength of the Spanish military and naval forces in the area of the Philippines, the disposition of the Spanish fleet, and the general status of the Spanish army. Their concern was heightened by the judgment of the German military attaché in Madrid that if there had been a conflict between the ships at Yap, war would already have come.[58]

But war was avoided and a peaceful solution was found, most fortunately for Spain. Elduayen sought to extricate himself from an untenable situation by promising the Germans shipping stations, coaling places, and provision depots if the Germans recognized Spanish sovereignty.[59] Bismarck, on his part, chastened by the kaiser's concern for Alfonso, which he also shared, initiated the move for arbitration. By this time he was also aware that the Spaniards had had technical priority in the occupation of Yap, although led to that action by the German plans, and that the German naval officer there had obeyed his orders explicitly but unwisely in view of the circumstances concerned. Bismarck was also later to say that he had figured that a week's warfare in the Far East would cost more than twice as much as German commerce there was worth for an entire year. As a consequence, he had restrained the German navy, which was itching for a shooting match to give its ships some genuine target practice.[60]

Bismarck, never very appreciative of the Spaniards, was highly critical of their behavior in this crisis. "They have conducted that affair in a very foolish manner," he said. He held Cánovas particularly responsible, saying he had "contradicted his promises because they were purely verbal and not written," and had shoved responsibility for affairs on the shoulders of the minister of foreign affairs, whom Cánovas said was the only official spokesman of the Spanish government for foreign affairs. As for the king, Bismarck considered him a dead man, "and I shall regret that, because the king was the only honest man with whom I have had dealings in Spain."[61]

And, indeed, Alfonso, whatever umbrage he may have felt at the outset, had been the major force in Spain for moderation. Early in September Solms had learned of the monarch's concern for the situation and of his sharp reproof of Salamanca for the return of his German decorations. But not until September 4 was the German envoy able to meet personally with the king in the garden at La Granja. The king listened attentively to all of Solms's explanations, only commenting that he had been brought up to believe the Carolines were Spanish, although the documents did not prove it. But he emphasized, "I am, however, no Napoleon, who lets himself be forced into war. I will never allow myself to be pushed into war against Germany and I can only repeat to you that I have the most unshakeable confidence in his majesty the Kaiser, the Crown Prince, and the German government." And he added plaintively. "What must you think of the people I have to rule!" In the period that followed the king emphasized repeatedly his opposition to war and by the middle of September Solms was able to report his quieting of the agitation. Morphy, who saw Solms at that time, paid tribute to the king's "statesmanlike qualities" and "clarity and firmness of judgment" in the crisis.[62]

Eventually both parties accepted Bismarck's suggestion of arbitration by Pope Leo XIII. The pope's award recognized Spanish sovereignty in the Carolines, but left the Marshall and Gilbert Islands subject to German occupation, and guaranteed free and unobstructed German commercial rights in the Carolines, along with rights of property ownership and the concession of a naval and coaling station. Spain never enjoyed the fruits of her possession—she was to have serious controversies with the United States over the Carolines and sell them to Germany in 1899 after the Spanish-American War.[63]

Spain was also in difficulty with the United States during 1885. As has been noted, the Cánovas ministry had begun with a modification of the *modus vivendi* arranged between the two countries in respect to trade with Cuba and Puerto Rico, but with the promise that the new government would negotiate a full commercial treaty relating to the subject.[64] John W. Foster, the American envoy, was given unusual full powers to negotiate such a treaty. The Spanish government was under great pressure to improve conditions on the island, which the German consul in Havana described as "a situation of complete degeneration, not to say barbarism, in which a large part of the island finds itself." And, noted the consul, there remained the old basic complaints—"the complete lack of ability and boundless corruption of the officials," the high tariffs, the bad condition of those under the patronage system against whom stocks and chains were still employed. That this estimate had justification was reflected in the Cortes debates of June and July, 1884, with the Cánovas government proclaiming its determination to make every sacrifice to retain the island and improve conditions there. But in the face of the agitation of the Cuban representatives, the Spanish government assumed increased power over Cuban affairs, including its budget, debt arrangements, and paper money.[65]

By June 30, 1884, Foster was finally able to initiate negotiations with Cánovas. Obviously these negotiations offered the best chance for the improvement of Cuban conditions, with a better market for the sale of sugar, tobacco, and other Cuban and Puerto Rican products and a potential reduction of the cost of living there. But Foster soon found that Elduayen was not really interested in tariff reduction—he still connected the tariffs strongly with the obtaining of governmental revenues in Cuba and opposed any kind of significant concessions. Foster approached Cánovas on the subject, stressing the difficulties existing in Cuba and the anger sure to be engendered there if a treaty were not concluded, and Cánovas appointed a special commissioner to represent Spain for the negotiations, apparently bypassing Elduayen.[66]

The commissioner was none other than Salvador Albacete, who had been minister of overseas territories under Martínez Campos, when Cuban reforms had been so paramount. Albacete proved to be a tough negotiator. He and Foster engaged in twenty-four conferences before they finally arrived at a treaty which seemed to promise much relief for the Cuban economy as well as trade advantages for the United States.[67]

But before the treaty was presented to the United States Senate, extracts from it were published in the *New York Times* with it quickly being disclosed that a copy of the treaty had been sold by a Spanish official for $2,000. Before the scandal was over with, the Spanish Senate held a "6,000 duros debate" in which the role of Dionisio López Roberts, count of Romera, the secretary of the Senate, who had signed the treaty, was weighed. Again one of the Silvela brothers, this time Francisco, opposed the action of Romera, while Elduayen defended it.[68]

There were, of course, rumors that Elduayen had encouraged the premature release of the treaty after having effectively delayed its negotiation in order to sabotage it. And this did occur. In the face of serious opposition from the Senate, President

Grover Cleveland, who had replaced Chester A. Arthur under whom the negotiations were concluded, withdrew it from Senate consideration and sent Foster back to Madrid to seek modification. Again Elduayen showed no interest in negotiations and, although Cánovas still professed sympathy, there is serious question whether the protectionist-minded prime minister really desired results.[69] And by 1886 the United States and Spain were again to be arguing over the differential flag rates—the different charges applied to goods arriving in Cuba in other than Spanish ships.[70]

Similarly, perhaps partially because England had supported Germany so strongly in the Yap affair, Spanish relations with that country were at an extremely low ebb. Elduayen sabotaged a *modus vivendi* agreed upon with England preliminary to a commercial treaty which would have given Great Britain most-favored-nation status and defended actions of Spanish authorities in Havana which went so far as to violate the diplomatic immunity of the British consul general there. The latter dispute was settled only after the strong and direct protests of the British Foreign Minister Lord Salisbury. They also sought to tax the British legation in Madrid and threatened to sequester furniture for nonpayment.[71]

The government's foreign policy had, therefore, come very close to breaching very friendly relations with Germany, had brought very cool relations with Great Britain, the United States, and Italy, and apparently, in view of later events, had not really won the strong favor of France.

Nor was the government's position at home free from justified opposition. As has been noted, the debate over the government's handling of university questions continued well into 1885.[72] Added to this troublesome concern was the storm of protest which erupted in Catalonia over a reform of the Civil Code of Laws, which threatened to overturn regional legal arrangements, based heavily on the dispositions of the Roman Law in respect to family and property institutions. The virulence of the protest was increased by the negotiations with England looking to most-favored-nation trading status for that country, a move which the

Catalans believed would be disastrous for their industry. The Centre Catalá convened representatives of cultural, political, and economic societies on January 11, 1885, and they drew up a petition which came to be called the "Memorial de Greuges" (grievances). A commission was appointed to see the king, who received them in audience on March 10. The Catalans spoke of their respect for Spanish unity, but claimed their foral privileges, the preservation of their regional administrative system, the use of the Catalan language in the schools, emendation of the proposed civil law, and preservation of their industry. The king's response was vigorously favorable. Although he emphasized that he was a constitutional monarch, implying that he could not deal directly with their grievances, the king paid respect to the energy of the Catalans and their industrial contributions to Spain, proclaimed himself a protectionist and individualist, and promised to study the manifesto of the commission.[73]

The critical implications of the king's comments were self-evident and the Catalans, on their part, continued to collect signatures and declarations in behalf of the maintenance of their local customs and language. Undoubtedly this protest had a negative effect on the negotiations for commercial treaties with Great Britain, the United States, and France. But Catalan discontent tended to aid the efforts of the government's opponents to reestablish unity.[74]

There was also criticism of the government for the existing unemployment and more importantly for the return to the system of government "irregularities" (graft). The most serious revelation of these "irregularities" occurred in respect to the municipal government of Madrid, where an investigation disclosed such flagrant wrongs that the entire city council and the mayor were replaced, but without legal process being instituted against those involved. As a result all of the opposition united against the government and confronted Romero Robledo with an unprecedented defeat, the opposition winning in thirty-two boroughs to the government's eighteen. These results encouraged the opposition in the provinces also.[75]

By the middle of May 1885, discontent had reached serious

levels among such Conservative party members as Manuel Silvela, who told Solms, "Corruption and bad economics have reached a level which the people can't stand." The opposition concentrated on Romero Robledo, Pidal, and Elduayen. But Silvela found the king giving the appearance of being "dispirited and disgusted," too much under the influence of bad companions, too much interested in hunting and gambling.[76] Although the German envoy was inclined to agree at this point, he was to note a little later that the king had been strongly devoting himself to army affairs, visiting the garrisons around Madrid, breakfasting with the officers, and making exercise marches with them. The king told the former Liberal foreign minister, the marquis of la Vega de Armijo, "If I always listened to the opposition, I would have to change the ministry every six months."[77]

In the midst of political dissent cholera began to make giant strides across the southern provinces of Spain, taking a heavy toll in Murcia and Valencia and making minor inroads in Madrid itself. This occasioned several kinds of political debate. One related to the harsh sanitary procedures instituted by Romero Robledo, which occasioned a serious demonstration in Madrid, where shops were closed and a protest march held, with republicans taking advantage of the situation to raise cries against the king. For the merchants of Madrid "business as usual" was more important than the dangers of cholera, and when a delegation from the merchants saw the monarch a week later in a sort of apology for their actions, his tone with them was sharp and critical—they had caused more deaths than the cholera![78]

A second controversy centered around the king's strong efforts to make a personal trip to the cholera area in Murcia. A threat of resignation by his ministry followed and the king consulted both the count of Toreno and Sagasta in respect to alternate ministries, but both refused to accept with the approval of the king's trip as a precondition. That the king's attitude found sympathetic reception abroad was underscored in a telegraphic advisory from Bismarck which told Solms not to advise the king, but that if he asked Bismarck's opinion, he would advise him to make the trip—there was as much danger, he thought, in Madrid as in Murcia.[79]

As a compromise measure Cánovas and Romero Robledo made the official visit to Murcia, where they distributed 80,000 pesetas for immediate needs, but stayed only twenty-four hours and carried their own foodstuffs with them. Although criticized at the time, modern medicine suggests this was a wise precaution.[80]

Still a third controversy occasioned by the cholera epidemic related to the anti-cholera injections being given by a Dr. Jaime Ferrán y Clua of Barcelona. A student of the work of Pasteur, Ferrán had been commissioned in 1884 by the city council of Barcelona to study the cholera epidemic in Marseilles and Toulon. After work in France he returned to his own small and primitive laboratory in Tortosa, where he claimed to have isolated the cholera vibrios (bacteria) and to be able to give preventive injections such as those for smallpox.[81]

A distinguished medical committee including doctors from France and the United States visited the area to investigate his claims, but their reports were inconclusive. The American doctor was more skeptical than the French member of the committee, although both were critical of Ferrán's secrecy in respect to the formulation of his vaccine. As a consequence, there were variant standards of usage—military authorities sponsoring inoculations and civil authorities opposing. Ferrán was to complain that government indifference had prevented the efficacious usage of his vaccine.[82]

In the long run the logic of Ferrán's work was upheld by scientific study, but the debate over whether the live antigens he used should be employed has continued and many later inoculations have caused serious reactions on the part of those to whom they were given. The studies of the time did indicate that some of his vaccine was contaminated, not so remarkable in view of the small amount of government aid he was given, but a judgment that his vaccine "probably killed more people than it protected" is not upheld by the statistics of the medical commission which investigated. A combination of the doctor's youth (he was thirty-three at the time), his primitive laboratory apparatus, his secretiveness in respect to the preparation of the vaccine (he "had a family to support"), and Spanish misoneism, which feared the new and untested technique, prevented a fair trial. Very probably the resignation a little later of the director of sanitary affairs in Spain, Alberto Bosch, reflected the popular judgment that the government should have tried anything which promised to check the ravages of this terrible disease.[83]

By the end of June Romero Robledo himself was admitting that he was the most unpopular man in Spain due to his sanitary policies, and there were continuing rumors of cabinet crises and reports that the duke of Sesto and Cánovas were still handling the king like a child.[84] At seven o'clock on the morning of July 2 the king proclaimed his independence by taking the train from Madrid to the nearby town of Aranjuez, where the cholera had made serious inroads. He was accompanied only by an adjutant and went without notifying the cabinet. There he found the people despondent, visited the hospitals and lazarets, and ordered the sick soldiers moved into the royal palace there. He had left a note to Cánovas asking pardon, but saying he felt it was his duty to go. In Madrid the news of the king's coup closed the sessions of the Cortes and filled the streets with a populace applauding him for his courage and independence.[85]

In later accounts there was the report that the king on receiving the severe admonitions of Cánovas for having so risked his life, responded, "This is often the result of the heroic deeds of men; they praise me and scold me for having risked that which I don't have, the life which escapes from me minute by minute."[86] For from this point on the king entered into an increasingly critical period of the virulent tuberculosis which was to cost him his life, keeping the seriousness of his illness secret as his ministers desired, and engaging in public functions as damaging to his health as the brief visit to Aranjuez.

Shortly after this incident the expected cabinet change came, Cánovas and most of the ministry remaining while Romero Robledo and the minister of the navy Antequera resigned. Antequera, who had resigned because of opposition to naval reforms, was replaced by Vice Adm. Manuel de la Pezuela y Lobo and the place of Romero Robledo was taken by Raimundo Fernández-Villaverde, known as "an excellent official, loyal, of great personal courage," but considered as reactionary and severe as Romero Robledo himself.[87]

There were, as always, continuing rumors of republican moves and conspiratorial activities and Villaverde took prompt and effective action against minor conspiracies in Gerona and Zaragoza.[88] These rumors were to increase as well as the substance behind them during the summer, while the king's health worsened so that by the time of the difficulties over the Carolines the king was again subject to "catarrh" with coughing and fever attacks.[89] Solms believed that the ministry used the question of the Carolines to divert public opinion and found the republican movement becoming serious.[90] There were also Carlist dangers since Cándido Nocedal, the leader of the Traditionalists, had died on July 18 and Don Carlos himself took over the leadership of the movement in an effort to avoid the divisions which had existed. Obviously the death of Alfonso with only a female heir would give the movement new life.[91]

In the midst of the Yap affair Solms was becoming quite critical of Cánovas as well as Elduayen, regarding him as typical of the group in Spain who displayed great energy as they moved up from "the lower spheres," but when they got to the top were no longer able to maintain the moral leadership they had once exerted. Even with all of the Liberal hue and cry against Germany, he felt a Sagasta ministry might improve matters and quiet people down, "although experience teaches that on the whole everything remains as it was."[92]

Solms saw the king only at a distance. In October he reported that the king's "youthful freshness had disappeared by August and that the Queen's doctor said he now 'looked like a corpse and had the expression of death on his face.'"[93] At the end of October he attended the races in Madrid and Solms found him "very suffering—his walk and posture were very weak."[94] By the middle of November the king at rest in the Pardo appeared better and Solms learned of plans for the king to go to San Lucar in the south of Spain.[95] But the recovery was short-lived. By November 20 in the midst of cold and rainy weather the king was very ill again[96] and after lengthy consultations of the doctors (still officially to the end with the notable exception of the queen's Austrian doctor denying tuberculosis), the king entered into the death stages on November 25. During the night he sent the queen, his personal physician, and his secretary, Count Morphy away, later calling out the words, "what a struggle!" with which this book began, then sleeping more easily and being found only after he had been dead at least half an hour. In later stories of the illness it was indicated that the king had been well aware of the nature of his illness, that he had kept secret his weakness after hard riding or hunting expeditions and hidden the blood-filled handkerchiefs, so that the room servants remarked on how many had been lost. It was also revealed that Cánovas had known from the king's personal physician of the seriousness of the king's illness, had been told that a warmer climate might lengthen his life for a year or two, but had sworn the physician to secrecy and taken the risk of the king's death to prevent adding fire to republican propaganda.[97]

It was, perhaps, fitting that the last friend to see the king and to talk with him at length just two days before his death was Solms.[98] If there was one thread of continuity in the king's life, it was his great admiration for Germany, for the kaiser, for Bismarck, for the German army and his friendship with Solms himself. It is not clear from the dispatches whether Solms was able to tell the king that the kaiser himself had directed the German signature to the protocol which would end the Yap affair. But certainly Solms must have been able to assure him that there would be no difficulties.

The king met him standing in the middle of the room and offered his hand. His face was pale and bloodless, his eyes and voice weak. Solms hastened to finish his business, but the king kept him to talk. "I thought I was very strong physically," he said, "and 'I have burned the candle at both ends.' I have discovered too late that it is not possible to work all day long with the head and amuse oneself all night! I shall give that up in the future." He would, he said, go to San Lucar and recover, perhaps come back for skiing in the Casa de Campo. He rejoiced in the marriage of his sister and the pregnancy of his wife— "Who would have thought it! I had already completely given up the hope of still having children!" But he added, "I am much sicker than people believe. If someone said to me, 'Tomorrow you will die,' that would be quite all right with me—but at twenty-eight years old to be so completely weak and so washed out is a terrible fate, if it should go on for long."

And in one final comment on the Yap affair and Spanish concerns about it, he declared, "I can assure you that not only the Spanish people but also all my ministers, without exception, were completely crazy." The king coughed softly at the end of their conversation, placed his handkerchief before his mouth and then bade Solms a gracious farewell. Solms had been with him over an hour while the duke and duchess of Montpensier, Generals Echagüe and Blanco, Count Morphy, and the duke of Sesto waited outside. The king's fondest recollections during the interview had been those of his visit to the kaiser at Bad Homburg— if he could go again this year, he said, he knew he would feel better.

Alfonso had ruled one month less than eleven years—he never reached the twenty-eighth birthday he anticipated in his conversation with Solms. His reign had been marked by constant rumors of revolts, earthquakes, cholera, and disillusionment, but he had provided stability for the throne, a balance wheel for the government, and a leadership which weakened the revolutionary disposition of the military.

His Austrian wife became regent and during her reign came the promotion of the respective Spanish and German legations to embassy status which her husband had sought as well as a semi-attachment of Spain to the Triple Alliance. His son, born after his death to become Alfonso XIII, was to share much of his father's admiration for Germany. But Spanish traditions had been too strong for Cánovas to become a true Bismarck or the king to equal the status of the German kaiser.

10

Retrospect and Judgment

 HE ELEVEN YEARS of Alfonso XII's reign had been
filled with political difficulties and turmoil. At the
age of seventeen the king had begun his role as
Spain's first constitutional monarch. He found it a
difficult task. As the years passed, he came to know
the leading personalities in the maelstrom of Spanish politics. With this knowledge had come considerable disillusionment and at times disgust. And it
also became clear that the role of a constitutional monarch in
Spain was to be very different from that exercised in England.
Although affairs followed the normal course of parliamentary
procedures after elections had been held, the nature of Spanish
elections under the Constitution of 1876 and the procedures instituted by Romero Robledo provided the governing party with
such an overwhelming majority that the only recourse of the
opposition was to make speeches in the Cortes, publish critical
stories in the newspapers, and engage in political agitation. The
judgment as to when this agitation was sufficiently dangerous
and the governing party no longer capable of a reasonably popular conduct of government lay in the hands of the monarch. In
the final analysis he decided whether the government should
resign or continue.

Through this basic control over the life or death of a government, the king also possessed a potentially very strong influence on governmental decisions. He presided over the cabinet sessions. He could and on occasion did refuse to ratify decisions. But he exercised this power very sparingly, at first because of his deference to Cánovas to whom he owed his throne and the stabilization of a chaotic political system. Both in that early period and later he also regarded his position as one in which he should, except in conditions of extreme urgency, defer to the responsible ministers. Under the Liberals he felt somewhat freer but still refrained from intervention into the normal course of politics. His personal inclinations were favorable to the liberalization of politics, but the rapid dissolution of liberal unity left him with no recourse but a return to the Conservatives. The second Cánovas period was disillusioning and the king's last two years were unhappy ones.

There was another area in which the king also had great potential influence—the military. From the first, advisers at home and abroad pushed the monarch to take a role of leadership over the army. The king followed this advice with some reluctance at first. In the early years he took part in the victory parade after the Carlist War, attended some reviews, but did not display real interest. But his first major governmental change came as the result of potential military difficulties—the political revolt of Martínez Campos and his friends. His incipient interest in military affairs was greatly increased after his visit to Germany and it became obvious that he hoped to create in Spain an army which would add to his international prestige. He pursued the cause of military reform avidly but achieved only a portion of what he sought—the army was at least partially depoliticized but not greatly strengthened. The king's constitution was overstrained by his efforts—a few more years and vital changes might have been accomplished.

The personality of the king was a winning one. He clearly possessed a personal charisma which charmed the emperors of Austria and Germany, most of the diplomatic representatives from abroad, and many of his potentially republican opponents.

He had a high degree of talent in public speaking in a country where this was a mark of great distinction. His goodwill and sincerity, his genuine patriotism, his calmness and moderate judgment were revealed again and again during his brief reign. But he also had a proclivity for personal indulgence which cost him heavily physically. Perhaps this reflected in part a search for release from a political situation which often disturbed him deeply. Then, too, habits begun when he assumed the throne at such an early age became entrenched and were to some degree a reflection of a society in which the theater, the *tertulia* at the café, a tendency to seek amusements even in the midst of difficult times were proclivities of both high and low society. Was it really to be expected that a young monarch would live the life of a monk in such a country?

Judgment on the king is simpler than that on Cánovas. He has long enjoyed a great prestige among Spanish historians. The contemporary Spanish historian Jesús Pabón y Suarez de Urbina relates that his whole early life was filled with the respect for Cánovism which predominated in Spain.[1] Others, such as José Luis Comellas, follow the earlier biographers of Cánovas in a strong defense of "the Cánovist system."[2] Ferrán Soldevila mixes praise and cautious criticism, writing of Cánovas's "skill and his harshness, his pride and intransigence, his prudence and decisiveness, his will power and his pessimism, his cultivated spirit and his joy in action and in struggle, and, above all, his lordly prestige, which gained him 'more respect than sympathy' and went along with a certain slovenliness in dress."[3]

But the great Spanish philosopher José Ortega y Gasset labeled the Restoration "a panorama of fantasies and Cánovas the great impressario of fantasmagoria." He paid respect to Cánovas's intellectual accomplishments but labeled him "a professor of corruption" who corrupted even the incorruptible, a leader who took over the role of the good Lord in constructing the opposing Liberal party, "a species of good devil or of poor devil, with which he completed his paradisical picture."[4]

Ortega's judgment is too harsh. No political leader can divorce himself from the traditions and mores of his country. Cánovas lived in a country which, in spite of economic progress, remained weak and backward in the Europe of the late nineteenth century. But the directing classes of the country sought to insulate themselves from this realization. They enjoyed the brilliant social life of the day, the high level of the theater, the parade of literary and intellectual celebrities in the academies, the animated conversations in the cafes. These were a part of a continuing Spanish tradition that the days of the Golden Age still lived on, that Spain remained a great nation except for her political backwardness, that she was being robbed of a position in international affairs that should accord with that of a major power. Perhaps Cánovas's major strength was the recognition that these days were past, that Spain must content herself with modest accomplishments, that politics was the art of achieving the possible.

But these very realistic presentiments were not accompanied by a search for innovation or renewal. This was underscored in the events relating to Cuba, as noted above. Even Concepción Arenal's pilgrimage for penitentiary reform gained nothing but kind words from the monarch. Ricardo de la Cierva finds Cánovas's major weakness in his failure to open paths to a larger role in Spanish life for the new classes which began to appear upon the scene. He believes that Cánovas began to realize the need for state intervention in social and economic life in 1889, but regards this as too late to be effective.[5] But none of Cánovas's rather dreary *discursos* provided real inspiration for a changed course of public policy or a renewal of public morale.[6] The king's Bismarck was rather like the monarch himself—finding relief from his own cynicism in the café society of the day or in his very creditable literary and historical pursuits.[7] Neither he nor the king displayed the energy, self-discipline, and drive for accomplishment of their German counterparts.

This story contains no clear lessons for the present monarch. He rules in a country very different from that of Alfonso XII and one much less able to shelter itself behind the Pyrenees from the influence of the outside world. But it may be hazarded that much still remains the same—the same deep divisions in the

Liberal camp, the same excessive bureaucratic influence, the same concern for potential military pronunciamientos, the same entrenched opposition to basic reform. Perhaps all that the history of Alfonso XII's reign offers is the example of an honest and well-meaning ruler who ought to have been blessed with better ministers and a more tolerant and cooperative political establishment.

Appendix

Solms's Dispatch Recounting His Last Visit with King

Alfonso XII of Spain, GFO, Reel 71

A10951—30 November 1885

SOLMS IN MADRID TO HIS EXCELLENCY, PRINCE VON BISMARCK, *No. 368*,
26 November 1885

I am the last friend whom His Highness the most honorable
King Alfonso accorded the honor of a reception.

The duke of Sesto announced me on the twenty-third of this month
at 11:30 and led me into the king's private room located on the second
floor, which was decorated with Gobelins [tapestries] and covered with
a thick carpet. The king was already standing in the middle of the
room, gave me his hand, and motioned me to a chair while he sank
down on an easy chair. I had not seen His Majesty close at hand since
the races of October 24 and although he already at that time seemed
frighteningly pale and weak, I found him looking still more colorless.
His face was completely white and bloodless, his lips blue, his mouth
not fully closed, his eyes very lifeless, likewise his voice and his entire
bearing.

The business portion of the conversation, which I cut as short as
possible, was quickly taken care of and I thought His Majesty would
dismiss me at once. But this did not occur.

The king turned to his travel plans; said he would go to San Lucar
and hoped that the mild air would restore him again, since his illness
consisted only in anemia. He still had no appetite ever and because the
sea air had always been good for him, he wanted to make some little
excursions to the closest ports. If it should go better, he was still thinking of coming back for the skiing in the Casa de Campo and perhaps
also still to hunt a little. Toward the end of January he would come

back to Madrid and the preparations for the marriage of his sister, which would take place on February 10.

I took the opportunity to congratulate His Highness on this happy event, whereon he remarked, "Eulalia has in this way the good fortune to remain in her homeland, which is seldom the portion of a princess. She will be very rich and can travel around the world wherever she wishes, either as a princess or incognito." I interjected that the young prince had become somewhat freer, especially when the duke of Montpensier was not close by. It would be very good if one transferred him to the hussars at Aranjuez. His Majesty answered, "I have given him too much leave for his bride; he must spend more time with his comrades!"

Upon my congratulations to the approaching delivery of Her Majesty the Queen, the king said: "Who would have thought it! I had already completely given up the hope of still having children!"

In respect to his health, the king said in passing: "I thought I was very strong physically and 'I have burned the candle at both ends.' I have discovered too late that it is not possible to work all day long with the head and amuse oneself all night! I shall give that up in the future."

I allowed myself to remind His Majesty that I had often said he slept too little. Four to five hours sleep and many nights not even going to bed was not in the long run to be stood.

His Majesty then said, "I am much sicker than people believe. If someone said to me, 'Tomorrow you will die,' that would be quite all right with me—but at twenty-eight years old to be so completely weak and so washed out is a terrible fate, if it should go on for long."

Upon this I said to His Majesty that at his age he still had strength enough to restore his blood, but that would not go quickly and therefore a longer absence from Madrid was absolutely necessary. I found him [I said] looking better than I expected, namely his ears again had more color and were not so transparent as earlier.

The king seemed pleased to hear this and he stated: "I shall be away from Madrid as much as I can; I will be here only for the marriage of my sister and the delivery of the queen and then go at once to La Granja. I will live entirely according to my health, since as long as I am sick I can concern myself about nothing. I will come on the thirtieth to Madrid. Just think, Camison suggested to me that I go to the opera so that the people would see that I was not so sick; [he said] it would not hurt me."

I was absolutely horrified by this idea and said: "Your Majesty will surely not do that; the people here have no concern for anything but public opinion. All the opera glasses would be, with the usual indiscretion, turned upon Your Majesty; that would make even a well person nervous!"

"I will indeed take care that I don't go to the opera.—If I could attend a maneuver with you this year rather than sitting here, I would feel much better!"

I had already often noticed that the days spent in Homburg were a favorite memory of His Majesty and answered thereby: "The pleasure of attending our maneuvers would still be often available to Your Majesty, since Your Majesty knows how welcome a guest you are with us!"

His Majesty then inquired very fully concerning the health of His Majesty the Kaiser and the Kaiserin and His Royal Highness the Crown Prince, the wife of the Crown Prince, and of Prince William.

His Majesty then reminded me of our last conversation on September 4 in La Granja. I then came to speak about the very friendly note, which I delivered to Sr. Elduayen on that day and on the senseless manner and way in which people had published the news from Yap and had interpreted it in a manner which had as good as nothing to do with the question in dispute. With this I told His Majesty that His Majesty the Kaiser or His Imperial and Royal Highness the Crown Prince had remarked to Count Benomar [the German envoy in Berlin] that there were only two sensible Spaniards, the one was His Majesty the King, the other Count Benomar!

This seemed to make the king very happy, since he answered rather livelily, "I can assure you that not only the Spanish people, but also all my ministers, without exception, were completely crazy."

Meanwhile, the duke and duchess of Montpensier had arrived to breakfast with His Majesty. Since I knew the painful punctuality of the company and also wished to avoid keeping the king talking too much, I asked whether I shouldn't withdraw. His Majesty answered in a cheerful tone: "No, I have asked Sesto to receive them; it won't hurt my uncle at all, if he has to wait for once."

I remarked that the excessive punctuality would often burden His Majesty in San Lucar. It was said that the duke determined the activities for the days of the week beforehand and if the program said, "Friday from three to five o'clock will be horseback riding," then there had to be horseback riding no matter how bad the weather was. Also it wasn't always so very warm in San Lucar. We had run into very cold weather there.

The king said his uncle had consideration for him and had also recently brought in heaters everywhere.

Finally, His Majesty asked me whether I had read the brochure which had just appeared concerning society in Madrid: "Morphy and I have come out well, but Sesto very badly."

I told His Majesty that I would probably share the same fate as the latter, since I had refused to receive the author, a correspondent of the *Figaro* and a native-born Spaniard; Morphy on the contrary had in hand his loan notes, which made the author cautious.

At the end of the conversation the king coughed softly and put his handkerchief before his mouth; then he stood up and gave me his hand and dismissed me in the most gracious manner.

As I walked into the next room, I found the duke and duchess of Montpensier, whom I congratulated on the engagement of the Infante, and the Generals Echagüe and Blanco, Count Morphy, and the duke of Sesto. They asked me in the rather hasty greeting how I had found the king.

Since I was the first friend whom the king had received in a long time and knew how anxiously the court and the royal family concealed the true state of the king, I answered shortly, the king seemed to me more lively than I had expected.

If I had known that the king suffered not from anemia but from tuberculosis, as has now become gradually known, I would still from the impression which he made upon me have given him scarcely a week to live.

It was at once commonly spread about in Madrid that I had found His Majesty looking considerably better.

It appears that remarks were made to His Majesty that he had extended his conversation with me too long (it lasted over an hour), since the king told the Infanta Isabella it had pleased him to see me, he had enjoyed himself, and I had also brought him good news.

I have allowed myself to relate even the less significant matters of this conversation in detail because they may have a certain interest as the last words which His Majesty the King had with me and for that matter with any friend.

Notes

CHAPTER 1. *Revolution and Restoration*

[1] Maximiano García Venero, *Alfonso doce: El rey sin ventura* (Madrid: Ediciones S. C. L., 1960), p. 274. The words were also reported by the German envoy in Madrid at the time, Graf Klaus Eberhard zu Solms-Sonnenwalde, in his dispatch, No. 362, Nov. 25, 1885. Germany, Auswärtiges Amt, I.a.B.o., "Schriftwechsel mit der Gesandtschaft zu Madrid sowie mit anderen Missionen und fremden Kabinetten über die inneren Zustände und Verhältnisse Spaniens," National Archives, Doc. Film 3547, Reel 61. (Hereinafter cited GFO, for German Foreign Office, with appropriate reel numbers. As indicated in the bibliography, the titles of some sections of the German Foreign Office materials vary, but the reel numbers indicate the series concerned and in the interest of brevity in the notes the author has not sought to distinguish among the series in his citations. Please consult the bibliography for the proper designations.)

[2] García Venero, *Alfonso doce*.

[3] For a somewhat diffuse and uneven biography of Isabella see Pierre de Luz, *Isabel II, reina de España*, trans. Gabriel Conforto Thomas (Madrid: Editorial Juventud, 1940). Also unsatisfactory is Pedro de Répide, *Isabel II, reina de España*, Vidas españolas e hispanoamericanas del siglo XIX, vol. 20 (Madrid: Espasa-Calpe, 1932). More scholarly but excessively apologetic is Carmen Llorca Vilaplana, *Isabel II y su tiempo* (Alcoy: Editorial Marfil, 1959).

[4] The standard work on the subject is E. Jones Parry, *The Spanish Marriages, 1841–1846: A Study of the Influence of Dynastic Ambition upon Foreign Policy* (London: Macmillan, 1936). See also De Luz, *Isabel II*, pp. 102–24; Llorca Vilaplana, *Isabel II*, pp. 69–81.

[5] Llorca Vilaplana, *Isabel II*, p. 83. Fernando Díaz-Playa in *Otra historia de España* (Barcelona: Plaza & Janes, 1972), p. 332, adds a little verse suggesting that Francisco "orina en cuclillas como una señora."

[6] Many observers made the obvious comment that a proper marriage might have calmed Isabella's tempestuous nature. As it was, the queen

reacted harshly against the mother's despicable marriage arrangements, making her personal life such a scandal that Metternich was to exclaim, "Queen Isabella is revolution incarnate, in its most dangerous form." Elizabeth Wormeley Latimer, *Spain in the Nineteenth Century* (Chicago: A. C. McClurg and Company, 1898), pp. 277–78.

[7] See the details in José María Moreno Echevarría, *Isabel II: Biograofia de una España en crisis* (Barcelona: Ediciones 29, 1973); cf. Eric Christiansen, *The Origins of Military Power in Spain, 1800–1854* (Oxford: Oxford University Press, 1967). See also Stanley G. Payne, *Politics and the Military in Modern Spain* (Stanford, Calif.: Stanford University Press, 1967), pp. 14–30; Raymond Carr, *Spain, 1808–1939* (Oxford: Oxford University Press, 1966), pp. 210–304.

[8] The most friendly and understanding portrait of Isabella's personality is that of Llorca Vilaplana, *Isabel II*, pp. 9–11, which emphasizes "her profound humanity," her generosity and goodness of heart, but recognizes her excessive emotionalism and absence of willpower. Sor Patrocinio received a pension from Isabella while in exile. Manuel Espadas Burgos, *Alfonso XII y los orígenes de la restauración* (Madrid: C.S.I.C., Escuela de Historia Moderna, 1975), p. 235.

[9] See photograph in Ferrán Soldevila, *Historia de España*, vols. 7, 8 (Barcelona: Ediciones Ariel, 1963–64), 7:131; cf. one on p. 102.

[10] Garcia Venero, *Alfonso doce*, p. 17.

[11] When this chapter was originally written, the excellent analysis of Queen Isabella's role in exile by Manuel Espadas Burgos, *Alfonso XII y los orígenes de la restauración*, had not yet been published. Although some of Espadas Burgos's analysis of Hispano-German relations during that period is faulty, the work is a mine of new information, heavily based on previously unexploited correspondence in the royal archives. Much of the contents of this chapter has been recast in the light of the new materials. For the queen's finances, see pp. 249–62 and appendixes 6–9.

[12] Carlos Marfori, her last favorite, remained her closest adviser during the exile period and a continuing source of criticism. Espadas Burgos, *Alfonso XII*, p. 225. In November 1875 she sent him to Madrid to consult with her son, probably in respect to her return, but he was arrested and sent to the Philippines, much to the displeasure of Isabella. Within a month, however, Isabella had found a replacement, one Ramiro de la Puente, who was also to be a cause of embarrassment. Chlodwig, Fürst von Hohenlohe-Schillingsfürst, in Paris to Auswärtiges Amt, Nov. 12, 1875, No. 234, GFO, Reel 54; Melchior Gustav,

Graf von Hatzfeldt-Wildenburg to A.A., No. 208, Dec. 27, 1875, Confidential, GFO, Reel 54.

[13] Espadas Burgos, *Alfonso XII*, p. 220. Isabella had also for a time sought an agreement with the pretender, ibid., pp. 210–12. The Marqués de Lema stresses the strong influence of Marfori and of a life-long companion of the royal consort, Antonio Ramos de Meneses, leading to an incident in which Francisco himself cast doubt upon the validity of the queen's abdication. *De la revolución a la restauración*, 2 vols. (Madrid: Editorial Voluntad, 1927), 2:713.

[14] Espadas Burgos, *Alfonso XII*, pp. 238–42. At one point Francisco threatened to take Isabella into the French courts over the matter!

[15] Ibid., pp. 234–35. See also his letter from England to his mother in respect to Francisco in Marqués de Lema, *De la revolución*, 2:744–45.

[16] During the remainder of his life Francisco lived outside Paris at Epinay, but his body was returned to Spain and buried in El Escorial. He did, of course, return for certain state occasions such as the marriage of Alfonso.

[17] See story of the queen's reluctant decision and the Infanta Paz's description of the act itself, Espadas Burgos, *Alfonso XII*, pp. 225–30. The abdication was, as the queen stated in her notification to her countrymen, signed in the presence of the royal family, the representatives of the Spanish nobility, and various generals and public figures.

[18] As detailed in the following chapter, Isabella gave open evidence of her hurt feelings when she was forbidden to accompany her son on his return to Spain and did, indeed, go so far as to threaten the revocation of her abdication.

[19] García Venero, *Alfonso doce*, pp. 69–74. Sesto became head of the king's household after the restoration and remained intimately associated with him until his death.

[20] Ibid. Morphy became the king's private secretary and like Sesto remained one of his closest confidants until his death.

[21] The best English account of the reign of Amadeo and the republic which followed is Joseph A. Brandt, *Toward the New Spain* (Chicago: University of Chicago Press, 1933), pp. 136–326. Cf. Alvaro Figueroa y Torres, Conde de Romanones, *Amadeo de Saboya, el rey efímero: España y los orígenes de la guerra Franco-Prusiana de 1870*, Vidas españolas e hispanoamericanas del siglo XIX, vol. 46 (Madrid: Espasa-Calpe, 1935).

[22] Espadas Burgos's thesis of anti-Germanism on the part of Alfonso and of Cánovas is very much undercut by the documentation provided in later chapters. *Alfonso XII*, pp. 36–41. Moreover, the rendition of

Cánovas's discurso of Nov. 26, 1870, into an anti-German one does not seem justified by a full reading of it. See Antonio Cánovas del Castillo, *Problemas contemporáneas*, 3 vols. (Madrid: Pérez Dubrull [vols. 1, 2] and M. Tello [vol. 3], 1884–90), 1:5–52.

23 Espadas Burgos, *Alfonso XII*, pp. 177–87. Alfonso's letter to his mother on Jan. 2, 1873 shows his political astuteness at that early date —"I am sorry he has given up the direction of policy, because though as a friend he could not be good, as an enemy he would be the worst." Ibid., p. 190.

24 Actually the marriage of Alfonso and María de las Mercedes was a part of the contract for Montpensier's temporary leadership of the Alfonsist cause, but would be strongly opposed by Isabella after the Restoration. For a probably invented description of the romance see García Venero, *Alfonso doce*, pp. 113–15.

25 Espadas Burgos, *Alfonso XII*, pp. 305–9. See biography by Wenceslao Ramírez de Villa-Urrutia, the Marqués de Villa-Urrutia, *El general Serrano, Duque de la Torre*, Vidas españolas del siglo XIX, vol. 1 (Madrid: Espasa-Calpe, 1929), p. 62, which suggests Serrano's *privanza* was still based on rumor.

26 Villa-Urrutia, *El general Serrano*; cf. Melchor Fernández Almagro, *Historia política de la España contemporánea*, vol. 1, *Desde la revolución de septiembre hasta la muerte de Alfonso XII* (Madrid: Pegaso, 1956), p. 238.

27 The literature on Cánovas is extensive. The best biography remains that of Melchor Fernández Almagro, *Cánovas, su vida y su política* (Madrid: Ediciones Ambos Mundes S.S., 1951) on which the more recent one of José Luis Comellas, *Cánovas* (Barcelona: Ediciones Cid, 1965), is heavily based although more readable. Preceding Fernández Almagro's biography were those of Charles Benoist, *Cánovas del Castillo: La restauración renovadora* (Madrid: Ediciones Literarias, 1931); V. C. Creuz, *Antonio Cánovas del Castillo: Sa carrière, ses oeuvres, sa fin. Étude biographique et historique* (Paris: F. Levé, 1897); Antonio Espina, *Cánovas del Castillo* (Madrid: Pegaso, 1947); Antonio María Fabié, *Cánovas del Castillo: Su juventud, su edad madura, su vejez* (Barcelona: Gustavo Gili, 1928); Adolfo Pons y Umbert, *Cánovas del Castillo* (Madrid: Hijos de M. G. Hernández, 1901) and a number of semibiographical studies noted in the bibliography.

28 Llorca Vilaplana, *Isabel II*, pp. 191–93; Espadas Burgos, *Alfonso XII*, pp. 380–82.

29 Espadas Burgos, *Alfonso XII*; cf. Fernández Almagro, *Cánovas*, pp. 233–36. Isabella continued, for example, to maintain correspondence

with General Concha although, as will be seen, Cánovas was strongly opposed to a military pronunciamiento.

30 See biography by Benjamin Jarnés, *Castelar, hombre del Sinaí*, Vidas españolas e hispanoamericanas del siglo XIX, vol. 45 (Madrid: Espasa-Calpe, 1935); cf. Brandt, *Toward the New Spain*, pp. 293–326.

31 Brandt, *Toward the New Spain*, pp. 323–26. A detailed analysis of Pavía's career and place in Spanish history is provided in Arthur Houghton, *Les origines de la restauration des Bourbons en Espagne* (Paris: Plon, Nourrit et cie, 1890), pp. 60–108. Pavía was, of course, not a monarchist but a conservative republican still hoping to preserve a unitarian republican government.

32 Houghton, *Les origines*, pp. 95–110; cf. Ildefonso Antonio Bermejo, *Historia de la interinidad y guerra civil de España desde 1868*, 3 vols. (Madrid: R. Labajos, 1875–77), 3:886–908; Marqués de Lema, *De la revolución*, 2:625–35; Fernández Almagro, *Historia política*, 1:209–14.

33 Soldevila, *Historia de España*, 7:89–90, uses the term but points out that there were some evidences of provincial opposition to the coup.

34 Fernández Almagro, *Historia política*, 1:215–19; cf. Houghton, *Les origines*, pp. 113–17; Brandt, *Toward the New Spain*, pp. 327–28. The official proclamation of the new government did specifically use the term "el gobierno de la república." See Diego Sevilla Andrés, *Consituciones y otros leyes y proyectos políticos de España*, 2 vols. (Madrid: Editorial Nacional, 1969), 1:573–77.

35 Houghton, *Les origines*, pp. 119–267, summarizes this period under the title "the hesitations of Marshal Serrano." The biography of the general by the Marqués de Villa-Urrutia, *El general Serrano*, is unsatisfactory for this period, pp. 215–33, as is also Espadas Burgos, *Alfonso XII*, pp. 92–96.

36 Espadas Burgos, *Alfonso XII*, pp. 310–11.

37 Ibid., p. 329; Bermejo, *Historia de la interinidad*, 3:914.

38 Houghton, *Les origines*, pp. 133–36. Houghton describes his own experiences in traveling through Carlist territory, with little disturbance involved except a series of transit taxes. Cf. Tomás Domínguez Arévalo, Conde de Rodezno, *Carlos VII, Duque de Madrid*, Vidas españolas del siglo XIX, vol. 4 (Madrid: Espasa-Calpe, 1929), pp. 159–63; Edgar Holt, *The Carlist Wars in Spain* (Chester Springs, Pa.: Dufour Editions, 1967); Roman Oyarzun, *La historia del carlismo* (Madrid: Alianza, 1969). France continued during the Serrano period to deny giving aid to the Carlists, although the Spanish foreign minister, the marqués de la Vega de Armijo was convinced that they were. Report of Marqués

de la Vega de Armijo's charges, July 16, 1874, and denial by Vernouillet, chargé d'affaires for France in Madrid to Decazes, Telegram, August 7, 1874 in France, Ministère des Affaires Étrangères, Commission de Publication des Documents Relatifs aux Origines de la Guerre de 1914, *Documents Diplomatiques Français, 1871–1914*, 1st ser., 1871–1900, 16 vols. in 17 (Paris: Imprimerie Nationale, 1929–59), 1:341, n. 3, 344. (Hereinafter cited as DDF.)

[39] Houghton, *Les origines*, pp. 137–57. The siege of Bilbao has been graphically portrayed by María Estibaliz Ruiz de Azua y Martínez de Ezquerecocha, *El sitio de Bilbao en 1874: Estudio del compartimiento social de una ciudad en guerra, Historia general del señorio de Bizcaya*, supplement 4 (Bilbao: Editorial La Gran Enciclopedia Vasca, 1976).

[40] Houghton, *Les origines*, pp. 157–65. At the time Cánovas said to a friend that if Serrano had been defeated, he would have been no use to his cause. But if he returned with laurels, then they would have to decide what course of action must be taken. Andrés Borrego, *Datos para la historia de la revolución, de la interinidad, y del advenimiento de la restauración* (Madrid: Imprenta de la Sociedad Tipográfica, 1877), p. 148.

[41] Copy of a private letter from Hatzfeldt to State Secretary, dated Paris, July 10, 1874, No. 267, GFO, Reel 49. Events described in Houghton, *Les origines*, pp. 175–80; cf. detailed account in Bermejo, *Historia de la interinidad*, 3:971–74.

[42] Houghton, *Les origines*, pp. 187–88.

[43] Soldevila, *Historia de España*, 7:96–97. He suggests that a thousand persons were deported to the Philippines. *La Iberia* on November 21, 1874, proclaimed, "The press, organ of the opinions of the country, should give an example of patriotism. If its mission in normal times is to present and discuss all those reforms in which the general public is interested and to aid with its counsels those who govern for the good administration of the state, in extraordinary circumstances such as we encounter today, it [the duty of the press] reduces itself to not presenting any obstacle to those men who rule us, leaving free to them the pathway along which they must guide us safely for the realization of patriotic purposes." And on November 27, 1874, dealing with difficulties involving students and professors at the Central University, *La Iberia* proclaimed: "The public professorship is a form of priesthood, and for that reason any negligence, any defect, however small, in the fulfillment of its duties may produce fatal consequences." The professors, it suggested, were "converting the temple of science into the

podium of politics," and making the examinations so easy, the students
were too free to cause difficulties.

⁴⁴The biography by the Conde de Romanones, *Sagasta o el político*,
Vidas españoles del siglo XIX, vol. 7 (Madrid: Espasa-Calpe, 1934),
devotes less than three pages to the Serrano period!

⁴⁵Comments on Sagasta's character from Ricardo de la Cierva, *Historia básica de la España actual, 1800–1975* (Barcelona: Editorial Planeta,
1974), p. 110. As reported below, during the later controversy over the
control of the party *La Iberia* was able during a relatively brief period
of time to marshal 30,000 signatures of support for Sagasta. See the
August 6, 1875, issue.

⁴⁶There is frequent reference in the German dispatches to the hostility of the Carlists and the aid given them by France, e.g., Memo,
A.A., Berlin, Aug. 2, 1874, A 3033, GFO, Reel 49; Bülow, A.A. to
Hans Lothar von Schweinitz in Vienna, No. 506, 514, Oct. 25, 1874,
GFO, Reel 51; Richard Lindau, consul in Bayonne, to Wesdehlen,
Paris, Oct. 25, 1874, GFO, Reel 51. There are also numerous references to the strengthening of the Serrano regime, Count Andrassy in
Vienna to Graf Karolyi in Berlin, Feb. 10, 1874, copy, GFO, Reel
48; Memo, A.A., Berlin, Aug. 2, 1874, A 3033, GFO, Reel 49. For the
false reports of a new Hohenzollern candidacy see memo of Bernhard
von Bülow to the Kaiser, June 4, 1874, A 2112, GFO, Reel 48, in
which he recounts efforts to allay the rumors that have circulated in
Spain for some time with the name of Friedrich Karl mentioned. These
were always stated in such an indefinite or unbelievable fashion that
direct denial did not seem necessary and recently they had derived
from the Carlist camp. But Bülow had taken the unusual action not
only of sponsoring articles in the *Norddeutsche Allgemeine Zeitung* but
also of placing a general dispatch with the Wolff bureau. A little later
a Foreign Office official in Berlin found in an interview with Ignacio
José Escobar of *La Epoca* that he at least was convinced that Germany
had no special interests in Spain. Memo, Sept. 24, 1874, von Philipsborn (director of Department II of Foreign Office, Legal and Commercial Affairs), A 4009/12/13, GFO, Reel 50. Espadas Burgos takes the
reports of French sources and republican agents as proving this very
unlikely German interest in another Spanish Hohenzollern candidacy,
Alfonso XII, pp. 20–23. There was also justifiable German indignation
over the Carlist execution of a retired German Captain Albert Schmidt,
who had been in the area in a nonmilitary capacity. See Bülow to
Kaiser, July 19, 1874, A 2864/2841, GFO, Reel 49 and July 20, 1874,

A 2898/2915, GFO, Reel 49, in which the kaiser had authorized the sending of German warships to the Spanish coast.

[47] Austen Henry Layard was a close friend of Serrano and had earlier sponsored recognition, but in the actual fact Germany took the lead. The Germans suspected that Layard feared Serrano was really working for Alfonso. Schweinitz in Vienna to A.A., No. 32, Feb. 9, 1874, GFO, Reel 48. Actually the original suggestion of recognition probably derived from Berlin. See Andrassy in Vienna to Graf Karolyi in Berlin, Feb. 10, 1874, Copy, Unnumbered, GFO, Reel 48. For the development of the German policy of recognition and its acceptance by Great Britain and Austria, see Julio Salom Costa, *España en la Europa de Bismarck: La política exterior de Cánovas, 1871–1881* (Madrid: C.S.I.C., Escuela de Historia Moderna, 1967), pp. 87–99. President Thiers of France had early expressed favor for Serrano but directed that the government should wait to see the permanence of the regime before extending recognition. A little later, however, the French began to attack the naming of Count Hatzfeldt as German envoy and allege a new Hohenzollern or Saxon candidacy for the throne of Spain. Thiers to M. de Bouillé, ambassador in Madrid, cipher dispatch, March 26, 1873; Duc Decazes, minister of foreign affairs, to de Goutant-Biron, French ambassador in Berlin, Telegram, May 29, 1874, DDF, 1:229–30, 33.

[48] Brandt, *Toward the New Spain*, p. 335. The American minister, Caleb Cushing, was particularly concerned with the phrase, "conservative principles," rather strangely so in view of his later stance in respect to the Cánovas government. United States, Department of State, Cushing to Fish, No. 100, Sept. 16, 1874, Dispatches from U.S. Ministers to Spain, Doc. Film 436, Microcopy No. M 31, Reel 64 (Hereinafter cited U.S. State Dept. with reel numbers).

[49] Espadas Burgos, *Alfonso XII*, pp. 42–43.

[50] Ibid., p. 40; cf. Dr. Manuel Izquierdo Hernández, *La historia para todos: Historia clínica de la restauración*, diary of Col. Juan de Velasco (Madrid: Editorial Plus-Ultra, 1946), pp. 57–59.

[51] Bülow to Hatzfeldt in Madrid, No. 171, Oct. 25, 1874, A 4386, GFO, Reel 51.

[52] Bülow to Schweinitz in Vienna, Nos. 506, 514, Oct. 25, 1874, A 4386, GFO, Reel 51.

[53] Bülow to Alvensleben in St. Petersburg, No. 548, Oct. 30, 1874, Secret, A 4386, GFO, Reel 51.

[54] Schweinitz to A.A., Vienna, No. 320, Oct. 18, 1874, Secret;

Alvensleben, St. Petersburg, to A.A., Telegram, No. 51, Nov. 9, 1874, GFO, Reel 51.

55 Espadas Burgos, *Alfonso XII*, p. 33, dated June 5, 1874.

56 Ibid., p. 104, Sept. 1873.

57 Ibid., pp. 106–22; see also Velasco's diary, Izquierdo, *Historia clínica*, pp. 59–67. Carlos Cardell y Pujalte attributes Alfonso's respect for the nature of constitutional monarchy to this brief stay in England, *La casa de Borbón en España* (Madrid: Agemundo, 1954), p. 361. But Alfonso never seems to have expressed much admiration for England or its government.

58 Espadas Burgos, *Alfonso XII*, pp. 116–21. Content of manifesto noted in following chapter.

59 Ibid., p. 370; cf. Fernández Almagro, *Cánovas*, pp. 258–59.

60 Espadas Burgos, *Alfonso XII*, pp. 371–72.

61 Fernández Almagro, *Cánovas*, pp. 259–60.

62 Ibid., pp. 258–59; Marqués de Lema, *De la revolución*, 2:692–93. Cánovas was unrealistic enough to think that under certain circumstances the king's presence might lead to an embrace between opposing Alfonsist and Carlist armies!

63 Goltz, Lisbon, to A.A., Telegram No. 12, Nov. 14, 1874, GFO, Reel 51.

64 I.e., Marqués de la Vega de Armijo, according to Wesdehlen in Paris to A.A., No. 196, Very Confidential; Minister of State Ulloa, reported Hatzfeldt to A.A., Telegram No. 14, Nov. 5, 1874; Hohenlohe in Paris to A.A., No. 199, Nov. 30, 1874; Hatzfeldt to A.A., No. 133, Nov. 29, 1874, linking both Ulloa and Sagasta to Montpensier and again in the matter of Ulloa, Hatzfeldt to A.A., No. 149, Dec. 18, 1874, GFO, Reel 51.

65 The most detailed accounting of Serrano's plan for ending the war and then a delay in which Alfonso might not be elected by the Cortes is found in a memo of Von Holstein on his conversation with the Marqués de la Vega de Armijo in Paris, Nov. 21, 1874, Annex to Wesdehlen in Paris to A.A., No. 196, Nov. 23, 1874, GFO, Reel 51. The interview contained a comment that other advisers might appear for Alfonso than Cánovas. Richard Lindau, the German consul in Bayonne, told the same story after the Restoration. Lindau to Hohenlohe, No. 373, Jan. 29, 1875, GFO, Reel 52. The story is confirmed by the British ambassador's (Layard's) report to Derby, No. 278A, March 9, 1875, Records of British Foreign Office, Public Record Office, 72:1408 (hereinafter cited BFO with appropriate reference num-

bers). Emilio J. M. Nogués in *Historia crítica de la restauración borbónica in España: Venticinco años de historia comtemporánea*, 3 vols. (Barcelona: La Enciclopedia Democrática, 1895–97), 3:49, asserts that Serrano's plan was to convoke an ordinary Cortes and reestablish the Constitution of 1869 before restoring Alfonso.

[66] Houghton, *Les origines*, pp. 253–67. Perhaps this view of Serrano is harsh. Bermejo gives him credit for reorganizing and strengthening the army, *Historia de la interinidad*, 3:913. But even Layard, his close friend, was to admit he had been "deficient in moral firmness, in political wisdom and foresight, and in knowledge of government." Layard to Derby, No. 13, Jan. 3, 1875, BFO 72:1405.

[67] See below, n. 80.

[68] Sketch which follows based on José Ibáñez Marín and Marqués de Cabriñana [Julio Urbina y Ceballos], *El general Martínez Campos y su monumento*, (Madrid: Establecimiento Tipográfico "El Trabajo," 1906).

[69] Ibid., pp. 59–64, 74.

[70] Ibid., pp. 93–106; see his proclamation to the people of Catalonia in Bermejo, *Historia de la interinidad*, 3:917–18.

[71] Ibáñez Marín, *El general Martínez Campos*, pp. 107–9.

[72] The details of the later coup emphasize the primary role of Gen. Fernando Primo de Rivera, who assured the Serrano government of the loyalty and nonpolitical stance of Martínez Campos but followed his pronunciamiento by taking over in Madrid. See report of Layard to earl of Derby, No. 138, enclosure, Jan. 28, 1875, BFO 72:1406. The character of Serrano in this period is emphasized by the fact that he placed absolute confidence in Primo. Borrego, *Datos para la historia de la revolución*, p. 176.

[73] Izquierdo, *Historia clínica*, pp. 71–72.

[74] Ibid., pp. 72–73.

[75] Espadas Burgos, *Alfonso XII*, pp. 348–49. Valmaseda also had only a few forces with which to work. See Marqués de Lema, *De la revolución*, 2:731.

[76] Borrego asserts that Serrano's minister of war, Francisco Serrano Bedoya, was perfectly aware that the Army of the Center was only waiting for the signal of a pronunciamiento and that Serrano himself in spite of all his military experience had left the direction of military affairs entirely in the hands of the minister. *Datos para la historia de la revolución*, p. 205.

[77] Fabié, *Cánovas*, p. 103.

[78] Houghton, *Les origines*, pp. 302–6.

[79] Ibid., pp. 328–34. Borrego hints that Serrano was as much concerned for possible liberal actions in the army as for the Carlists. *Datos para la historia de la revolución*, p. 205.

[80] This was part of the letter which Martínez Campos wrote to Cánovas before leaving for Sagunto. Fernández Almagro, *Historia política*, 1:246. In the debate over his action Izquierdo, *Historia clínica*, p. 89, gives equal credit to both Cánovas and Martínez Campos. A recent study by Diego Sevilla Andrés, *Historia política de España, 1800–1973*, 2 vols., 2d ed. (Madrid: Editora Nacional, 1974), 1:329–31, sets forth the same opinion of the necessity of Sagunto as does the author.

[81] Fernández Almagro, *Historia política*, 1:249.

[82] Ibid. His official telegram arrived the following morning.

[83] See diary of Colonel Velasco, Izquierdo, *Historia clínica*, p. 67.

CHAPTER 2 . *Cánovas: Pacification and Conciliation*

[1] García Venero, *Alfonso doce*, p. 138.

[2] Comments on king's arrival in Barcelona from Ferrán Soldevila, *Historia de Catalunya*, 2d ed. (Barcelona: Editorial Alpha, 1962), 3: 1385–86, and U.S., Department of State, Dispatches Addressed to the Department of State by United States Consular Representatives Abroad, 1789–1906, Barcelona, Microcopy T 121, Roll 7, Fred H. Schenck to Asst. Secretary of State, Nos. 21, 23, January 3, 6, 1875. Hereinafter cited U.S., Consular Dispatches, with city, film, and roll numbers. On the reception in Madrid *La Iberia* said that the supposed "paisanos" giving cheers for Alfonso and the duke of Sesto before the latter's house were really members of a squadron of militia and that the city was being *ordered* to light up for the king's return. Jan. 1, 2, 1875. But *El Imparcial's* description of the king's arrival seems to document genuine enthusiasm, Jan. 15, 1875. See photographs in Ferrán Soldevila, *Historia de España* 8:132, 135.

[3] Even the format of the decree establishing the "Ministry Regency" followed that of a royal decree. See *Gaceta de Madrid*, Dec. 31, 1874; cf. Modesto Lafuente y Zamalloa et al., *Historia general de España desde los tiempos primitivos hasta la muerte de Fernando VII*, vol. 25 (Barcelona: Montaner y Simón, 1922), pp. 4–5. His decision was, of course, confirmed by the king before he left Paris.

[4] The order of the words in the title was significant. This was one

important aspect of what Cánovas designated as a policy of "attraction," that is, of conciliation to political opponents.

⁵Text in Fernández Almagro, *Historia política*, appendix no. 16, vol. 1, pp. 536–39.

⁶Fernández Almagro, *Cánovas*, pp. 285–86.

⁷Ibid. The Moderado group was to display wide variations and deep divisions during the following period. A recent study contrasts the traditions of Jaimé Balmés and Donoso Cortés in respect to the attitude of the right in Spain with Balmés emphasizing the "possibility" of a cooperation with "the spirit of the age," whereas Donoso Cortes emphasized the imminence of inevitable catastrophe. The latter viewpoint had undergirded the attitude of the neo-Catholics Aparisi Guijarro and Cándido Nocedal, who had both gone to the Carlist camp during the revolutionary period. Essentially, Cánovas was seeking to promote a return to the Balmés tradition and to a considerable degree succeeded in doing so. See Richard A. H. Robinson, *The Origins of Franco's Spain: The Right, the Republic and Revolution, 1931–1936* (Newton Abbot: David & Charles, 1970), pp. 16–20.

⁸See life by Antonio Fabié y Escudero, *Biografía del excmo. señor D. Pedro Salaverría*, 2 vols. (Madrid: Imprenta de Fortanet, 1898).

⁹Espadas Burgos, *Alfonso XII*, pp. 371–73; Soldevila, *Historia de España*, 7:363.

¹⁰January 1, 1875. On the following day *La Iberia* did take note of the combination of Liberals and Traditionalists and express the hope that some of the advances of 1868 would be preserved.

¹¹*Gaceta de Madrid*, Dec. 31, 1874; cf. Ibáñez Marín, *El general Martínez Campos*, pp. 117–18.

¹²"Vieja y nueva política" (Conferencia dada en el teatro de la comedia el 23 de marzo de 1914), *Obras completas*, vol. 1, 1902–16 (Madrid: Revista de Occidente, 1950), p. 281.

¹³The German chargé, Maximilian, Graf von Berchem, reported at a later date that the king had insisted on the right of the duke of La Torre to return to Madrid over the opposition of the cabinet. Berchem to A.A., No. 129, June 15, 1875, GFO, Reel 53. Report of the interview, Layard to Derby, Nos. 278A, 279, March 9, 10, 1875, BFO 72:1408.

¹⁴E.g., Berchem to A.A., No. 108, April 29, 1875, GFO, Reel 53. The duchess spoke strongly against the generals "who had broken their promises" and engaged in treason against her husband. When von Hatzfeldt visited the duke and duchess in October, he found the wife's influence over her husband undiminished as was also her malice against

the regime—the regime had forbidden the duke to visit Andalucía as they had planned for fear regiments there might proclaim "Viva, Serrano!" Hatzfeldt to A.A., No. 170, Oct. 5, 1875, GFO, Reel 54.

[15] Castelar's real effectiveness was past by this time. He remained as a symbol of an ideal rather than a political force. See Jarnés, *Castelar, hombre del Sinaí*.

[16] Fernández Almagro, *Cánovas*, p. 283, pictures Martos as much impressed by Cánovas's plans before the Restoration, but his name was closely linked with that of Ruiz Zorrilla, although he remained in Madrid, "alejado de la política," until 1880. See article in *El Globo*, Dec. 1, 1878.

[17] He does have some significance with respect to a projected federalist constitution drawn up in Zaragoza in 1883 but is not again elected deputy until 1886.

[18] See life by Ruiz Gómez Chaix, *Ruiz Zorrilla: El ciudano ejemplar*, Vidas españolas e hispanoamericanos del siglo XIX, vol. 41 (Madrid: Espasa-Calpe, 1934). Exactly why a life of constant conspiracy qualifies Ruiz Zorrilla as "an exemplary citizen" escapes the logic of the author. His major ally in his efforts until 1890 was Nicolas Salmerón y Alonso, whose expulsion from his chair at the Central University is noted below.

[19] *El Imparcial*, Jan. 1, 1876, "El año 1875," reviewing the course of the dictatorship during the past year.

[20] For a summary of press guidelines issued by the government, see *Gaceta de Madrid*, Jan. 30, 1875; Reactions, *La Política*, Jan. 30, 1875; *El Imparcial*, March 10, 13, 18, 19, May 20, 1875. *El Imparcial* was, for example, suspended on May 22, 1875, for suggesting in an article that the actions of Cánovas were not in accord with the Sandhurst Manifesto promising that he (the king or Cánovas?) would never abrogate the fundamental rights of Spaniards. The long row of press suspensions which followed does not comport with Ricardo de la Cierva's comments on the freedom of the press under Cánovas. *Historia básica*, p. 114. Cierva notes the great influence and wide distribution of *El Imparcial*, pp. 106, 114; cf. Vicente Cacho Viu, *La institución libre de enseñanza*, vol. 1, *Origenes y etapa universitaria, 1860–1881* (Madrid: Ediciones Rialp, 1962), 1:294; Manuel Ortega y Gasset, *"El Imparcial": Biografía de un gran periódico español*, Introduction by Juan Pujal (Zaragoza: Librería General, 1956). For those readers not familiar with *El Imparcial*, it should be noted that the stance of this newspaper was a reasoned liberalism; it contained daily summaries of the press not only

in Madrid but elsewhere in Spain, with its own commentaries; and managed to squeeze in a great deal of the political gossip circulating in the capital even in the midst of stern press controls. The author used it as a major key to daily events supplementing it with the other newspapers at times of crisis or controversy.

21 *El Imparcial*, Jan. 4, 6, 7, 9, 1876.

22 Ibid., Nov. 18, 20, 1874; *La Iberia*, Nov. 21, 1874.

23 *Gaceta de Madrid*, Jan. 1, 22, 1875; *El Imparcial*, Jan. 1, 1876, "El año 1875."

24 *La Iberia*, May 7, 9, 30, 1875.

25 See comments on Romero Robledo's prestige in this period in José Francos Rodríguez, *En tiempo de Alfonso XII, 1875–1885* (Madrid: Renacimiento, 1917), pp. 20–21. Characterization by Aureliano Linares Rivas, *La primera cámara de la restauración: Retratos y semblanzas* (Madrid: J. C. Conde, 1878), pp. 167–75.

26 A detailed but not very impressive treatise is Vicente Villaspesa Calvache, *El funesto caciquismo y algo de su terapéutica* (Almería and Madrid: J. Fernández Murcia, 1908). A recent study by José Varela Ortega, "Los amigos políticos: Funcionamiento del sistema caciquista," *Revista de Occidente*, 2d ser., vol. 43 (Oct., Nov., Dec., 1973), pp. 45–74, breaks significant new ground with access to reports from the Ministry of the Interior. In two concise pages Manuel Tuñon de Lara indicates the basic relationship of the system to the existence of a feudal, landed estate, so that the only real remedy was basic social reform. *La España del siglo XIX* (Paris: Librería Española, 1968), pp. 209–10. See also Carr, *Spain, 1808–1939*, pp. 366–79. The recent study by Robert W. Kern, *Liberals, Reformers and Caciques in Restoration Spain, 1875–1909* (Albuquerque: University of New Mexico Press, 1974), although subject to some egregious errors in its representation of the political developments of the period, does provide a valid general view of the system. The author, however, finds some rationale in the assertion of Emiliano Aguado that in the Spain of the Restoration period the caciques were a necessary mechanism of the political scene. See his *Don Manuel Azaña Díaz*, (Barcelona: Ediciones Nauta, 1972), p. 28. Barring a new revolution, the republican thrust which probably had the largest support (although continuing to be deeply divided in philosophy) was excluded from real expression. So long as the monarchy and the church were maintained, the concept of social oligarchy was unavoidable. That which was unfortunate was not the centralization of government, which Kern criticizes so strongly, as much as the

self-satisfied attitude of both major parties. Corruption at all levels was the evil and, as will be seen, the king was aware of it, but had no viable way of remedying it. José Ortega y Gasset blamed the whole system on Cánovas, calling him a "professor of corruption," but he, too, was tied to the existing situation and traditions. *Obras completas,* 1:281–82.

[27] The continued concern for the effects of republican propaganda supports this thesis. The demonstrations of overwhelming support in Barcelona on a number of occasions and in Madrid on the death of republican General Lagunero show the latent strength of this ideal.

[28] See Clara E. Lida, *Anarquismo y revolución en la España del XIX* (Madrid: Siglo Veintiuno Editores, 1972), pp. 236–57, and her *Antecedentes y desarrollo del movimiento obrero español, 1835–1888: Textos y documentos* (Madrid: Siglo XXI de España, 1973), pp. 344 ff.; Manuel Tuñon de Lara, *El movimiento obrero en la historia de España* (Madrid: Taurus, 1972), pp. 269–92; Luis Gómez Llorente, *Aproximación a la historia del socialismo español hasta 1921* (Madrid: Editorial Cuadernos para el Diálogo, 1972), pp. 43–78. The author feels that the practical effects of these movements is best expressed by Jaime Vicens Vives in his *Approaches to the History of Spain*, trans. and ed. Joan Connelly Ullman (Berkeley: University of California Press, 1967), pp. 136–40.

[29] *Gaceta de Madrid*, Jan. 4, 24, 1875.

[30] Ibid., Feb. 4, 8, 1875.

[31] *El Imparcial* began its criticism of deportations on March 28, 1876, followed with stories on July 14, August 4, 5, 13, 14, 24, 1876. Government responses admitted 21 political deportations to Fernando Po and said others were common criminals. In the end, of the deportees at Ceuta apparently about 400 were amnestied. As noted above, there had been stories of 1,000 to 1,400 deportees under Sagasta. See review of matter by Cushing, who, as usual, defended the government strongly. Cushing to Fish, No. 337, April 10, 1875, U.S. Dept. of State, Reel 68.

[32] *La Política*, Feb. 5, 9, 1875. The generals were Izquierdo, Lagunero, and Carmona.

[33] Ibid., Oct. 10, 1875. The concept of "legal community" had been emphasized in the Assembly of Notables which initiated the move toward the drawing up of a new constitution. Fernández Almagro, *Historia política*, 1:299.

[34] See Juan del Nido y Segalerva, *Historia política y parlamentaria del excmo. sr. d. Antonio Cánovas del Castillo* (Madrid: Prudencio P. de

Velasco, 1914), pp. 326–38; cf. Richard Herr, *Spain*, The Modern Nations in Historical Perspective (Englewood Cliffs, N.J.: Prentice-Hall, 1971), p. 114.

35 British recognition of Alfonso was delayed while that government sought assurances of the government's intention to preserve religious toleration, which Cánovas provided. Layard to Derby, No. 148, Feb. 3, 1875, BFO 72:1406. Layard, of course, continued to be the main motive force for protests in respect to intolerant acts of the new regime. Assurances of Sweden's interest in Spanish religious freedom, deriving directly from the Swedish king, were conveyed to the German Foreign Office by their ambassador Graf F. von Eichmann, Stockholm, to A.A., No. 40, March 5, 1875, GFO, Reel 53.

36 The German Foreign Office expressed its concern for religious toleration to its representative in London. State Secretary von Bülow, No. 27, Jan. 2, 1875, and to its representative in St. Petersburg, No. 33, Jan. 2, 1875, GFO, Reel 52. The ambassador in St. Petersburg, Friedrich Johann, Graf von Alvensleben, reported the tsar's personal concern in the matter stating that Russia would not make recognition dependent upon Spain's religious policy, but might intervene later. Alvensleben to A.A., Jan. 14, 1875, copy, No. 19, Jan. 19, 1875, GFO, Reel 52.

37 When Fritz Fliedner, the representative of the German evangelical church in Spain, asked Cushing's help in respect to Spanish action disallowing civil marriages, Cushing replied in quite intemperate fashion in the negative. Cushing to Fish, No. 285, Feb. 23, 1875, and annex, U.S. Dept. of State, Reel 67. A second letter by Fliedner obtained such responses as, "You assume that your object is the promotion of religious liberty. I think it is a very different one, namely, the furtherance of sectarian propagandism," and denouncing, "the dictatorial interposition of foreign Governments." Cushing to Fish, No. 295, March 4, 1875, U.S. Dept. of State, Reel 67. And again in his dispatch No. 321, March 19, 1875, Cushing showed hostility to efforts to exert pressure on Spain. U.S. Dept. of State, Reel 67.

38 See Layard to Derby, No. 148, Feb. 3, 1875, BFO 72:1406. Also Georg Herbert, Graf zu Münster, in London to A.A., Telegram No. 7, Jan. 21, 1875, GFO, Reel 52, indicating Derby had assurances from the king; also Memo of Bülow to Kaiser, March 15, 1875, A 1386, GFO, Reel 53.

39 Hatzfeldt to A.A., No. 53, Feb. 27, 1875, GFO, Reel 53.

⁴⁰Bülow to Kaiser, unnumbered, March 6, 1875; State Secretary to Hatzfeldt, No. 74, March 8, 1875, GFO, Reel 53.

⁴¹Cánovas himself was to call the Moderados "Carlists less the king [Carlos]." In Congress of Deputies, March 8, 1876, answering speech of Alejandro Pidal y Mon. See Nido y Segalverva, *Historia política*, p. 450.

⁴²Although Linares Rivas called the Moderados a party which "only recalled our troubles" led by "prehistoric personalities" (*La primera cámara*, p. 94), both the English and German diplomatic representatives worried about its potentialities. Layard wrote that Cánovas by his efforts for conciliation was strengthening the clerical party which he considered the only real danger to the throne. He mentioned the activities of the women of the capital in their behalf including the wife of Martínez Campos. Layard to Derby, No. 302, March 19, 1875, BFO 72:1408; Nos. 16, 30, Confidential, 61, Jan. 13, 19, Feb. 9, 1876, BFO 72:1434. Augusto Conte also mentioned the activities of the ladies of the capital in his *Recuerdos de un diplomático* 3 vols. (Madrid: Gongora, 1901–3), 3:185. Similarly German reports of concern came to the Foreign Office from Münster in London, No. 28, confidential, Feb. 19, 1875, GFO, Reel 52; Berchem, chargé in Madrid, No. 106, April 28, 1875, GFO, Reel 53; No. 136, July 15, 1875, GFO, Reel 54; and with comments on dangers of "Moderado generals" Quesada, Martínez Campos, and Echagüe, No. 109, April 29, 1875, GFO, Reel 53; and Hatzfeldt to A.A., No. 159, Sept. 24, 1875, GFO, Reel 54. Hatzfeldt in the period that followed expressed his worries that Cánovas himself was moving to the Moderado side: No. 180, Oct. 26, 1875 and Nov. 13, 1875, Secret, A 5457, GFO, Reel 54.

⁴³*El Imparcial*, El año 1875," Jan. 1, 1876. The best history of the church during this period, still somewhat overly general, is that by José Manuel Cuenca Toribio, *Estudios sobre la iglesia española del XIX* (Madrid: Ediciones Rialp, 1973). See 93–94 for early actions of the Cánovas regime.

⁴⁴*Gaceta de Madrid*, Feb. 27, 1875. The role of Maldonado Macanaz in Orovio's actions is noted in *El Imparcial*, Aug. 28, 1876. The controversy and subsequent events are followed in detail in Cacho Viu, *La institución libre*, 1:282 ff.

⁴⁵Antonio Ramos Oliveira reports that Cánovas tried, but failed, to get Giner de los Ríos to compromise before the harsh action was taken against him. *Politics, Economics and Men of Modern Spain, 1808–*

1946 (London: Victor Gollancz, 1946), pp. 113–14. Lengthy citations of the protests of the professors concerned are reproduced in Antonio Pirala y Criado, *Historia contemporánea: Segunda parte de la guerra civil. Anales desde 1843 hasta el fallecimiento de don Alfonso XII*, 6 vols. (Madrid: Felipe González Rojas, 1893–95), 4:14–22. Both *La Iberia* and *El Imparcial* followed matters cautiously in this period of extreme censorship. See *La Iberia*, March 14, 17, April 7, 11, 1875; *El Imparcial*, Feb. 28, April 3, July 16, 19, Aug. 3, 1875. Cacho Viu notes that the protest had begun at Santiago, but under Giner de los Ríos's inspiration, *La institución libre*, 1:285 ff.

⁴⁶ See complaints of *La Iberia*, Nov. 27, 1874, on the role of the university professors, ch. 1, n. 43. *La Iberia* was, of course, justified in suggesting that the measures now being used were more extreme than had ever previously been employed. March 15, 1875. Cushing had little sympathy for the professors, who had, he said, neglected their chairs for years in order to engage in politics. Dispatches to Fish, No. 345, April 12, No. 354, April 19, 1875, U.S. Dept. of State, Reel 68. Luis Silvela, who had tried to mediate the dispute, warned Giner de los Ríos that the actions of the professors concerned had not found general applause. Apparently unsympathetic at this point, he was himself involved in a later dispute over government intervention into university affairs. Cacho Viu, *La institución libre*, 1:316.

⁴⁷ For the king's attitude and that of Cánovas, see Pirala, *Historia contemporánea*, 4:14–22; Carr, *Spain, 1808–1939*, pp. 350–51. Most newspapers accepted the change of cabinet as in part related to Orovio's actions. E.g., *La Política*, Sept. 12, 1875, "El triunfo de la libertad"; *La Iberia*, Sept. 14, 1875, "La primera victoria."

⁴⁸ *La Iberia* (which had obtained a copy of the circular), Sept. 17, 18, 23, 1875; *El Imparcial*, Sept. 14, 16, 17, 1875. Hatzfeldt could not understand the action of Antonelli and Simeoni, which seemed to have the result of unifying public opinion, "if you can speak of public opinion in Spain," in opposition. Hatzfeldt to A.A., No. 150, Sept. 20, 1875, GFO, Reel 54. Later he reported the strong anger expressed by Minister of Justice Fernando Calderón Collantes in respect to the matter. Hatzfeldt to A.A., No. 168, Oct. 5, 1875, Secret, GFO, Reel 54.

⁴⁹ Cases involved the closing of a Protestant chapel at San Fernando, the disturbances of an evangelical service in Oviedo, of German church services at St. Andres, where a German teacher was arrested, and complaints over the seizure of evangelical Bibles being sold in Sala-

manca. See Layard to Derby, No. 178, Feb. 10, 1875, BFO 72:1406;
Berchem to A.A., No. 122, May 25, 1875, GFO, Reel 53; May 31,
1875, A 2730, GFO, Reel 53; No. 140, Aug. 6, 1875, GFO, Reel 54.
As noted, the major German Protestant worker in Spain was Pastor
Fritz Fliedner, who had been sent to Spain in 1870 by the Committee
for the Advancement of Evangelism in Spain. By 1875 the committee
claimed twenty-five congregations with more than 10,000 members as
well as three schools in Madrid with 130 students. Petition to Bismarck, March 6, 1875, GFO, Reel 53. One of the reports in the German Foreign Office files designated Fliedner as an industrious book-
seller—a "hauswirt Pastor." F. Kohler to Fliedner, Feb. 10, 1875,
copy, GFO, Reel 52. In spite of his complaints about treatment, he
did remain in Spain and continue to sell books! The work of the English, American, and Scotch societies was much more extensive but
perhaps best summarized as "not insignificant enough to be ignored nor
strong enough to be greatly feared." From John David Hughey, "Spanish Governments and Protestantism, 1868–1931" (Ph.D. dissertation,
Columbia University, 1951), which is somewhat more detailed than his
book, Religious Freedom in Spain: Its Ebb and Flow (London: Carey Kingsgate Press, 1955). Protestant newspapers such as La Luz and El Bien
Público were to run into serious government action since they constituted opposition to the established religion. One evidence of the public
mood was reported in an article, "El Fanatismo," by El Imparcial, July
23, 1875, which related that a boy of sixteen who had failed to remove
his hat when the religious procession of a brotherhood in Seville passed
by was struck so hard on the head by one of the brotherhood that he
was near death. And later El Imparcial reported the exhumation of
bodies buried in Catholic cemeteries that had only had civil marriage.
April 26, 1876.

[50] José M. Tallada Pauli, Historia de las finanzas españolas en el siglo XIX
(Madrid: Espasa-Calpe, 1946), p. 99.

[51] See analysis in Jerónimo Bécker, Historia de las relaciones exteriores
de España durante el siglo XIX: Apuntes para una historia diplomática, 2 vols.
(Madrid: Editorial Voluntad, 1926), 3:273–74; Fabié y Escudero, Salaverría, 2:657–660.

[52] Fabié y Escudero, Salaverría, 2:660–907, examines Salaverría's
procedures; cf. Tallada Pauli, Historia de las finanzas, pp. 104–5.

[53] It seems clear that the burdens on real estate and the level of indirect taxes were excessive. Tallada Pauli, Historia de las finanzas, p. 111.

[54] Ibid., pp. 112, 123.

[55] The increasing savagery displayed by the Carlists in this period of their decline is described in Bermejo, *Historia de la interinidad*, 3:986–1007. The Carlist general Rafael Tristany reported the difficult situation of the Carlists in Catalonia, and Antonio Dorregaray in command of the Army of the Center told of many people in his area who had in three months time paid thirteen trimesters of taxes. Pirala, *Historia contemporánea*, 3:640–41, 561–62.

[56] Pirala, *Historia contemporánea*, 3:317 ff., 597–98; Bermejo, *Historia de la interinidad*, 3:1152; cf. Carlos Martínez de Campos y Serrano, Duque de la Torre, *España bélica: El siglo XIX*, (Madrid: Aguilar, 1961), p. 270, who does, of course, pay just due to the heroism of the Carlists.

[57] Fernández Almagro, *Historia política*, 1:260–61. The doubts of German observers as to the potential influence of Cabrera are reflected in Hatzfeldt to A.A., No. 76, March 9, 1875; No. 77, March 22, 1875; Lindau in Bayonne to Hohenlohe in Paris, April 23, 1875, A 2129, GFO, Reel 53. José Ramón Alonso suggests that Cabrera's action had some value in the Maestrazgo but nowhere else. *Historia política del ejercito español*, (Madrid: Editora Nacional, 1974), p. 387.

[58] *El Imparcial*, April 22, 1876; *Diario*, Congreso, 1:638–39, 662–63, 772, April 21, 1876.

[59] Pirala, *Historia contemporánea*, 3:678–84; Bermejo, *Historia de la interinidad*, 3:1049–51. Rodezno, *Carlos VII*, pp. 194–95, notes that the Carlists captured two thousand weapons and the complete equipment of several Alfonsist battalions. The Carlists took joy in the fact that "the youngster," Alfonso, came within an ace of losing his life, see Martínez de Campos y Serrano, *España bélica*, p. 262. The king told Berchem of his close call. See Berchem to A.A., No. 138, July 29, 1875, GFO, Reel 54.

[60] See reports of Münster in London to A.A., No. 28, Feb. 19, 1875, GFO, Reel 52; Hohenlohe in Paris to A.A., No. 186, Aug. 7, 1875, GFO, Reel 54; Hatzfeldt to A.A., No. 156, Sept. 20, 1875, GFO, Reel 54. The Germans were much disturbed by a proposal emanating from Portugal during this period that Concert of Europe arrangements be revived and France commissioned to end the Carlist War and safeguard Alfonso's throne. The Germans could not understand how France, which had been supposedly favoring the Carlists, could now reverse her stand and send armies against them. Needless to say, the Germans did not buy the idea. See special section in GFO, Reel 92, relating to this proposal, especially, Bülow in Ems to von Philipsborn, No. 1, Confidential, June 9, 1875; No. 3, Confidential, June 13; No.

20, June 26; Hohenlohe in Paris to Philipsborn, No. 162, Secret, July 5, 1875.

⁶¹ Hatzfeldt suggested that profit rates of 35 percent were being made in the war and, hence, the government was not anxious to conclude it. Hatzfeldt to A.A., No. 198, Dec. 7, 1875, GFO, Reel 54.

⁶² See Martínez de Campos y Serrano, *España bélica*, p. 266. On Martínez Campos's campaign in Catalonia see Pirala, *Historia contemporánea*, 3:597 ff.; Bermejo, *Historia de la interinidad*, 3:1111, 1177–81, 1236–1333. Ibáñez Marín, *El general Martínez Campos*, pp. 246–53, indicated again Martínez Campos's irritation with the efforts of General Quesada to hold back his action. The German chargé, Berchem, also attributed Martínez Campos's success to his "eigenmächtig" action, but pointed out that a long siege operation would have left Alfonso in the position of Serrano—the "temperament of the nation cannot stand that sort of delays." Berchem to A.A., No. 145, Aug. 27, 1875, GFO, Reel 54; similar, Lindau at Bayonne to Hohenlohe in Paris, Aug. 28, 1875, Anlage to Hohenlohe to A.A., No. 199, Sept. 2, 1875, GFO, Reel 54.

⁶³ The British ambassador, Layard, wrote home that Martínez Campos in his campaign to the French frontier had taken a serious gamble, but got away with it. For three days he was out of touch with the government and wound up dependent on French supplies. But the government had to portray the expedition as a great military exploit. Layard to Derby, Nos. 60, 66, February 9, 14, 1876. BFO 72:1434.

⁶⁴ In respect to his political position see ch. 2, n. 42. The general's letters of May 13 and August 31, 1875, to Isabella are reproduced in two appendixes of Juan Ortega y Rubio, *Historia de la regencia de María Cristina Habsbourg-Lorena*, 3 vols. (Madrid: Felipe González Rojas, 1905), 1:517–19.

⁶⁵ See summary of end of Carlist War by Layard, Layard to Derby, No. 107, March 1, 1876, BFO 72:1435; Rodezno, *Carlos VII*, pp. 214–15. Both Layard and Hatzfeldt reported that Martínez Campos got a more enthusiastic reception in Madrid than did the king. Layard to Derby, No. 149, March 23, 1876, BFO 72:1436; Hatzfeldt to A.A., No. 39, March 23, 1876, GFO, Reel 55.

⁶⁶ For the Basque story see Enrique Terrachet Sauca, *La agonía de los Fueros, 1844–1878, a través de los acuerdos de la Deputación Foral y Juntas Generales de Guernica, Historia general del Señorío de Bizcaya*, vol. 9 (Bilbao: Editorial La Gran Enciclopedia Vasca, 1973). For Catalonia, Ferrán Soldevila, *Historia de Catalunya*, 2d ed., vol. 3 (Barcelona: Editorial Alpha, 1962), p. 1387.

[67] On meeting with Sagasta see *La Política*, "El banquete de ayer," June 18, 1875; *La Iberia*, June 18, 1875. Berchem reported on this meeting in his dispatch to the German Foreign Office, No. 131, June 28, 1875, GFO, Reel 53; related the king's promise of greater influence after the Cortes, No. 139, Aug. 6, 1875, GFO, Reel 54; and reported some doubts on part of king of returning to Cánovas after the Jovellar ministry, No. 191, Nov. 17, 1875, GFO, Reel 54. Layard was not won over by the king until a conversation reported in his No. 236, May 2, 1876, BFO 72:1436, after which he blamed the king's lack of influence on Cánovas, Nos. 264, 268, May 20, 1876, BFO 72:1437.

[68] García Venero, *Alfonso doce*, pp. 143–44; Izquierdo, *Historia clínica*, p. 202.

[69] See Layard to Derby, No. 149, March 23, 1876, BFO 72:1436.

[70] García Venero, *Alfonso doce*, pp. 157–61. José de Carvajol, an ex-minister of the republic, reported the king's sadness and boredom in the palace and the controls exercised by Cánovas, Fernández Almagro, *Historia política*, 1:287. Hatzfeldt said that an "unbelievable story" that the duke of Sesto had simply had a girl who was following the king shot was widely accepted in Madrid. Private letter to A.A., Sept. 21, 1875, A 4572, GFO, Reel 54.

[71] Marqués de Lema, *De la revolución*, 2:779–84. The Marqués de Bedmar told the German ambassador in St. Petersburg that he had had a difficult time in persuading Isabella not to accompany her son and had got the Duc Decaze's promise to stop her by force if necessary. Alvensleben in St. Petersburg to A.A., No. 136, May 27, 1875, GFO, Reel 53.

[72] Fernández Almagro, *Cánovas*, pp. 302–5 and letter of Cánovas to queen, April 14, 1875, appendix 9, pp. 645–50; of Juan de la Pezuela to queen explaining king's decision, appendix 13, pp. 660–62; of Isabella to Cánovas, April 23, 1875, appendix 14, pp. 662–77.

[73] Berchem to A.A., No. 103, April 24, 1875, GFO, Reel 53.

[74] Hohenlohe to Kaiser, No. 159, June 29, 1875, GFO, Reel 53.

[75] Lindau to Hohenlohe, No. 607, Aug. 4, 1875, GFO, Reel 54.

[76] Hohenlohe to A.A., No. 185, Aug. 6, 1875, GFO, Reel 54.

[77] Rodezno, *Carlos VII*, pp. 198–202; cf. Pirala, *Historia contemporánea*, 3:728 ff. Her correspondence with Carlos was marked by affectionate phrases and continued into November 1875. See also John D. Bergamini, *The Spanish Bourbons: The History of a Tenacious Dynasty* (New York: G. P. Putnam's Sons, 1974), p. 388.

[78] Hohenlohe in Paris to A.A., No. 234, Nov. 12, 1875, GFO, Reel

54; Hatzfeldt to A.A., Nov. 13, 1875, Secret, A 6457. GFO, Reel 54.

[79] Hatzfeldt to A.A., No. 208, Secret, Dec. 27, 1875, GFO, Reel 54.

CHAPTER 3. *Constitution, Cortes, and Controversy*

[1] José Luis Comellas calls Cánovas's development of the theory of an internal constitution the "heart" of his system. *Historia de España moderna y contemporánea, 1464–1974* (Madrid: Ediciones Realp, 1974), p. 408. Full text of Sandhurst Manifesto in Nido y Segalerva, *Historia política*, pp. 400–402. Emphasis added.

[2] *El Imparcial*, Jan. 9, 1875; *La Política*, Jan. 30, Feb. 24, 1875.

[3] Jan. 14, 1875.

[4] Jan. 13, 1875.

[5] See breakdown in *La Iberia*, May 22, 1875.

[6] The story is followed in detail in Carlos Navarro y Rodrigo, *Un período de oposición* (Madrid: Imprenta de los Hijos de J. A. Garcia, 1886), pp. 2–12, in Pirala, *Historia contemporánea*, 4:28–57, and in columns of rival Constitutional newspapers *La Iberia* and *La Política*.

[7] *La Política*, May 12, 1875.

[8] *La Iberia*, April 29, May 1, 1875; *La Política* began its reports on May 3, 1875, denying that there was a basic difference between the two formulas.

[9] *La Política*, May 3, 1875.

[10] *La Iberia*, May 4, 5, 6, 7, 8, 9, 1875.

[11] Ibid., May 12, 1875; *La Política*, May 12, 1875.

[12] *La Iberia*, May 16, 1875; *La Política*, May 17, 1875.

[13] *La Iberia*, May 17, 1875; *La Política*, May 18, 21, 24, 29, June 1, 1875.

[14] In letter of May 2, see *La Política*, May 12, 1875.

[15] *La Política*, Jan. 5, 13, 14, 22; Feb. 2, 1875.

[16] E.g., July 8, "La política del Sr. Cánovas"; July 16, 1875, "El Sr. Cánovas y *La Iberia*."

[17] *La Iberia*, Aug. 6, 1875.

[18] *La Política*, May 21, 1875.

[19] He became the president of the commission designated to present the constitution to the Cortes.

[20] Early in August they issued a manifesto directed against the "free religion principle" embodied in the draft. *El Imparcial*, Aug. 8, 1875.

[21] The favorable response to this change was noted in ch. 2, n. 47.

22 See ch. 2, n. 48.

23 *El Imparcial*, July 18, 1875.

24 April 10, 1877.

25 *Diario*, Congreso, 1875–76, vol. 3, apéndice primero al núm. 68, p. 2.

26 *La Iberia*, July 13, 15, 23, 1875.

27 *El Imparcial*, Aug. 4, 6, 8, 1875.

28 Ibid., July 21, 24, Aug. 17, 21, 1875.

29 Ibid., Dec. 3, 1875. For the election procedures and results see Miguel Martínez Cuadrado, *Elecciones y partidos políticos de España, 1868–1931*, (Madrid: Taurus, 1969), 1:211–31.

30 *La Iberia*, Nov. 7, 8, 11, 1875. *La Política* still denounced Sagasta for holding to a constitution which he himself had voided for eight months. Nov. 8, 1875. Considered significant in leading to the action of the Constitutionalists was the meeting between Sagasta and the king which had taken place on June 17. See *La Iberia* and *La Política*, June 18, 1875.

31 *La Iberia*, Dec. 14, 15, 1875.

32 Dec. 14, 15, 18, 1875.

33 *La Iberia*, which printed reports from provinces on Jan. 8, 20, 28, 1876.

34 Layard to Derby, No. 32, Jan. 20, 1876, BFO 72:1434.

35 Layard to Derby, No. 106, March 1, 1876, BFO 72:1435.

36 Summary in Nido y Segalerva, *Historia política*, pp. 439–520. Fabié says Cánovas presented the original draft to the cabinet on Jan. 25, 1876. *Cánovas*, p. 117.

37 Noted not only in *El Imparcial*, April 9, 21, 1876 and *La Iberia*, July 21, 1876, which found Cánovas the "soul, mind, and word" of his party, but in the report of Layard to Derby, No. 264, May 20, 1876, BFO 72:1437, in which Layard finally recognized that Cánovas had shown "great ability, energy, and eloquence in managing his majority in the Cortes," but suggested that his fellow cabinet members had been of little use to him—when they spoke, said Layard, "he has been generally obliged to unsay, or to explain away, what they have said." And as a consequence, "The whole burden of the defence of his policy and measures has fallen upon his shoulders." Layard felt he had failed to make a favorable impression on public opinion. Count Hatzfeldt made similar comments, No. 32, March 23, 1876, GFO, Reel 54.

38 A copy of the constitution is found in Pirala, *Historia contemporá-*

nea, 4:778–84; and Sevilla Andrés, *Constituciones*, 1:597–612. The latter source also presents the *dictamen* or formal defense of the constitution, pp. 589–96.

[39] Soldevila, *Historia de España*, 8:157.

[40] Martínez Cuadrado, *Elecciones y partidos políticos*, 1:225, 243. The proportion of voters to inhabitants, notes Diego Sevilla Andrés, was approximately the same as that in England during the same period. See his *Historia política de España, 1800–1973*, 2d ed., p. 356.

[41] See debates of Constitutionalist deputy José Luis Albareda and Sagasta with Francisco de Paula Candau, who was also a member of the dissidents and of the commission which presented the constitution to the Cortes. *Diario*, Congreso, 3:1531–53, May 18, 1876. Candau pointed out that Sagasta himself had talked of the need for amendment of the Constitution of 1869 to provide greater governmental controls.

[42] Posada Herrera had tremendous prestige during this period but there was little public evidence to justify it. Evidently his real forte lay in private conversations and conciliation. See Linares Rivas, *La primera cámara*, pp. xi, 5–10; *El Imparcial*, Aug. 25, Oct. 13, 1876.

[43] Pidal y Mon was only thirty at the time of this debate but already leader of the so-called "Catholic Union." In 1884, as noted later, he would bring his followers into Cánovas's party and become minister of development in the last cabinet under Alfonso.

[44] *Diario*, Congreso, 3:1377–87, May 12, 1876. The author finds Alonso Martínez's exposition much more reasoned and convincing than that of Cánovas. Linares Rivas was to say that if all that were needed to be the leader of a great party were "intelligence, knowledge, and respectability," Alonso Martínez would have been one. Unfortunately, more was required in Restoration Spain. *La primera cámera*, pp. 103–10. Cánovas's speech on Article 11 is found in *Diario*, Congreso, 3:1390–91, May 12, 1876.

[45] See ch. 3, n. 41.

[46] *Diario*, Congreso, 5:3133–34, July 15, 1876.

[47] *El Imparcial*, Sept. 7, 10, 12, 13, 1876.

[48] Ibid.

[49] The protests of the English and German diplomatic representatives had begun earlier and took on greater scope with the affair of the hospital at Cádiz discussed below.

[50] Relation of Constitutionalist deputy in Cortes, Nov. 25, 1876, *Diario*, Congreso, 6:3545–47.

[51] *Gaceta de Madrid*, Oct. 23, 1876. See Layard's commentary, Layard

to Derby, No. 442, Oct. 24, 1876, BFO 72:1439; No. 447, Oct. 26, 1876, BFO 72:1439.

[52] *La Iberia* on Sept. 22, 1876, published a report from a newspaper in Cologne quoting Cánovas as saying the sub-governor would not only be removed but brought to the tribunals.

[53] Ibid., Oct. 8, 15, 1876; cf. *El Imparcial*, Oct. 13, 1876.

[54] *La Iberia*, Sept. 13, 1876.

[55] *El Imparcial*, Oct. 16, 1876.

[56] Ibid., Oct. 29, 1876. *La Iberia*, Oct. 31, 1876, criticized Alonso Martínez's elastic interpretation of the article.

[57] *El Imparcial*, Sept. 29, Oct. 3, 1876. *La Iberia*, as to be expected, was hostile to the group, Oct. 3, 1876.

[58] *El Imparcial*, Nov. 4, 1876; Jan. 11, 1877.

[59] Alonso Martínez's speech, *Diario*, Congreso, 6:3666–71; Cánovas's reply, ibid., pp. 3671–76. The major speech against the government was delivered by José Luis Albareda, ibid., pp. 3644–50.

[60] Ibid., p. 3664.

[61] *El Imparcial*, Nov. 11, 15, 1876. Hatzfeldt attributed the firing to a reference in the text suggesting the probable illegitimacy of Alfonso, but said the text had been used for years and the sudden and arbitrary action was not wise. Hatzfeldt to A.A., No. 157, Nov. 16, 1876, GFO, Reel 55.

[62] *Diario*, Congreso, 6:3680–81.

[63] Layard to Derby, No. 543, Dec. 22, 1876, BFO 72:1440; Ernst Kropf, German consul at Cádiz, Dec. 13, 1876, annex to Hatzfeldt to A.A., No. 204, Dec. 18, 1876, GFO, Reel 57.

[64] Layard to Derby, No. 531, Dec. 11, 1876, BFO 72:1440.

[65] Reference to Kaiser's marginalia, Bülow to Kaiser, Dec. 29, 1876, Unnumbered, GFO, Reel 55.

[66] Hatzfeldt to A.A., No. 205, Dec. 15, 1876, GFO, Reel 55.

[67] Bülow to Kaiser, Jan. 3, 1877, Unnumbered, GFO, Reel 55.

[68] Jaime Vicens Vives with Jorge Nadal Oller, *An Economic History of Spain*, trans. Frances M. López-Morillas (Princeton, N.J.: Princeton University Press, 1969), pp. 615–97; cf. Comellas, *Historia de España moderna*, pp. 415–18. Although the author would agree with Joan Connelly Ullman (*The Tragic Week: A Study of Anticlericalism in Spain, 1875–1912* [Cambridge: Harvard University Press, 1968], pp. 10–11) that both Liberal Conservatives and Constitutionalists followed policies favorable to the industrialization of Spain, he is not sure that one can securely assign groups such as the Andalusian landowners to the Lib-

eral Conservatives and Castilian wheat growers to the Constitutionalists. The events relating to Cuba, discussed below, show the great strength of the Liberal Conservatives among the wealthy classes in Catalonia, and in that controversy they strongly defended the interests of the wheat growers. The "behind the scenes" story of the relation of economic groups to politics is yet to be written.

[69] Vicens Vives, *Economic History*, pp. 717–46.

[70] William L. Giro to Dwight T. Reed, consul general in Madrid, June 7, 1884, U.S. Consular Dispatches, Alicante, T357, Roll 3; John F. Quarles to Assistant Secretary of State, No. 24, July 12, 1878, U.S. Consular Dispatches, Málaga, T217, Roll 11.

[71] John F. Quarles to Assistant Secretary of State, No. 24, July 12, 1878, U.S. Consular Dispatches, Málaga, T217, Roll 11.

CHAPTER 4. *The Foreign Policy of Cánovas del Castillo*

[1] See ch. 1, nn. 52, 53, 54.

[2] Quotations from Cushing's dispatches of Feb. 15, 1875, No. 268, U.S. Dept. of State, Reel 67; July 19, 1875, No. 449, U.S. Dept. of State, Reel 70; January 14, 1876, No. 769, U.S. Dept. of State, Reel 74.

[3] Layard wrote, "The opinions of Mr. Cushing on these matters, which he has been in the habit of expressing somewhat openly, agree more with those of the Russian Minister than of any other member of the Diplomatic Body in Madrid. They have afforded great pleasure and satisfaction to the Spanish Government, and this is probably the object that Mr. Cushing has had in view, hoping to be thus enabled to settle in a satisfactory manner the questions pending between Spain and the United States." Layard to Derby, No. 62, Confidential, Feb. 9, 1876, BFO 72:1434. *La Epoca*, one of the principal government newspapers, wrote on January 4, 1876, "Mr. Cushing at the advanced age of 78 years appears to be as much alert and gifted with the same vivacity as when he was in Spain approximately half a century ago" and designated him as the ablest and most experienced of the diplomatic representatives. Claude M. Fuess, *The Life of Caleb Cushing* (New York: Harcourt, Brace, 1923), provides no information suggesting Cushing's financial involvement in the Cuban claims settlement, but Martin Duberman, *James Russell Lowell* (Boston: Houghton Mifflin, 1966), p. 285, speaks of the suspicions in respect to this matter.

[4] They led off the round of recognitions. On Aug. 21, 1875, Berchem reported the granting of Russian decorations to Cánovas and members of the cabinet. Aug. 21, 1875, A 2964, GFO, Reel 54.

[5] Particular comments are found in Berchem to A.A., No. 123, June 1, 1875, GFO, Reel 54; No. 144, Aug. 27, 1875, A 5457, GFO, Reel 54; Hatzfeldt to A.A., No. 180, Oct. 26, 1875; Nov. 13, 1875, Secret, A 5457 GFO, Reel 54; No. 194, Nov. 17, 1875, GFO, Reel 54; Tümpling to A.A., No. 120, July 25, 1876, GFO, Reel 55.

[6] More sophisticated analyses (but perhaps not more accurate) of Cánovas's foreign policy are found in Leonor Meléndez Meléndez, *Cánovas y la política exterior española* (Madrid: Institute de Estudios Políticos, 1944), pp. 41–115; Salom Costa, *España en la Europa de Bismarck*, pp. 414–22.

[7] Sister M. Celine Esther Parent, "Caleb Cushing and the Foreign Policy of the United States, 1860–1877" (Ph.D. dissertation, Boston College, 1958), pp. 234–43; Fernández Almagro, *Historia política*, 1: 203–6.

[8] Fernández Almagro, *Historia política*, 1:203–6.

[9] Brandt, *Toward the New Spain*, pp. 303–9.

[10] See Bécker, *Historia de las relaciones exteriores*, 3:216–19 and Parent, "Caleb Cushing," pp. 265–77. Negotiations began in the first month of the Restoration, reached their conclusion on April 21, 1875, with the receipt of the sum concerned. See Cushing to Fish, No. 356, April 21, 1875, U.S. Dept. of State, Reel 68. There was the case of Burriel which continued to be a problem never solved—he was promoted and decorated and never punished. See Parent, "Caleb Cushing," pp. 277–82.

[11] The assertion that the insurrectionists were now thinking more and more of independence rather than autonomy is strongly supported by Herminio Portell Vilá, *Historia de Cuba en sus relaciones con los Estados Unidos y España*, 4 vols. (Miami, Fla.: Minemosyne Publishing, 1969), 2:199–536. He is, of course, a Cuban patriot seeking to emphasize the significance of the idea of independence from the earliest period possible. The enthusiasm which surrounded Martínez Campos's brief period as captain general of Cuba would seem to raise serious doubts that the quest for independence had gained the allegiance of anywhere close to a majority of Cubans at that time. The Spanish government emphasized the racial aspects of the struggle and made a clear impression on foreign representatives with this approach. See Layard to Derby, Feb. 12, 1876, BFO 185:585; Cushing to Fish, No. 777, Jan.

16, 1876, U.S. Dept. of State, Reel 76; Hatzfeldt to A.A., Nos. 209, 214, Dec. 27, 28, 1875, GFO, Reel 95; Hatzfeldt to A.A., No. 13, Jan. 3, 1877, GFO, Reel 95. Philip S. Foner, *A History of Cuba and its Relations with the United States*, vol. 2, provides a detailed account of the role of black forces in the Ten Years War.

[12] Fernández Almagro, *Historia política*, 1:319–20. The Marqués de la Habana, José Gutiérrez de la Concha, returned to be one of the first Spanish generals to oppose the continued wasting of troops in Cuba. See Layard to Derby, No. 515, Dec. 6, 1876, BFO 72:1440.

[13] Fernández Almagro, *Historia política*, 1:320–22.

[14] Ibid., pp. 323–24. Major resources were furnished by the Compañía Transatlántica, whose president was Antonio López y López, first Marqués de Comillas, who also became the president of the new bank. Cushing, who was shocked at the interest rate involved, reported the involvement of Manuel Calvo, "one of the wealthiest of the Peninsulars in Cuba" along with Zulueta, López, Salamanca, and others. Cushing to Fish, No. 1084, Aug. 12, 1876, U.S. Dept. of State, Reel 79.

[15] Fernández Almagro, *Historia política*, 1:322–24. Layard reported the military failure of Jovellar with his difficulties being enhanced by high taxation in Cuba and shortly afterward suggested the real worries of the Spanish government in respect to Cuba. Martínez Campos took over at a time of virtual crisis. Layard to Derby, No. 199, Confidential, April 14, 1876, BFO 72:1436; No. 264, May 20, 1876, BFO 72:1437.

[16] Background and slight effect of the note detailed in Allan Nevins, *Hamilton Fish: The Inner History of the Grant Administration* (New York: Dodd, Mead and Company, 1936), pp. 874–84.

[17] E.g., Cushing to Fish, No. 815, Feb. 9, 1876, U.S. Dept. of State, Reel 75; No. 820, Feb. 19, 1876, U.S. Dept. of State, Reel 76. See also Parent, "Caleb Cushing," pp. 260–65.

[18] See comments of Fish in Nevins, *Fish*, pp. 880–82.

[19] Cushing to Fish, No. 777, Jan. 16, 1876, U.S. Dept. of State, Reel 76.

[20] Hatzfeldt to A.A., Nos. 209, 214, Dec. 27, 28, 1875; No. 13, Jan. 3, 1877, GFO, Reel 95.

[21] Story of incident, German Foreign Office Memorandum to all embassies, Jan. 21, 1875, GFO, Reel 52.

[22] Bismarck to Hatzfeldt, No. 19, Jan. 16, 1875, GFO, Reel 52.

[23] See memorandum of von Bülow to Kaiser, Jan. 18, 1875 and memorandum of Bismarck to Kaiser, Jan. 20, 1875, GFO, Reel 52.

24 Bismarck to von Hatzfeldt, Jan. 16, 1875, cipher telegram No. 19, GFO, Reel 52; Bülow to Hatzfeldt, No. 26, Jan. 23, 1875, GFO, Reel 52.

25 Hatzfeldt to A.A., No. 10, Jan. 25, 1875, GFO, Reel 52. The German navy was not satisfied yet, however, and Bülow complained on March 6, 1875, to the head of the German admiralty, Albrecht von Stosch, about aggressive statements of the captain of the *Nautilus*, the German warship on the scene. A1251, Secret, GFO, Reel 53. Damages of 345,000 reales were received on April 9, 1875, Hatzfeldt to A.A., Telegram No. 61, April 9, 1875, GFO, Reel 53, and the exchange of salutes finally took place on April 28, 1875. Berchem to A.A., Telegram No. 69, April 28, 1875, GFO, Reel 53.

26 See "Joló" in *Diccionario de historia de España*, 2d. ed., 2:555–57; Bécker, *Historia de las relaciones exteriores*, 3 : 273–76.

27 Bécker, *Historia de las relaciones exteriores*, 3 : 276–87.

28 The Germans seemed to show more interest in the Sulus than the British, but in the face of the evident concern of Cánovas and the personal intervention of Alfonso, the Germans accepted a conciliatory settlement. Memorandum of German Foreign Office, June, 1976, A 3260; Private letter of von Bülow to Hatzfeldt, Feb. 6, 1877; Private letter of von Hatzfeldt to Bülow, Feb. 12, 1877; Münster in London to A.A., No. 29, Feb. 24, 1877; Hatzfeldt to A.A., No. 67, Feb. 18, 1877; Hatzfeldt to A.A., Private letter, March 12, 1877. All in GFO, Reel 55. Copy of agreement, Calderón Collantes to Layard, Nov. 11, 1876, BFO 185:585. But Hatzfeldt was still wondering in October 1877 why Spain tried to keep the Sulus when they were so subject to uprisings of the native Mauris, who were still causing difficulty for Spain, No. 185, Oct. 4, 1877, GFO, Reel 56.

29 See speech of German Gamazo referred to in ch. 5.

30 Hatzfeldt to A.A., No. 205, Dec. 25, 1875, GFO, Reel 95.

31 Covered in Hatzfeldt to A.A., No. 207, Confidential, Oct. 31, 1877; No. 208, Confidential, Oct. 31, 1877. GFO, Reel 56.

32 Bismarck to State Secretary, Varzin, Nov. 15, 1877, A 6822, GFO, Reel 56. Instructions to Hatzfeldt following Bismarck's comments were sent Nov. 25, 1877, Secret, "eigenhändig," A 7316, GFO, Reel 56.

33 Bismarck to Bülow, Varzin, Nov. 21, 1877, GFO, Reel 56.

34 Rachel Challice, *The Secret History of the Court of Spain during the Last Century* (London: John Long, 1909), p. 223, tells of first marriage. On marriage proposal, Memo of Bülow on conversation with Kaiser

at Baden Baden, Oct. 18, 1877, A 6320, GFO, Reel 56. When Hatzfeldt again raised the question, Bülow noted that he should not have done so. Hatzfeldt to A.A., No. 24, Private, Nov. 26, 1877, and Bülow to Bismarck, No. 43, Dec. 2, 1877, A 7052, GFO, Reel 56.

35 Bülow to Bismarck, No. 54, Secret, Dec. 22, 1877, GFO, Reel 56.

36 Bülow told Hatzfeldt, No. 3, Jan. 4, 1878, that the kaiser was not against the marriage but that it was a private matter. By March 3, 1878, it was clear that Isabella had been involved in the negotiations, Bülow to Hatzfeldt, No. 88, March 3, 1878. Hatzfeldt reported in No. 73, Secret, April 15, 1878, that Silvela had received the negative report in respect to the marriage and Bülow informed him that it was the prince's own decision which had thwarted the marriage proposal. Bülow to Hatzfeldt, No. 91, May 1, 1878, GFO, Reel 56.

37 Bismarck to Bülow, Dec. 13, 1877, Varzin, A 7316, GFO, Reel 56. Germany, he suggested, should treat the approach like that of a loving friend who brings up something which for the present cannot be accepted.

38 When Hatzfeldt talked with Merry y Colon shortly after the interview, he found him uninformed. Hatzfeldt to A.A., No. 221, Confidential, Nov. 15, 1877. A little later he learned Merry would not be the ambassador if embassy status were granted. Hatzfeldt to A.A., No. 233, Secret, Dec. 5, 1877. But by Dec. 22 Merry had received instructions with a note from Silvela formally setting forth the proposal. Bülow to Bismarck, No. 54, Secret, Dec. 22, 1877, and note from Silvela to Merry, Dec. 12, 1877, A 7461–7516, GFO, Reel 56.

39 Hatzfeldt to A.A., No. 253, Secret, Dec. 31, 1877, with Bismarck's marginalia, GFO, Reel 56.

40 Hatzfeldt to A.A., No. 16, Secret, Jan. 15, 1878, GFO, Reel 56.

41 Ibid.; Bülow to Bismarck, No. 3, Berlin, Jan. 24, 1878; Bismarck to Bülow, Varzin, Jan. 26, 1878, A 535; Notes of Silvela to Merry y Colon, Jan. 15, 1878, A 559. GFO, Reel 56.

42 Hatzfeldt to A.A., No. 20, Feb. 1, No. 24, Feb. 9, 1878, GFO, Reel 56.

43 By June 17, 1878, Hatzfeldt was, indeed, reporting to his home government that he felt there had been a swing away from Germany and that in spite of hard work he was not accomplishing anything in respect to the religious question. Hatzfeldt to A.A., Private letter, A 3781, GFO, Reel 56.

44 Hatzfeldt to Bülow, No. 242, Secret, Dec. 15, 1877, GFO, Reel 56.

45 Hispano-French relations are treated fully and thoroughly in Salom Costa, *España en la Europa de Bismarck*, pp. 184–252, 275–91, 296–310, 397–409.

46 Ibid., pp. 409–14. The author has read through the English diplomatic dispatches of this period but does not feel it worthwhile to trace the continuing process of negotiations over commercial differences.

CHAPTER 5. *The King and the Parties*

1 *El Imparcial*, Nov. 2, 1876.

2 Ibid., Dec. 21, 1876.

3 Ibid., Feb. 6, 1877.

4 Ibid., April 10, 1877. Text of law in Sevilla Andrés, *Constituciones*, 1:613–23.

5 *El Imparcial*, April 11, 1877. These events demonstrated the prescience of the Marqués de la Vega de Armijo, who had warned in the constitutional commission that the constitutional provisions for the Senate carried the danger of establishing excessive conservatism. See Raul Bertelson Repetto, *El senado en España* (Madrid: Instituto de Estudios Administrativos, 1974), p. 428.

6 Rundown of press in *El Imparcial*, April 7, 12, 1877.

7 Ibid., April 25, 1877.

8 Ibid., Feb. 11, 1877.

9 Ibid., April 3, 1877.

10 Ibid., April 27, 1877.

11 Ibid., Jan. 16, 1877.

12 Ibid., March 7, 1877.

13 Ibid., Jan. 12, 1877.

14 Ibid., Feb. 5, 1877. The political explanation was also given by Layard in his dispatch to Derby, No. 94, Feb. 14, 1877, BFO 72:1468, and in Pirala, *Historia contemporánea*, 4:124. For the story of the later rumor see pp. 228–29.

15 No less than eight newspapers were denounced during the first half of March 1877. *El Imparcial*, March 14, 15, 1877.

16 Ibid., Feb. 9, 1877.

17 Ibid., April 24, 1877.

18 *Diario*, Congreso, vol. 1, 1877, pp. 12–13.

19 Ibid., pp. 121–28, May 9, 1877.

[20] Ibid., pp. 128–31, May 9, 1877.

[21] Ibid., pp. 155–58, May 11, 1877.

[22] Ibid., pp. 159–67, May 11, 1877.

[23] Ibid., pp. 181–89, May 12, 1877.

[24] Ibid., pp. 192–98, May 14, 1877.

[25] Ibid., pp. 224–26, May 14, 1877.

[26] *La Política*, June 12, 1877.

[27] *El Imparcial*, July 12, 15, 1877.

[28] Ibid., Sept. 25, 27, 1877.

[29] *El Diario Español*, Oct. 23, 1877.

[30] *El Imparcial*, Aug. 3, 1877.

[31] Ibid., July 29, Aug. 8, 1877.

[32] Ibid., Aug. 28, 1877.

[33] Ibid., Dec. 28, 1877. *La Epoca* on Oct. 13, 1877, reported the story of an interview with Posada Herrera who was supposed to have said he was coming to Madrid not to preside over the Congress but to preside over the Center. *La Epoca* expressed its justified doubts.

[34] *El Imparcial*, Jan. 31, 1878.

[35] Ibid., Feb. 14, 1878.

[36] Pirala, *Historia contemporánea*, 4:132–36; Hatzfeldt to A.A., No. 78, March 11, 1877; No. 97, May 6, 1877, GFO, Reel 55.

[37] In the matter of the position of Cánovas and Silvela, see Layard to Derby, No. 108, Feb. 27, 1877, BFO 72:1468; Hatzfeldt to A.A., No. 63, Feb. 17, 1877; von Thielen to A.A., No. 167, Aug. 8, 1877, GFO, Reel 55; Hatzfeldt to A.A., No. 183, Sept. 30, 1877, No. 236, Dec. 5, 1877, GFO, Reel 56. Germany was lukewarm on the marriage. After a memorandum to the kaiser, Hatzfeldt was told to follow the lead of the rest of the diplomatic corps—the marriage was a cause neither for pleasure nor displeasure for Germany. Bülow to Kaiser, Dec. 12, 1877, A 7229; Bülow to Hatzfeldt, Dec. 13, 1877, A 7242, GFO, Reel 56. One sign of French favor was the expulsion of Don Carlos from France. Reported, Hohenlohe to A.A., No. 91, May 23, 1877, Telegram, GFO, Reel 55.

[38] The German representatives followed the controversy in detail. Most embarrassing to the Spaniards was Isabella's interview with the German chargé in which she indicated she would have preferred a German wife for her son. De la Puente was blamed for stirring her up to unseemly action. Von Thielen to A.A., No. 155, Secret, July 12, 1877, GFO, Reel 55; von Thielen to A.A., unnumbered, Confidential,

Sept. 23, 1877, GFO, Reel 56; von Thielen to Bülow, Private Letter, Very Confidential; Hatzfeldt to A.A., No. 181, Sept. 28, 1877; Hatzfeldt to A.A., No. 15, Secret, Oct. 6, 1877, GFO, Reel 56.

39 Hatzfeldt reported her departure on Nov. 13, 1877, in a private letter to Bülow, A 6902, GFO, Reel 56.

40 *El Imparcial* reported the events on Jan. 7, 9, 1878. Also reported by Hatzfeldt to A.A., No. 254, Secret, Dec. 31, 1877, GFO, Reel 56, with added comment that Isabella was supposed to have given a German journalist a manifesto against her son. Clippings from *Pall Mall Gazette* of Dec. 26, 1877, and Dec. 29, 1877, included.

41 Copy of her letter given in *El Mundo Político*, Jan. 8, 1878, with defense of queen.

42 The German representative in Lisbon on Dec. 13, 1877, had, indeed, mentioned the possibility of the son placing his mother in a sanatorium, No. 48, GFO, Reel 56, and an unidentified German press clipping in the German Foreign Office files carried a note that "die arme vielgeschmähte Frau" might be put in a sanatorium.

43 *El Imparcial*, Jan. 15, 1878.

44 Lafuente, *Historia general*, 25:55–57; *El Imparcial*, Dec. 13, 1877.

45 *El Mundo Político*, Jan. 3, 4, 1878; report of sale of copies for forty reales, *El Imparcial*, Jan. 5, 1878. *La Paz* began publication again on Jan. 8, 1878, after forty-five day's suspension only to be denounced again on Feb. 19. *El Imparcial*, Jan. 8, Feb. 19, 1878.

46 *El Mundo Político*, Feb. 21, 1878.

47 *El Imparcial*, Jan. 15, 16, 1878.

48 García Venero, *Alfonso doce*, p. 180; description of Francisco de Asis from Martin Hume, *Modern Spain*, *1788–1898* (New York: G. P. Putnam's Sons, 1900), p. 528.

49 Quoted, Bergamini, *The Spanish Bourbons*, p. 294. The king at the diplomatic reception for the occasion also emphasized how happy he was to be marrying a *Spanish* princess. Hatzfeldt to A.A., No. 243, Dec. 17, 1877, GFO, Reel 56.

50 Francos Rodríguez, *En tiempo de Alfonso XII*, pp. 67–78.

51 Hatzfeldt reported that 50,000 persons stood before the palace in Madrid at the time of the death. Hatzfeldt to A.A., unnumbered, June 28, 1878, A 3967, GFO, Reel 56.

52 See Izquierdo, *Historia clínica*, pp. 124–31. He does not mention the miscarriage on the part of the queen reported by Hatzfeldt, No. 96, June 16, 1878, GFO, Reel 56.

53 Lowell to Evarts, No. 95, July 3, 1878, U.S. Dept. of State, Reel

84: "Meanwhile the wildest and I may say the most atrocious rumors were current among the vulgar, so atrocious, indeed, that I will not shock you with a repetition of them." The Republican newspaper *La Correspondencia de Barcelona* reported on June 27, 1878, that the Duque de Montpensier came and after inquiring of the cause of his daughter's death, said he was sorry he had not stayed with her. It paid for the story with forty day's suspension. Another story, surfacing in the German *Deutsche Montagsblatt* of Oct. 28, 1878, reported that the tutor for the Montpensiers had said in an interview that the princess of Asturias had forgotten her sister-in-law was ill (!) and fired a pistol in the next room resulting in a nervous paroxysm from which the queen never recovered! The German Foreign Office arranged a counteracting article in the *Norddeutsche Allgemeine Zeitung* of Nov. 1, 1878. Conde de Benomar in Berlin to State Secy., Oct. 29, 1878, Confidential, A 6101; Benomar to State Secy., Personal, Nov. 2, 1878, A 6172 (thanking him for the article), GFO, Reel 56.

[54] García Venero, *Alfonso doce*, p. 195.

[55] A recent movie and a television program in the series "Sombras recobradas" dealt with the theme.

[56] *El Imparcial*, Oct. 10, 23, 1877.

[57] Ibid., Jan. 2, 4, 1878. In this same period the sub-governor of Mahon was still active. The Protestant newspaper *El Bien Público* was denounced, freed, and denounced again. Ibid., Jan. 13, 1878. Hatzfeldt's report of Alcoy and of Cánovas's promise to look into it, Hatzfeldt to A.A., No. 10, Jan. 15, 1878, GFO, Reel 56. Hatzfeldt informed Pastor Fliedner of the interview. A second report of Hatzfeldt indicated the obvious influence carried by Fliedner. No. 49, March 20, 1878, GFO, Reel 57.

[58] Lionel Sackville-West, who had replaced Layard as the British ambassador, reported on Sept. 15, 1878, that he had met with a "liberal spirit" from Spanish authorities and promise of royal clemency, No. 172, BFO 72:1501. But he received letters from A. J. Arnold, the assistant secretary of the Evangelical Mission in London to Mr. R. Bourke, M.P., No. 524, Oct. 15, 1878, and from the Synod of Pirth and Stirling to the Foreign Office, No. 557, Oct. 16, 1878, BFO 72:1519, complaining of Benoliel's treatment in prison. A letter of the Evangelical Alliance, Nov. 6, 1878, reported that Benoliel had finally received his pardon on October 30, BFO 72:1519.

[59] In his dispatch of Sept. 15 noted above Sackville-West said that the Benoliel case showed that charges of "so-called religious persecution"

were often misrepresented by sectarian zeal in England, and Derby had earlier commented to Salisbury (No. 10, Jan. 5, 1878, BFO 72:1517) that English missionaries expected too much. They could not expect to sell Bibles on the open street in a country where most of the people were "bigoted Roman Catholics."

[60] *El Imparcial*, Jan. 12, 1877.

[61] *El Imparcial*, Oct. 21, 22, 24, 25, 26, 27, 31, Nov. 3, 1877. Hatzfeldt found Manuel Silvela concerned by Calderón Collantes's influence and a little later he reported Calderón Collantes's support of intolerant action in the little town of Commuñas near Toledo, where stones were thrown at the house of the Protestant pastor (he had supposedly disturbed a religious procession) and the house later seized. Since the house belonged to Pastor Fliedner, who clearly had much influence with the German Foreign Office, Hatzfeldt interceded with Cánovas and got it released. But he was much disturbed by Calderón Collantes's Ultramontanism. Hatzfeldt to A.A., No. 59, April 3, 1878; No. 71, May 1, 1878; No. 87, June 1, 1878, GFO, Reel 57. *La Epoca* on Oct. 22, 31, Nov. 4, 1877, tried to soften opposition criticism by assuring critics, with Cánovas's blessing, that there was no intention of returning to the conditions of the Constitution of 1845.

[62] *El Imparcial*, Jan. 30, 1878.

[63] Ibid., Feb. 12, 1878. This, of course, provided the last step needed for what Comellas has called the "turno organizado," the planned change of parties. *Historia de España moderna*, p. 409.

[64] *El Imparcial*, Feb. 16, 1878.

[65] *Diario*, Congreso, 1878, 1:172–77, Feb. 28, 1878.

[66] Ibid., pp. 177–79, 181–82, Feb. 28, 1878.

[67] Ibid., pp. 125–36, Feb. 26, 1878.

[68] Ibid., pp. 245–60, 264–67, March 7, 8, 1878.

[69] Ibid., pp. 267–72, March 8, 1878.

[70] Ibid., 2:520–37, March 21, 1878; 2:919–34, April 9, 1878; 6:2752–70, July 14, 1878.

[71] Ibid., 2:934–38, April 9, 1878; *El Imparcial*, Nov. 12, 1878.

[72] July 26, 1878.

[73] Sept. 22, 1878.

[74] Nov. 16, 1878.

[75] Nov. 19, 1878.

[76] Lowell to Evarts, No. 108, Aug. 26, 1878, U.S. Dept. of State, Reel 87. Lowell had fished for the appointment to Spain, a political plum which he obtained in 1877. But his wife, while in Madrid almost

suffered the fate of Mercedes—death from typhus. Her stronger constitution carried her through several crises, but Lowell was much relieved to exchange Madrid for London in May 1880. See Claire McGlinchee, *James Russell Lowell* (New York: Twayne Publishers, 1967), pp. 97–100; Duberman, *James Russell Lowell*, pp. 284–301.

[77] The scorecard was given by *El Imparcial*, March 30, 1878, noting thirteen denunciations by then; *La Iberia* recorded fourteen more since May 7 on June 11, 1878; *El Imparcial* reported thirteen in July by July 14, 1878, and five more in the first half of August, *El Imparcial*, Aug. 16, 1878; on two days in October, the tenth and eleventh, there were three more and three more on November 9 and 10 (*El Imparcial*, Oct. 13, Nov. 10, 1878), and they still continued.

[78] Soldevila, *Historia de España*, 8:158.

[79] Ibid., p. 157.

[80] *Diario*, Congreso, 3:1900–1962, May 25–27, 1878. The extremity of the situation in Barcelona, aggravated by severe drought conditions, the resultant closing of industries with consequent unemployment, and the necessity of establishing soup kitchens, government corruption, the gas war that closed shops and forced restaurants to use oil lights, and the harsh repression of the government are graphically related by the lively German consul who had moved from Bayonne to Barcelona after the Carlist War. Richard Lindau to Hatzfeldt, Feb. 22, March 15, May 17, July 2, Dec. 10, 1878. *Anlagen* to Hatzfeldt to A.A., No. 44, Feb. 27, 1878; Unnumbered, March 17, 1878, A 1974; No. 89, June 2, 1878; No. 685, July 4, 1878, GFO, Reel 56.

[81] *La Iberia*, July 8, 1878.

[82] *El Imparcial*, April 9, 28, 1878.

[83] Hatzfeldt was among the strongest critics of Cánovas's moderation. He should simply have ended the *fueros* with a stroke of the pen, he said. Hatzfeldt to A.A., No. 150, Nov. 7, 1876; No. 207, Dec. 18, 1876, GFO, Reel 55. The problem of the Basque *fueros* is well depicted in Soldevila, *Historia de España*, 8:160–67.

[84] Comment made while he was in Vienna. Von Schweinitz to A.A., No. 68, Secret, Feb. 20, 1877, GFO, Reel 55. German dispatches indicate strong hostility to Carlos and pressure against any favorable reception.

[85] The debate over the Basque *fueros* in 1876 had been a bitter one. The law of July 21, 1876, had placed the Basque provinces under military and tax obligations like the rest of Spain, but after much controversy a solution had been reached in 1877 allowing the provincial

deputations to be responsible for the raising of taxes. H. Butler Clarke, *Modern Spain, 1815–1898* (Cambridge: Cambridge University Press, 1906), p. 405.

⁸⁶ See Carr, *Spain, 1808–1939*, pp. 390–93; Herr, *Spain*, pp. 118–19. American consular reports indicated that economic conditions in Catalonia were seriously depressed in 1878 but made considerable recovery in 1880, sparked by better grape and wheat crops and the beginning of the importation of crude petroleum to be refined in Spain. Fred H. Schenck, Barcelona, to Asst. Secy. of State, No. 142, Aug. 25, 1878; No. 232, Nov. 1, 1881, U.S. Consular Dispatches, Barcelona, Roll 8.

⁸⁷ See notes of German consul cited above, n. 80, and Antonio Ramos Oliveira, *Politics, Economics and Men of Modern Spain, 1808–1946*, p. 383.

⁸⁸ Ibid., pp. 128 ff.

⁸⁹ See debates in Cortes noted above, ch. 5, n. 70.

⁹⁰ See Herr, *Spain*, pp. 116–23. Francos Rodríguez, *En tiempo de Alfonso XII*, pp. 57, 104–6, notes a growing sense of despair and prevalent conversations on the cost of living in the years 1877–79.

⁹¹ Juan Antonio Cabezas, *Concepción Arenal o el sentido romántico de la justicia*, Vidas españolas y hispanoamericanas del siglo XIX, vol. 59 (Madrid: Espasa-Calpe, 1942), pp. 200–218.

⁹² Phrase used by *El Imparcial*, Oct. 14, 1877.

⁹³ Ibid., July 8, Nov. 27, Dec. 6, 1878; Jan. 10, Feb. 2, 21, 1879.

⁹⁴ *Diario*, Congreso, 1878, 2:564–67. In this period Silvela was also complaining about the "atonía política." See María Carmen García-Nieto, Javier María Donezar, and Luis López Puerta, *Restauración y desastre, 1874–1898*, Bases documentales de la España contemporánea, vol. 4 (Madrid: Guadiana, 1972), pp. 71–73.

C H A P T E R 6. *Martínez Campos Versus Cánovas*

¹ Von Thielen to A.A., No. 123, Sept. 30, 1878; Solms to A.A., No. 166, Confidential, Dec. 23, 1878, GFO, Reel 56. Sackville-West to Foreign Office, No. 162, Confidential, Sept. 5, 1878, BFO 72:1501.

² *El Imparcial*, Nov. 2, 13, 1878; von Thielen to A.A., No. 137, Oct. 26, 1878; No. 145, Nov. 14, 1878, GFO, Reel 56. Silvela in his conversation with von Thielen said Oliva was not a socialist, but he believed the attempt had been prepared by Federalist Republicans in Paris.

³ See ch. 5, n. 52.

⁴ Sackville-West to Foreign Office, No. 162, Sept. 5, 1878; No. 176, Very Confidential, Sept. 19, 1878, BFO 72:1501.

⁵ García Venero, *Alfonso doce*, p. 202.

⁶ To be intensified during the period of Liberal government, as seen below.

⁷ Conte, *Recuerdos de un diplomático*, 3:347–48.

⁸ Conte was able to report back that she was marked by her grace and freshness, with nice eyes, an elegant figure, and tiny hands which seemed too small to play the piano as well as she did. She was well educated in history and literature, spoke French, English, and Italian as well as German, and was quickly to learn Spanish. Conte, *Recuerdos de un diplomático*, 3:387–91.

⁹ Lowell to Evarts, No. 221, Dec. 15, 1879, U.S. Dept. of State, Reel 89.

¹⁰ The marriage, said Lowell, awakened neither the sympathies nor the animosities connected with the first marriage. He believed the personality of the archduchess would win support if she could overcome the natural coolness involved in her being a foreigner. Lowell to Evarts, No. 219, Nov. 16, 1879, U.S. Dept. of State, Reel 89; cf. Julian Cortes Cavanillas, *María Cristina de Austria: Madre de Alfonso XIII* (Madrid: Ediciones Aspas, 1944), pp. 39–40. María Cristina found life difficult in the palace where her consort's adventures were well known. Eventually she had Elena Sanz and her sons sent to Paris only to be confronted with Alfonso's enchantment with "la Biondina," an Italian contralto "of second class," whom she also finally managed to get sent away, pp. 49–52.

¹¹ Antonio Ballesteros y Beretta, *Historia de España y su influencia en la historia universal* (Barcelona: Salvat Editores, 1956), 11:334; Fernández Almagro, *Historia política*, 1:315, doubts Serrano's involvement in any plot; *El Imparcial*, Aug. 10, 1878.

¹² Solms to Bülow, No. 167, Secret, "Eigenhändig," Dec. 28, 1878, GFO, Reel 56.

¹³ Cánovas's concerns are reflected in conversations with Solms. He indicated that it would be well if he were replaced. It would be of advantage to the king to have a different party—there were dangers to the dynasty in staying too long with those who had become too much accustomed to their lucrative state offices. Solms to A.A., No. 166, Confidential, Dec. 23, 1878, GFO, Reel 56.

¹⁴ *El Imparcial* on July 2, 1878, spoke with disdain of the possibility

of "twelve to fifteen years" of Cánovist government. When Romero Robledo spoke in the Cortes about the government being "young and robust," the Constitutionalists posed the question, "and the royal prerogative?" Ibid., Nov. 10, 1878. And when the king talked with Sagasta early in January 1879 and spoke favorably of the Constitutionalists, they exulted. Ibid., Jan. 12, 1879.

¹⁵ The opposition of Francisco Silvela to the government budget has already been noted. Late in May he resigned his position as vice-president of the Congress. *El Imparcial*, May 29, 30, 1878. By this time another majority vice-president, Moreno Nieto criticized the government education bill (ibid., April 25, 1878) and majority deputy Álvarez Bugallal was reported hostile to Romero Robledo (ibid., Aug. 29, 1878).

¹⁶ Portell Vilá, *Historia de Cuba*, 2:529; 3:24. The figures were set forth in a manifesto of General Jovellar in the *Gaceta de la Habana* of June 14, 1878—of the losses the Spanish army suffered 80,000 deaths —presumably the other 120,000 were civilians. Figures given in report of German consul in Havana, Feigel, to A.A., No. 42, June 15, 1878, GFO, Reel 95. In the later Cortes debates it was revealed that the Cuban debt included costs of actions in Santo Domingo and Mexico. Ruiz Gómez, May 27, 1880, *Diario*, Senado, 1879–80, 4:1978.

¹⁷ Cushing to Fish, Nos. 321, 336, Oct. 3, 10, 1876, U.S. Dept. of State, Reels 80, 81.

¹⁸ Ibáñez Marín, *El general Martínez Campos*, pp. 129, 158.

¹⁹ Ibid., pp. 314–16.

²⁰ T. Ochando, *El general Martínez Campos en Cuba: Reseña político-militar de la última campaña, noviembre de 1876 a junio de 1878* (Madrid: Imprenta de Fortanet, 1878), passim.

²¹ Ibid.

²² *El Imparcial*, June 22, 1878, reported Martínez Campos had been given dictatorial powers to negotiate peace. In the Cortes debates there was disagreement over the extent of the concessions which could be offered. Frederico Ochando, one of Martínez Campos's agents in the negotiations, read a telegram from Jovellar authorizing a wide range of concessions to the insurrectionists who surrendered, including recognition of military status. He believed, but the Cánovas government denied, that Jovellar acted directly on the authorization of the government. *Diario*, Congreso, 4:1702–3, Feb. 6, 1880; Denial by Elduayen, *Diario*, Congreso, 4:1703. Melchor Fernández Almagro reported that

Cánovas was in disagreement with several clauses of the accord, *Cánovas*, p. 353.

23 The impression in Madrid was that financial resources were more important than military in ending the war. Even before the Restoration, General Concha, then in command in Cuba, had told the home government that the insurrection could not be halted by action on the field of battle—only a general amnesty and better administrative arrangements offered a chance of success. (Reported, Hatzfeldt to A.A., No. 209, Dec. 27, 1875, GFO, Reel 95.) Now, in the midst of Martínez Campos's campaign, Hatzfeldt again reported that financial lures rather than military action were being used: "Although decisive actions were supposed to follow immediately after the arrival of General Martínez Campos, up until now, so far as is known here, only one encounter with the insurgents has taken place—which appears to have been for the [government] troops unsuccessful and rather bloody. It is commonly taken for granted here that Martínez Campos, faithful to the system followed in the Carlist Wars, will seek there, too, to win the chiefs of the insurgents over by financial advantages." The Cuban loan, thought Hatzfeldt, and it was confirmed by former Minister of State Ulloa, had been made chiefly for this purpose and this was Spain's last real chance to end the difficulties in Cuba. Hatzfeldt to A.A., No. 13, Jan. 3, 1877, GFO, Reel 95.

24 Although Portell Vilá, *Historia de Cuba*, does not believe in a decline of annexation ideas, the records of Fish's and Cushing's correspondence indicates at least a temporary backing away from it and some action against Cuban insurrectionists in the United States. E.g., Cushing to Fish, No. 748, Jan. 4, 1876; No. 849, Feb. 21, 1876, U.S. Dept. of State, Reels 74, 76; Nevins, *Fish*, pp. 878–86.

25 Salamanca's opposition to the peace began in the Congress of Deputies on May 7, 1878, and continued throughout the whole discussion of the Cuban question. The phrase quoted derived from the session of July 15, 1879, and charges that Salamanca was using "stolen" documents were made the following day. *Diario*, Congreso, 1879–80, 1:622, 647.

26 Text, *El Imparcial*, July 14, 1879; Ibáñez Marín, *El general Martínez Campos*, pp. 332–33.

27 Fernández Almagro, *Historia política*, 1:334–35. Maceo, the "Bronze Titan," had rejected the terms of the Peace of Zanjón in his famous "Protest of Baraguá" and continued to be Spain's most dan-

gerous opponent. But see Leonardo Griñal Peralta, *Antonio Maceo: Análisis carácterológico* (La Habana: Editorial Trópico, 1936), pp. 126–29, for a description of the quasi friendship between Maceo and Martínez Campos.

[28] William Fletcher Johnson, *The History of Cuba*, 3 vols. (New York: B. F. Breck & Co., 1920), 3:300, lists a number of these supposed secret agreements and José Martí also spoke of "secret arrangements of Zanjón" in letters to Eligio Carbonell, Jan. 10, 1892; Fernando Figueredo, Jan. 15, 1892; Serafín Bello, Jan., 1892, *Obras completas*, 74 vols., ed. Gonzalo de Quesada y Miranda et al. (La Habana: Trópico, 1936–53), 66:98, 101, 109. The author is inclined to accept Martínez Campos's repeated denials and assume that further reforms were suggested in oral conversations but not given written form.

[29] Martínez Campos's telegrams and portions of his private communications with Cánovas and Minister of War Ceballos were read into the Cortes records during the lengthy debates which followed his fall. See debates in Congress of Deputies of July 16, 1879, *Diario*, Congreso, 2:658, and Senate debates of March 11, 1880, *Diario*, Senado, 3:1225–29, 1231–32. Most are reproduced in Ibáñez Marín, *El general Martínez Campos*, pp. 335–75.

[30] According to *El Imparcial*, Jan. 13, 1880.

[31] Portell Vilá, *Historia de Cuba*, 3:17–25.

[32] The worries of the Cánovas government were reflected in the reports of the new German ambassador Graf zu Solms-Sonnenwalde. Manuel Silvela, the minister of foreign affairs, informed him of Martínez Campos's recall on Jan. 29, 1879, saying it had been only intended to have the general stay a year in Cuba; Silvela did not mention any charge of maladministration, but Cánovas did so several weeks later with the comment that the general wanted to place too heavy demands on Spain. In March after the cabinet change Silvela added the statement, "We are completely ruined by Cuba and in a terrible embarrassment." Solms to A.A., No. 11, Jan. 29; No. 21, Feb. 25; No. 25, March 13, 1879, GFO, Reel 57.

[33] The Cortes debates after the fall of Martínez Campos revealed that Cánovas had seen both men before they accepted their posts. Francisco Silvela, the minister of the interior, had also consulted him. *Diario*, Senado, 2:1192–93, March 9, 1880.

[34] Martínez Campos had never met Albacete before this time. Statement, *Diario*, Senado, 2:1185, March 9, 1880. Characterization, Fabié, *Cánovas*, p. 123.

35 For Martínez Campos's earlier position see ch. 2, nn. 42, 64. The Moderados in their first party meeting displayed some support for him and shortly afterward the prominent Moderado, the Conde de Valmaseda, was named captain general of New Castile. *El Imparcial*, March 21, 24, 1879.

36 Sept. 11, 1878.

37 Enrique de Tapia, *Francisco Silvela, gobernante austero* (Madrid: Afrodisio Aguado, 1968). The treatment of this government period, pp. 95–110, is quite superficial but underscores the differences with Romero Robledo noted below.

38 *El Imparcial*, May 21, 23, 1879. See also debates in Congress of Deputies, June 26, 1879, *Diario*, Congreso, 1:307–19.

39 *El Imparcial*, March 12, 1879; cf. Fernández Almagro, *Historia política*, 1:337–38.

40 *El Imparcial*, March 28, 1879.

41 *El Imparcial* stressed the difference, Dec. 28, 1879, but its own columns had recorded more than forty-five press denunciations under Martínez Campos. Lowell also recorded the continuance of censorship, domiciliary visits, and arrests. Lowell to Evarts, No. 202, Sept. 29, 1879, U.S. Dept. of State, Reel 89.

42 *El Imparcial*, May 31, 1879. The "Conservative" aspect of the party was subordinated until the elections of 1884.

43 Ibid. Reports of the statement varied slightly.

44 Ibid., June 3, 1879.

45 Reported from *Los Debates*, *El Imparcial*, April 27, 1879.

46 "There are," warned Constitutionalist deputy Navarro y Rodrigo, "embraces that smother individuals and protectorates that assassinate governments." *Diario*, Congreso, 1:363–64, July 31, 1879. By the opening of the Cortes, American Minister James Russell Lowell was already aware of the plan underfoot—"the desire being to neutralize or rather to annihilate Martínez Campos with as little inconvenience to the majority and with as much apparent undesignedness as possible." A little later he spoke of Martínez Campos's "good sense, good feeling and honest purpose," but compared him with General Grant in his political inexperience and wondered whether he might have the courage to dissolve the Cortes again and perhaps go on to reform the peninsula as well as Cuba! Lowell to Evarts, June 2, Aug. 19, 1879, Nos. 186, 192, U.S. Dept. of State, Reel 88,

47 *Diario*, Congreso, 4:1713–14, Feb. 6, 1880.

48 Ibid., 1:247–48, 621–67, June 26, July 15, 16, 1879.

⁴⁹ Ibid., 1:307–19, July 1, 1879. Silvela dealt conciliatorily with Romero Robledo on this occasion—there were to be more serious differences in 1885 and 1891.

⁵⁰ Labra, July 3, 1879, *Diario*, Congreso, 1:358–59; Martínez Campos, July 12, 1879, ibid., pp. 564–7. Labra was born in Cuba and served as a deputy for several districts of Cuba from this point forward giving urgent support to the cause of emancipation and reform. But he stayed in the peninsula even after Cuba finally achieved the independence he had advocated.

⁵¹ *El Imparcial*, July 13, 17, 27, 1879. During the course of the debates Cánovas had proclaimed, "General Martínez Campos and I . . . know each other so well that . . . nothing, absolutely nothing can separate us." *Diario*, Congreso, 1:367, July 3, 1879.

⁵² *El Imparcial*, Aug. 17, 1879. The German ambassador reported that Romero Robledo was the son-in-law of a Cuban planter and placed Cánovas among the Málagan sugar growers (which Cánovas later denied). Writing shortly after the resumption of Cortes debates, he prophesied: "at any rate it will now depend on the patriotism of the Spaniards, on the willingness of the individual to make the necessary sacrifice in behalf of the whole, whether Cuba remains a Spanish possession." Hatzfeldt to A.A., No. 118, Nov. 14, 1879, GFO, Reel 95.

⁵³ *El Imparcial*, Oct. 12, 1879. *La Epoca* described his reception with a chorus of 300 and an orchestra of 40 and visits to port works and steamers with Senator Puig, the Marqués de Monistral, and "empresa López." Oct. 5, 10, 1879.

⁵⁴ *El Imparcial*, Oct. 11, 15, 22, 1879; *La Epoca*, Oct. 12, 13, 15, 1879.

⁵⁵ *El Imparcial*, Aug. 17, 18, 20, 1879.

⁵⁶ The new insurrection broke out late in August but public notice did not come until reopening of the Cortes. Fernández Almagro, *Historia política*, 1:344–45; cf. Hugh Thomas, *Cuba, the Pursuit of Freedom* (New York: Harper & Row, 1971), p. 269.

⁵⁷ Those opposed to reform exaggerated the size and scope of the insurrection and attached names to it of those not directly involved. Although José Maceo, his brother, was involved, Antonio Maceo gave support only from outside Cuba as did also Máximo Gómez. It was a Cuban general acting under General Blanco, Martínez Campos's successor, who was most prominent in suppressing the insurrection. See Luis Estévez y Romero, *Desde el Zanjón hasta Baire: Datos para la historia política de Cuba* (Habana: Tipografía La Propaganda Literaria, 1899), pp. 55–56.

⁵⁸ *Diario*, Congreso, 2:1083 ff., Nov. 14, 1879.

⁵⁹ Reported, *El Imparcial*, Nov. 15, 1879. In the Congress of Deputies Albacete stated that he must keep "la mas exquisita reserva" in respect to the form they would take. *Diario*, Congreso, 2:1088, Nov. 14, 1879.

⁶⁰ Ibid., p. 1091. The American minister, James Russell Lowell, noted the growing opposition to reform and asserted, "The only firm conclusion I have been enabled to draw is that the gravity of the Cuban question is hardly yet understood in Spain, that one of the very few persons who seems to have some conception of it is General Martínez Campos, and that everything will depend on the ability he may show of impressing his opinion on others either by force of argument or by political pressure." Lowell to Evarts, No. 216, Nov. 11, 1879, U.S. Dept. of State, Reel 89.

⁶¹ *El Imparcial*, Nov. 17, 1879. At a luncheon meeting of about twenty persons including a number of Cuban representatives.

⁶² *El Imparcial*, Nov. 21, 1879. The emancipation draft did not seem to comport with Martínez Campos's prediction in a letter to General Blanco, Oct. 26, 1879, that the emancipation law would convince "the colored people that the Spanish nation is not only not *slavist* and marches rapidly to the extinction of the differences between races, but also that it pays more attention to the Negro race than the insurrectionists did at the beginning of the war." Fernández Almagro, *Historia política*, 1:573, appendix 25.

⁶³ *El Imparcial*, Nov. 21, 1879.

⁶⁴ Ibid., Nov. 23, 1879. As late as Nov. 24 Martínez Campos expressed his belief that there was no crisis, only "bad intelligence" among party members, which he expected to be resolved. *Diario*, Congreso, 3:1224–41.

⁶⁵ *El Imparcial*, Nov. 28, 1879.

⁶⁶ Ibid., Dec. 8, 1879. Manuel Silvela, brother of Martínez Campos's minister of the interior and former minister of foreign affairs under Cánovas, told the German envoy that he had helped on the compromise on the slavery issue and was also making good progress on the tax matters when Cánovas suddenly lost patience and put up Orovio and Toreno to sabotage the general. Solms to A.A., No. 3, Jan. 7, 1880, GFO, Reel 58. Lowell reported that nothing he had seen in Madrid matched the excitement surrounding the fall of the Martínez Campos government. If, he said, Cánovas's intention had been to neutralize the general, "it has wholly failed of its object, for during his administra-

tion and especially since the crisis he has shown himself so honest, rightminded, manly, and magnanimous that his popularity is now far greater than when he came back from Cuba." No. 22, Dec. 15, 1879, U.S. Dept. of State, Reel 89.

[67] *El Imparcial*, Dec. 8, 1879, reported complete suppression of the insurrection in Las Villas.

[68] Ibid., Dec. 8, 19, 1879. In the eyes of both domestic and foreign observers the king was, during this period, making efforts to free himself from the tutelage of Cánovas and to push toward the alternation of governments. See, e.g., Sackville-West to Salisbury, Nos. 8, 202, Jan. 14, July 20, 1880, BFO 72:1565. Sackville-West considered that the situation actually endangered the throne.

[69] *El Imparcial*, Dec. 8, 9, 1879.

[70] His comments on Dec. 10, 1879, were relatively brief; the real fireworks came in March 1880. *Diario*, Senado, 1:537–38, 540.

[71] The incident became known as the "Sombrerazo." If the *Diario* is accurate, Cánovas's departure had been properly explained. *Diario*, Congreso, 3:1276–80, Dec. 10, 1879. Cf. *El Imparcial*, Dec. 11, 12, 13, 1879.

[72] *El Imparcial*, Jan. 27, 1880; *Diario*, Congreso, 3:1527–31. The law for the abolition of slavery in Cuba was passed while the Constitutionalists, Democrats, and most Cuban delegates were absent.

[73] Spanish historians have too often searched for the rhetoric rather than the facts, ignoring, for example, the carefully prepared speeches of Servando Ruiz Gómez, *Diario*, Senado, Dec. 13, 1879, 1:583; May 26, June 1, 2, 1880, 4:1974–80, 2017–2111, 2116–23.

[74] The major debates came in the Senate although related to Cánovas's somewhat rude handling of the matter in the Congress. See *Diario*, Congreso, Feb. 6, 7, 1880, 4:1712–17, 1725–30, 1731–34, 1736. *Diario*, Senado, March 9, 11, 13, 15, 2:1178–97; 3:1224–37, 1278–82, 1295–1309.

[75] *El Imparcial*, March 12, 1880. Solms found the whole affair like "a great theatrical event"—Martínez Campos did well but got confused after an hour and a half! Solms to A.A., No. 30, March 14, 1880, GFO, Reel 58.

[76] Fernández Almagro, *Historia política*, 1:349. Martínez Campos's own conception of abolition was never clearly spelled out. For a discussion of the effects of this law see Franklin W. Knight, *Slave Society in Cuba during the Nineteenth Century* (Madison: University of Wisconsin Press, 1970), pp. 172 ff.

[77] *El Imparcial*, Dec. 24, 1879.

[78] Ibid., Dec. 26, 27, 1879.

[79] Ibid., Jan. 31, 1880.

[80] Speeches of Bernardo Portuondo, Feb. 4, 24, 1880, *Diario*, Congreso, 3:1661–70, 1990–92.

[81] Albacete in Congress, Feb. 12, 14, 20, 1880, *Diario*, Congreso, 4:1779–83, 1806–10, 1892–1902.

[82] Virtually stated by Silvela in Congress, Feb. 7, 1880, *Diario*, Congreso, 4:1721–2.

[83] Ruiz Gómez, *Diario*, Senado, May 26, 1880, 4:1979–80. Details of contract stated by Elduayen, *Diario*, Congreso, 3:1680, Feb. 5, 1880.

[84] Text of budget, *Diario*, Congreso, Apéndice primero al número 105, Feb. 19, 1880. The reforms were stated late, page 11 of the dictamen, and after many reservations. Sagasta was to say that the language of the reforms undercut their effect. *Diario*, Congreso, 5:2225, March 5, 1880.

[85] *Diario*, Congreso, vol. 5, see assertion of Cuban wealth, p. 8, rejection of *cabotaje*, pp. 9–10.

[86] On charges signatures of the Cuban senators were purchased by special concessions, General Sanz, *Diario*, Senado, 4:1274, March 13, 1880; Marqués de la Habana, ibid., 1311, March 15, 1880.

[87] Castro in Congress, May 20, 1880, *Diario*, Congreso, 4:1851.

[88] The general's brother Miguel Martínez Campos asserted that new payments had been made for the cancellation of this already profitable loan. *Diario*, Congreso, 5:2607–18, April 3, 1880.

[89] See discussion of failure of ratification of this treaty in ch. 9. A second treaty of 1891 was also to fail of ratification.

[90] Bernardo Portuondo, *Diario*, Congreso, 3:1665, Feb. 4, 1880. Statements of other Cuban deputies were almost as rapturous.

[91] Most of the generals spoke in Martínez Campos's behalf in the Cortes. A subordinate issue was the dismissal of generals sympathetic to Martínez Campos who had tried to resign active posts so that they could take part in the political opposition.

[92] The father of one of Cánovas's biographers, Antonio María Fabié, was also a supporter of the general. See Fabié, *Cánovas*, p. 127; *Diario*, Congreso, 6:3068–69, April 19, 1880.

[93] Martos was president of the directive committee of the Progressive Democratic party but did not succeed in unifying groups to the left of the Constitutionalists.

[94] Discussed more fully in ch. 7.

⁹⁵ Fernández Almagro, *Historia política*, 1:353–54.

⁹⁶ Ibid., pp. 376–77.

⁹⁷ Dispatches in order mentioned: Solms to A.A., No. 6, Jan. 9, 1880, GFO, Reel 58. Sackville-West to Salisbury, No. 202, July 20, 1880, BFO 72:1566. Solms to A.A., No. 92, June 14, 1880; von Bülow memo, No. A 3890, Ems, June 28, 1880; Solms to A.A., No. 139, July 31, 1880; No. 15, Feb. 8, 1881, GFO, Reel 58. Sevilla Andrés in his second edition of his *Historia política* emphasizes the role of the king, 1:359.

⁹⁸ Fernández Almagro, *Historia política*, 1:378.

⁹⁹ On the supposed *cabotaje* experiment, Estévez y Romero, *Desde el Zanjón hasta Baire*, pp. 122–23. Martínez Campos again carried reform ideas to Cuba in 1895, but found little support for them either in Cuba or in Spain. General Weyler, the Duque de Rubí, who replaced him, called the Peace of Zanjón "excessively benevolent" and labeled Martínez Campos's policies "absurd." *Mi mando en Cuba, 10 de febrero 1896 a 31 octubre 1897: Historia militar y política de la última guerra separatista durante dicho mando*, 5 vols. (Madrid: F. González Rojas, 1910–11), 1:73, 101.

¹⁰⁰ Portell Vilá, *Historia de Cuba*, 3:109.

¹⁰¹ As Hugh Thomas shows, the sugar industry in Cuba had been quite adversely affected by the latter part of the Ten Years War and entered in the 1880s into a crisis situation which weeded out many of the small planters. *Cuba, the Pursuit of Freedom*, pp. 271–80.

¹⁰² *Diario*, Congreso, 4:2057–70, Feb. 27, 1880. Some of Cánovas's language was also sharp, for example the phrase "insurrectos enemigos ireconciliables," ibid., p. 1736, Feb. 7, 1880.

¹⁰³ Fabié, *Cánovas*, p. 125.

C H A P T E R 7. *Liberal Interlude: The Trial of "Fusionism"*

¹ From dispatches of Sackville-West to Lord Granville, Nos. 26, 31, 34, Feb. 9, 15 (Confidential), 18, 1881, BFO 72:1595. The U.S. ambassador also felt that the change of government had been necessary to avoid revolution. Fairchild to Evarts, No. 114, Feb. 10, 1881, U.S. Dept. of State, Reel 91.

² The biography by the Conde de Romanones, *Sagasta o el político*,

is most unsatisfactory. The course of politics is well described in Fernández Almagro, *Historia política*, 1:379 ff., but the comments of the British and German ambassadors recorded below are more revealing.

³ Supposedly the king had the advice of Manuel Silvela in naming Martínez Campos as minister of war, but later events suggest he did not need it and relied fully on the loyalty of the general. See Solms to A.A., No. 89, Dec. 19, 1881, GFO, Reel 58.

⁴ Cabinet descriptions from Lafuente, *Historia general*, 25:155–56; Fernández Almagro, *Historia política*, 1:379; Solms to A.A., No. 16, Feb. 9, 1881, GFO, Reel 58. Venancio González was the son of a poor worker in Lisle, displaying more rural astuteness than Romero Robledo but less a salon figure. The memoirs of the distinguished Constitutionalist leader, Fernando de León y Castillo, Marqués del Muni, *Mis tiempos*, 2 vols. (Madrid: Sucesores de Hernando, 1921) are most disappointing, since they consist largely of his parliamentary speeches.

⁵ Villa-Urrutia, *El general Serrano*, p. 239; cf. Manuel Ferandis and Caetano Beirao, *Historia contemporánea de España y Portugal* (Barcelona: Editorial Labor, 1966), pp. 319–20.

⁶ Lafuente, *Historia general*, 25:155–56; Fernández Almagro, *Historia política*, 1:380.

⁷ Fernández Almagro, *Historia política*, 1:381. On Sept. 2, 1880, Alonso Martínez, with Sagasta's approval, had written a letter to the previous minister of grace and justice protesting the discrimination against the female heir. He thus became an early defender of women's rights. Pirala, *Historia contemporánea*, 6:521–23.

⁸ Fernández Almagro, *Historia política*, 1:381; cf. Lafuente, *Historia general*, 25:161.

⁹ See ch. 8, n. 16.

¹⁰ The German ambassador reported the changes in detail and critically. See his dispatches, No. 18, Feb. 22, 1881, No. 31, Confidential, April 25, 1881 (reporting both king and Cánovas had opposed the firing of lower ranking officials), GFO, Reel 58. *La Epoca*, of course, on March 20, 1881, complained of the "empleomanía" of the Liberals!

¹¹ See Martínez Cuadrado, *Elecciones y partidos políticos*, 1:263–78. Solms noted that only one-fourth to one-third of the eligible voters took part. No. 61, Aug. 31, 1881, GFO, Reel 58. *La Epoca* reported that in Madrid with 400,000 votes the candidate with the most votes was Posada Herrera, who received 3,076. Aug. 16, 1881. There was to be some ironic humor in the opposing speeches of the two election masters

on the floor of the Cortes: González defending the elections, Oct. 4, 1881, *Diario*, Congreso, 1:207–14; Romero Robledo challenging them, Oct. 5, 1881, *Diario*, Congreso, 1:225–30 et seq.

[12] June 22, 1881.

[13] *La Epoca*, July 2, 1881; cf. Gómez Chaix, *Ruiz Zorrilla*, pp. 115–21. The comments in respect to government efforts to persuade Ruiz Zorrilla to return to Spain are born out in Solms's conversation with the Marqués de la Vega de Armijo, No. 41, Jan. 18, 1881, GFO, Reel 58.

[14] Letter dated March 20, 1881, cited *La Epoca*, April 3, 1881.

[15] Cited by British ambassador Sir Robert Morier to Granville, No. 173, Nov. 15, 1883, BFO 72:1646.

[16] *La Epoca*, Oct. 31, Nov. 13, 1881.

[17] Ibid.

[18] Ibid., March 9, 10, 13, 16, 1881.

[19] Bécker, *Historia de las relaciones exteriores*, 3:343–49.

[20] Solms to A.A., No. 54, July 29, 1881, GFO, Reel 58.

[21] July 26, 1881. There was criticism of the political character of the letter, but by the opening of the Cortes Cánovas had decided to join with Pidal y Mon in criticizing the government's failure to defend the pope fully. See Pidal y Mon's amendment to reply to speech from throne subscribed to by Cánovas, *Diario*, Congreso, 2:674, Oct. 28, 1881. And Cánovas in his first speech under Sagasta strongly defended papal rights, ibid., pp. 996–1013, Nov. 15, 1881.

[22] Solms to A.A., No. 42, June 21, 1881, GFO, Reel 58.

[23] Solms to A.A., No. 33, March 30, 1882, GFO, Reel 58.

[24] Part of the king's conversation with Solms noted below, No. 86, Very Confidential, Dec. 16, 1881, GFO, Reel 58.

[25] Solms to A.A., No. 45, June 27, 1881, GFO, Reel 58. The American ambassador also took favorable note of the king's offer confirmed to him in a private conversation, although he assumed Jews were coming from Germany as well as Russia. Fairchild to Blaine, No. 164, June 20, 1881, U.S. Dept. of State, Reel 92.

[26] *La Epoca*, August 23, 25, 1881; Solms to A.A., No. 68, Sept. 18, 1881, GFO, Reel 58.

[27] *Diario*, Congreso, 1:2–4. There were reiterated references to the value of peace and quiet and "the ordered exercise of constitutional liberties." The king delivered it in a loud voice and with customary rhetorical gestures. Solms to A.A., No. 69, Sept. 21, 1881, GFO, Reel 58. The American chargé, Dwight T. Reed, was also disappointed

with the performance—nothing clear and concise had emerged from it all. Reed to Blaine, No. 97, Sept. 27, 1881, U.S. Dept. of State, Reel 93.

28 *La Epoca*, Sept. 20, 1881. In the Cortes Sagasta defended the retention of the parliamentary oath and the Constitution of 1876 subject to amending laws and supported the concept of democracy within the framework of monarchy. *Diario*, Congreso, 1:16–18, Sept. 21, 1881; 3:902–3, 950–53, Nov. 11, 1881; 3:962–63, Nov. 12, 1881.

29 Solms to A.A., No. 69, Sept. 21, 1881, GFO, Reel 58.

30 Fernández Almagro, *Historia política*, 1:385.

31 See reference in ch. 7, n. 24.

32 Fernández Almagro, *Historia política*, 1:387.

33 Ibid., pp. 387–88; cf. Lafuente, *Historia general*, 25:161–62. Strongest opposition in the Cortes to the industrial taxes and the change in sales tax provisions came from the Conservative deputy Rafael Atard Llobelle, *Diario*, Congreso, Dec. 5, 12, 19, 1881, 4:1563, 1732–33, 5:1973. It is clear that the tax provisions were not only revolutionary but complex, discriminating among classes of businesses and their locations, and hence difficult to defend. See *La Epoca*, Feb. 1 and 5, 1882.

34 Events described in Fernández Almagro, *Historia política*, 1:388; Lafuente, *Historia general*, 25:164–66; Pirala, *Historia contemporánea*, 6:571. Debate in Cortes, *Diario*, Congreso, 6:2274–86, 2290–98, March 21, 1882—Romero Robledo; reply of González, 6:2298–2307; Conde de Xiquena, 6:2327–32; Cánovas, 6:2332–34.

35 Richard Lindau, still on the scene as German consul in Barcelona, provided graphic descriptions of the difficulties in Catalonia. Lindau to Solms, March 30, 31, April 3, 1882, annexes to Solms to A.A., No. 35, March 31, 1882, No. 37, April 2, 1882, No. 39, April 6, 1882, GFO, Reel 58. The reports of the American consul, though less graphic, also documented the presence in Barcelona of some 4,800 troops and of severe government action against the workers. Schenck to Asst. Secy. of State, No. 248, April 1, 1882, U.S. Consular Dispatches, Barcelona, Roll 8.

36 Clarke, *Modern Spain, 1815–1898*, p. 381; Pirala, *Historia contemporánea*, 6:575–79. Although the treaty seemed to provide great advantages for Spanish wines, critics pointed out that French importers were using good Spanish wines to upgrade native products rather than placing them on the market, thus minimizing the value of tariff reductions. *La Epoca*, April 10, 1882. Bécker also considered the treaty disadvan-

tageous, *Relaciones commerciales entre España y Francia durante el siglo XIX* (Madrid: Jaime Ratés Martín, 1910), pp. 145–72. Balaguer and Cánovas in the Cortes, *Diario*, Congreso, 7:2780–97, 3015–16, April 17, 22, 1882. For the Catalan nationalist movement see Soldevila, *Historia de Catalunya*, 3:1388–89.

[37] See ch. 7, n. 24. Copy of reform project, *Diario*, Congreso, vol. 3, Nov. 22, 1881, appendix 2, pp. 2–9. Reference to the German example was strong. The major outcome of military reform in this period was the establishment of the General Military Academy in Toledo. As respects military service, the system of exemptions and paid substitutes left the army still short in numbers and quality. See Payne, *Politics and the Military in Modern Spain*, pp. 47–48.

[38] Solms to A.A., No. 88, Confidential, Dec. 7, 1881, GFO, Reel 58. The French reports on the Madrid Conference do not support the favorable view given by Fernández Almagro, *Cánovas*, pp. 362–65. See Jaurès to Freycinet, No. 37, Confidential, June 2, 1880; No. 38, June 5; Telegrams, June 6, 26, 1880, DDF, 3:127–29, 135–37, 155–56; and summary dispatch of Jaurès to Barthélemy Saint-Hilaire, No. 42, July 8, 1881, 4:54–55. Germany had under Bismarck's instructions gone "hand in hand" with the French in respect to the actions of the Conference. See *Die Grosse Politik*, Vol. 3, No. 664, 397–98, Interim director of German Foreign Office, Prince von Hohenlohe to Solms, Draft, Berlin, May 6, 1880; No. 665, 398–99, Hohenlohe to Solms, Draft, May 27, 1880. For the Madrid Conference and the expedition of 1882 (a warship accompanied a Spanish commission which claimed the territory with the Sultan acceding in 1883) see Bécker, *Historia de las relaciones exteriores*, 3:354–65, 426–29 and his *Historia de Marruecos: Apuntes para la historia de la penetración europea, y principalmente de la española en el Norte de África* (Madrid: Jaime Ratés Martín, 1915), pp. 331–50; Wallace R. Klinger, "Spain's Problem of Alliances: Spanish Foreign Policy from the Conference of Madrid, 1880 to the Mediterranean Agreement of 1907" (Ph.D. dissertation, University of Pennsylvania, 1944), pp. 11–12.

[39] Events described in Fernández Almagro, *Historia política*, 1:392–93; Lafuente, *Historia general*, 25:169–70; and in Solms to A.A., No. 14, Jan. 25, 1882; No. 18, Jan. 31, 1882; No. 20, Feb. 8, 1882; No. 21, Very Confidential, Feb. 9, 1882; No. 27, Confidential, Feb. 20, 1882, GFO, Reel 58. *La Epoca* was critical of the project, Jan. 17, 18, 19, 21, 1882. The Nocedals were even more Carlist than the pretender.

In 1887 Ramón broke with Carlos VII because of his alleged "liberalism"! Jesús Pabón y Suárez de Urbina *La otra legitimidad* (Madrid: Prena Española, 1969), pp. 54 ff.

[40] Solms to A.A., No. 106, Sept. 23, 1882, GFO, Reel 58.

[41] Solms to A.A., No. 27, Confidential, Feb. 20, 1882, GFO, Reel 58.

[42] Solms to A.A., No. 68, May 22, 1882, GFO, Reel 58.

[43] Solms to A.A., No. 102, Sept. 3, 1882; No. 107, Sept. 24; No. 116, Oct. 9; Chargé Goltz to A.A., No. 121, Oct. 21; Solms to A.A., No. 160, Dec. 3; No. 162, Dec. 7, 1882, GFO, Reel 58. Sagasta and Cánovas debated the government's position in the Congress of Deputies with Sagasta charging that the Conservatives were "good friends of the Dynastic Left" and Cánovas responding in an ambiguous fashion. *Diario*, Congreso, 1:360–75, Dec. 23, 1882.

[44] Solms to A.A., No. 160, Dec. 3, 1882, GFO, Reel 58. By April 2, 1882, *La Epoca* was often using the term "partido conservador."

[45] Solms dispatch of Dec. 3, 1882, see ch. 7, n. 43. In a drawing room speech to the diplomats the king expressed his pleasure at "the political parties which were grouping themselves around the monarchy." Morier to Granville, No. 13, Jan. 24, 1883, BFO 72:1644.

[46] Solms to A.A., No. 182, Dec. 29, 1882, GFO, Reel 59.

[47] Solms to A.A., No. 183, Confidential, Dec. 29, 1882, GFO, Reel 59.

[48] Solms to A.A., No. 4, June 4, 1883; No. 5, Jan. 9, 1883, GFO, Reel 59. Comment on Girón, Gómez Chaix, *Ruiz Zorrilla*, pp. 120–21. Pirala suggests that the crisis was occasioned most largely by Camacho's handling of his ministry. *Historia contemporánea*, 6:621–22.

CHAPTER 8. *Liberal Interlude: Crisis and Dissolution*

[1] Fernández Almagro, *Historia política*, 1:393.

[2] This description has sought to summarize the findings of Clara E. Lida, who has traced down the history of Andalusian anarchism in a series of publications beginning in 1968 with her doctoral dissertation at Princeton University, "Orígines del anarquismo español, 1868–1884." See her "Agrarian Anarchism in Andalusia: Documents on the Mano Negra," *International Review of Social History* 14, no. 3 (1969): 315–51; *Anarquismo y revolución en la España del XIX*; *La mano negra:*

Anarquismo agrario en Andalucía (Algarte, Vizcaya: Zero, 1972); and *Antecedentes y desarrollo del movimiento obrero español, 1835–1888: Textos y documentos*. The statutes and regulations of "La mano negra" are reproduced in *Antecedentes*, pp. 425–32 and in the article cited, pp. 345–52. Lida's work has overtaken recent Spanish studies in the area—see Diego Abad de Santillán, *Historia del movimiento obrero español* (Madrid: Editorial XYZ, 1967), pp. 253–66; Maximiano García Venero, *Historia de los movimientos sindicalistas españoles, 1840–1933* (Madrid: Ed. del Movimiento, 1961), pp. 229–63. In a lengthy dispatch, No. 38, March 12, 1883, Solms sent home a detailed description of the troubles in Spain and the Black Hand. Part of the difficulty, he said, stemmed from crop failures in the summer of 1882 and, although the government promised help, Camacho refused to suspend the grain tariffs. The price of wheat in Córdoba, Huesca, and Málaga was almost double that in Salamanca, Navarre, and Avila; rye almost quadruple; peas two and a half times. The government did help some 5,000 families to leave for Oran or America. Reel 59, GFO.

[3] Tuñon de Lara, *El movimiento obrero*, pp. 276–82; cf. Lida, *Antecedentes*, pp. 40–46, 423–25, et passim.

[4] Gómez Llorente, *Aproximación a la historia del socialismo español*, pp. 79–94.

[5] Lida, "Agrarian Anarchism," p. 316. Solms in the dispatch cited in n. 2 to this chapter noted the sending in of Col. José Oliver (apparently the same officer involved in putting down the student riots noted in ch. 9) and a strong contingent of the Guardia Civil and reported much of the detail of the organization of the Black Hand reproduced by Lida, as noted. In a later dispatch, No. 138, June 21, 1883, Reel 59, GFO, Solms was quite critical of the poor management and poor labor relations in Andalusia. Unlike Solms, the American consul in Málaga was a strong defender of the Guardia Civil. In a long dispatch in 1884 he praised their courage, courtesy, and efficiency and indicated he always felt inclined "to raise my hat to them." He admitted they sometimes arrested unfortunates guilty only of petty theft, but approved their actions against the gypsies and reported they always showed consideration in conducting their prisoners on the way to North Africa. H. C. Marston to Asst. Secy. of State, No. 117, July 22, 1884, U.S. Consular Dispatches, Málaga, Roll 13.

[6] Fernández Almagro, *Historia política*, 1:390.

[7] Solms to A.A., Nos. 7, 11, Jan. 15, 21, 1883, GFO, Reel 59.

[8] Solms to A.A., No. 62, Secret, April 6, 1883, GFO, Reel 59.

[9] Solms to A.A., No. 134, Confidential, July 14; No. 185, July 5, 1883, GFO, Reel 69.

[10] U.S. Ambassador John W. Foster to Frelinghuysen, No. 46, July 27, 1883, U.S. Dept. of State, Reel 96.

[11] The French received a corresponding indemnity for damages to French subjects during the Carlist wars and did not vote their indemnity until they were sure the Spanish Cortes would reciprocate. Pirala, *Historia contemporánea*, 6:613, 615. There had been questions in the Cortes on the delay in 1882, see *Diario*, Congreso, March 22, 1882, 6:2397–2404. As late as March 5, 1883, Romero Robledo was still opposing the payment to the French, *Diario*, Congreso, 7:1246–48. Cf. Bécker, *Historia de las relaciones exteriores*, 3:405–13; Solms to A.A., No. 83, April 30, 1883, GFO, Reel 59.

[12] Solms to A.A., No. 83, April 30, 1883, GFO, Reel 59.

[13] Solms to A.A., Nos. 94, 115, May 10, 29, 1883, GFO, Reel 59. The king had received a delegation from Valencia and received cheers from followers of Martos and enthusiastic comments from Martos himself.

[14] Solms to A.A., No. 132, Very Confidential, June 13; No. 137, Confidential, June 30, 1883; No. 215, June 27, 1883, GFO, Reel 59. Morier also felt that the cabinet had been unwise in starting procedures against *El Liberal*. Morier to Granville, No. 101, Confidential, June 12, 1883, BFO 72:1644.

[15] The king was to confess his errors in his last interview with Solms just before his death. See also Cavanillas, *María Cristina*, pp. 49–52; Agustín de Figueroa, *La sociedad española bajo la restauración* (Madrid: Ediciones Aspas, 1945), pp. 142–43.

[16] Solms to A.A., No. 105, Secret, May 17, 1883, GFO, Reel 69. The report of the interview which follows is taken from this lengthy and frank dispatch. The queen actually preceded the king in a visit to Germany and Austria, June 11–July 31, 1883, but family ties deprived the visit of any political significance. Pirala, *Historia contemporánea*, 6:633.

[17] Solms to A.A., No. 114, Confidential, May 28, 1883, GFO, Reel 69.

[18] Münster in London to A.A., No. 72, June 11, 1883, GFO, Reel 69. The king personally expressed his regrets to Morier at his inability to visit England, but Morier recorded a little later a cooler tone on the

part of the Marqués de la Vega de Armijo which he attributed to the abandonment of the visit. Morier to Granville, No. 112, July 21; No. 119, Confidential, July 31, 1883. BFO 72:1645.

19 Solms to A.A., No. 127, Very Confidential, June 8, 1883, GFO, Reel 69.

20 Ibid.; Morier also related later that the original plan had been for a state visit on the way to Germany but that this had been postponed due to the illness of President Grévy, but the president himself had not been told of this until later! No. 152 (A), Oct. 5, 1883, BFO 72:1645.

21 Bismarck to Kaiser, June 14, 1883, A 2675; Bülow to Bismarck, No. 1, June 19, 1883, A 2785, GFO, Reel 69.

22 See ch. 8, n. 9.

23 Solms to A.A., No. 156, July 18, 1883, A 3348; No. 168, Aug. 4, 1883, A 3679, GFO, Reel 69.

24 Lafuente, *Historia general*, 25:175.

25 Solms to A.A., No. 149, Confidential, July 14, 1883, GFO, Reel 59.

26 Lafuente, *Historia general*, 25:176.

27 Solms to A.A., No. 140, June 26, 1883, GFO, Reel 59; Fernández Almagro, *Historia política*, 1:408.

28 Fernández Almagro, *Historia política*, 1:399 ff.; Lafuente, *Historia general*, 25:179 ff.; Pirala, *Historia contemporánea*, 6:638–45. The recent article by Carlos Dardé Morales, "Los partidos republicanos en la primera etapa de la Restauración, 1875–1900" in José María Jover Zamora, ed., *El siglo XIX en España: Doce estudios* (Barcelona: Planeta, 1974), pp. 433–63, underscores the complexity and division of republican forces during this period.

29 Solms to A.A., Telegram No. 66 from San Ildefonso, Aug. 6, 1883; von Hatzfeldt to von Bülow, Cipher telegram No. 12, Aug. 6, 1883; Solms to A.A., Telegram No. 67, Aug. 7, 1883; Schmidthals in Portugal to A.A., No. 2, Aug. 7, 1883, GFO, Reel 59.

30 Lafuente, *Historia general*, 25:181. The German reports placed the uprising at nearby Najera, Solms to A.A., Telegram No. 69, Aug. 8; No. 70, Aug. 9, 1883, GFO, Reel 59.

31 Lafuente, *Historia general*, 25:182; Fernández Almagro, *Historia política*, 1:400. Lindau in Barcelona to A.A., Telegrams, No. 6, Aug. 9; No. 7, Aug. 10; No. 8, Aug. 11, 1883; Solms to A.A., Telegrams Nos. 72, 73, Aug. 10, 1883, GFO, Reel 59.

32 Solms to A.A., No. 175, Aug. 12; Telegram No. 80, Aug. 13; No. 177, Aug. 13, 1883, GFO, Reel 59. Morier also wrote of the "uni-

versal expression of disgust and shame" with which the events had been received by "the public, and by the press of all political shades." Morier to Granville, No. 123, Aug. 7, 1883, BFO 72:1645. The figures for the Spanish army are given emphasis by comparative statistics for the German army at that time with 18,139 officers for 427,000 men. See José Ramón Alonso, *Historia política del ejercito español* (Madrid: Editora Nacional, 1974), p. 397.

[33] Solms to A.A., No. 177, Aug. 13, 1883, GFO, Reel 59.

[34] Solms to A.A., No. 169, La Granja, Aug. 7, 1883, GFO, Reel 59.

[35] Solms to A.A., No. 177, Aug. 13, 1883, GFO, Reel 59. Morier also reported the king's irritation after he had believed the era of pronunciamientos was over and criticized the absence of practically all the ministers during the crisis. Morier to Granville, No. 122, Confidential, Aug. 6; No. 125, Aug. 9, 1883, BFO 72:1645.

[36] Solms to A.A., No. 189, Very Confidential, Aug. 21, 1883, GFO, Reel 59.

[37] Solms to A.A., No. 177, Aug. 13, 1883, GFO, Reel 59.

[38] Solms to A.A., Telegram No. 82, Aug. 17; Lindau to A.A., unnumbered, Aug. 21; Solms to A.A., No. 188, Aug. 21; No. 191, Aug. 22; No. 193, Aug. 23; No. 196, Aug. 28, 1883, GFO, Reel 59. Morier reported favorable receptions at Valencia, Zaragoza, and most other stops. All in all the outcome of the tour had been "to establish cordial relations between the Monarch and his people." He still felt, however, that the army was "rotten and unsound to the core." Morier to Granville, No. 135, Aug. 27, 1883, BFO 72:1645.

[39] Solms to A.A., No. 204, Sept. 2, 1883, GFO, Reel 59. Morier later reported regulations ordering that officers who had belonged to a corps in which an insurrection took place and was not at once put down should *ipso facto* be deprived of their posts—adding the comment that in 1874 this would have affected Martínez Campos himself. But he reacted strongly to the apologetic tone used in dealing with military orders of republican character—"That a Spanish Minister of War should feel it necessary as it were thus to offer an apology for removing from the service officers bound by secret oaths to insurrection certainly throws a strange and somewhat lurid light on the present constitution of His Catholic Majesty's army." Morier to Granville, No. 145, Sept. 5, 1883, BFO 72:1645.

[40] Morier, as well as many domestic observers, believed Spain was searching for "a Monarchical harbour of refuge for the young Royalty of Spain against the threatening dangers of Republican and Revolution-

ary propaganda from France." But he believed the bulk of Spanish liberals were friendly to France. Morier to Granville, No. 148, Sept. 11, 1883, BFO 72:1645. When the French ambassador in Berlin, Alphonse Chodran, Baron de Courcel, talked to the former ambassador to Spain now State Secretary Count Hatzfeldt, the latter warned that it seemed Spain was trying to follow France in her republicanism and that this would not be advantageous to France, since it would increase the concern of monarchical states. He added favorable comments on Alfonso's personal qualities, courage, and resolution to defend himself with energy. Courcel, of course, said France wanted to preserve good relations with all her neighbors, but also noted that Alfonso still intended to make his trip to Germany and he was sure plans were afoot for some sort of secret agreement or alliance. The French chargé in Madrid added later that neither the Marqués de la Vega de Armijo nor General Blanco, who were accompanying the king, were well disposed to France. Courcel to Challemel-Lacour, minister of foreign affairs, No. 138, Confidential, Aug. 14, 1883; Belle, chargé in Madrid, to Challemel-Lacour, No. 44, Sept. 4, 1883, DDF, 5:84–85, 96–97.

[41] Bismarck to A.A., Telegram No. 29, Aug. 29, 1883, GFO, Reel 69.

[42] Ibid.; Bismarck to Understatesecretary Busch, Sept. 10, 1883, GFO, Reel 69. Morier reported that Franco-Spanish relations were still strained by the Saida affair as well as by the suspicion of Zorrilla's activity in France and of the use of French money to support the insurrections. But France did allay Spanish concerns somewhat by prohibiting Zorrilla's return. Morier to Granville, No. 136, Aug. 28; No. 140, Aug. 30, 1883, BFO 72:1645.

[43] Fernández Almagro, *Historia política*, 1:409; Lafuente, *Historia general*, 25:188–89.

[44] Heinrich VII, Prinz Reuss in Vienna to A.A., No. 236, Sept. 12, 1883, GFO, Reel 69. Augusto Conte, who had arranged the king's second marriage and then remained in Vienna as ambassador, reported that the king while in Vienna showed he could still repeat the poems of Espronceda, Nuñez de Arce, and Campoamor, as well as of some foreign poets, but gave an air of being distracted and disappointed at the failure to effect reforms in Spain. *Recuerdos de un diplomático*, 3:488.

[45] Bülow in Merseburg to Bismarck, No. 1, Sept. 17, 1883; Bismarck to Bülow, Telegram No. 52, Bad Gastein, Sept. 21, 1883; Bülow to Bismarck, No. 2, Sept. 19, 1883 (reports concern of General von Albedzell also). GFO, Reel 69.

46 Fernández Almagro, *Historia política*, 1:409; Lafuente *Historia general*, 25:189; Pirala, *Historia contemporánea*, 6:665–66; Goltz, chargé in Madrid, to A.A., No. 227, Sept. 22; No. 231, Sept. 24, 1883, GFO, Reel 69. There was no direct description from within Germany of the king's reception and actions there.

47 Goltz to A.A., No. 227, Sept. 22; No. 231, Sept. 24, 1883, GFO, Reel 69.

48 Reported, Bülow in Paris to A.A., No. 323, Sept. 27, 1883, GFO, Reel 69; cf. Fernández Almagro, *Historia política*, 1:411. The French ambassador in Vienna was critical of the response of the French press, which occasioned unfavorable German and Austrian comment. "We are losing the friendship of Spain and the good opinion of the world." Foucher de Careil, Vienna, to Jules Ferry, No. 95, Sept. 28, 1883, DDF, 5:122.

49 Fernández Almagro, *Historia política*, 1:412–13; Bülow to A.A., Telegram No. 99, Sept. 29, 1883, GFO, Reel 59.

50 Morier reported that the Marqués de la Vega de Armijo had listened behind the door to Grévy's apology and that the French officially published record differed substantively from that which Grévy had actually said. Morier to Granville, No. 151, Oct. 3, 1883, BFO 72: 1645. Very active in seeking to repair the diplomatic damage was the Baron de Michels, who later became the French ambassador to Spain. Undoubtedly this helps to explain the favorable reception of Michels noted below. Pirala, *Historia contemporánea*, 6:667–76.

51 Morier reported the "almost frenzied welcome" given to the monarch. No. 151, Oct. 3, 1883, BFO 72:1645. German reports, Bülow, Paris, Telegram No. 1, Oct. 1; Nos. 330, 331, Oct. 1, 2, 1883; Goltz in Madrid, Telegrams No. 99, 100, 101, 103, 104, Oct. 1, 2, 3, 1883; No. 247, Oct. 3, 1883, GFO, Reel 59. French report, Belle, chargé in Madrid, to Challomel-Lacour, Telegrams, Oct. 1, 1883, DDF, 6:124–25.

52 The Marqués de la Vega de Armijo asked German reaction to the anti-German aspect of the treatment of the king. Hatzfeldt to Bismarck, Oct. 4, 1883, A 4858; No. 1, Oct. 4, 1883, A 4876; Memo of Bismarck, Friedrichsruh, Oct. 5, 1883, A 4898; Memo to Hatzfeldt, Oct. 5, 1883, A 4904. GFO, Reel 59.

53 German Foreign Office to Kaiser, Oct. 7, 1883, and to Goltz in Madrid, Oct. 7, 1883, A 4910, GFO, Reel 59.

54 Bismarck to Understatesecretary Busch, Friedrichsruh, Oct. 5, 1883, A 4905, GFO, Reel 59. He asked Busch to tell Count Benomar

that Spain could count in case of need not only upon sympathy but "upon a practical demonstration of this and no one in France has any doubt of this." The reservations attached not to Alfonso but to the fidelity of his subjects.

55 Morier to Granville, No. 156, Oct. 10, No. 158, Oct. 13, 1883, BFO 72:1645. Conte had characterized the Marqués de la Vega de Armijo as excessive in both his affections and his hates. *Recuerdos de un diplomático*, 3:490. The French chargé in Madrid reported a cool reception upon the part of the king when he first returned, but by a few days later he found the climate of opinion much better. When Baron Michels returned in November, the king went out of his way to deal with him in polite and cordial fashion. Belle to Challemel-Lacour, Telegrams, Oct. 5, 10, 1883; Michels to Ferry, No. 61, Confidential, Nov. 18, 1883, DDF, 5:127, 133, 147–48.

56 Bülow in Paris to A.A., Telegram No. 110, Oct. 13; No. 342, Oct. 11, 1883, GFO, Reel 59.

57 Goltz to A.A., Nos. 280, 281, 283, Oct. 13, 14, 15, 1883, GFO, Reel 59. The king's role in the change was strongly stressed.

58 Fernández Almagro, *Historia política*, 1:417–20. The American ambassador Foster had hoped the new government heralded "a new era of more liberal and enlightened principles of government" (Foster to Frelinghuysen, No. 80, Oct. 15, 1883, U.S. Dept. of State, Reel 97), but Morier considered Posada Herrera "a consummate trimmer, of great position and respectability," but reported almost immediately that he had completely failed in achieving the desired conciliation on the Left. Morier to Granville, Nos. 183, 184, 187, Dec. 12, 13, 16, 1883, BFO 72:1646.

59 Morier to Granville, No. 191, Dec. 19, 1883, BFO 72:1646.

60 Fernández Almagro, *Historia política*, 1:418–20. The Commission of Social Reforms continued into the Cánovas government and heard testimony from Pablo Iglesias and a written statement from Jaime Vera. Gómez Llorente, *Aproximación a la historia del socialismo español*, pp. 90–92.

61 Gómez Llorente, *Aproximación a la historia del socialismo español*, pp. 420–23; Lafuente, *Historia general*, 25:212–26.

62 Morier believed, inaccurately, that the visit was unexpected and caused "great embarrassment to the king." But he was impressed by the "dignified simplicity and gentleness" of the crown prince, which dispelled any idea he was being used by Bismarck for Machiavellian

purposes. Nos. 172, 177, 179, 180, Nov. 16, 24, Dec. 4, Dec. 8. 1883, BFO 72:1646. Although the French ambassador in Berlin noted exaggerated statements attributed to Alfonso in German newspapers, Hatzfeldt told him the king had probably spoken in more measured fashion. Michels was again received by the king and given the Cross of Charles III. Neither believed the visit had much effect upon internal politics in Spain, although the Spanish ambassador in Berlin said the crown prince had made a good impression with his grand air, affability, and expansive language. Courcel to Ferry, No. 191, Dec. 10, 1883; Michels to Ferry, No. 65, Dec. 12, 1883; Courcel to Ferry, Dec. 31, 1883, DDF, 5:161, 165–66, 193–94. Lafuente, *Historia general*, 25:209–10.

[63] Solms to A.A., No. 326, Nov. 18, 1883, GFO, Reel 60.

[64] Solms to A.A., No. 2, Jan. 4, 1884, GFO, Reel 60. Morier also reported that Serrano had been in secret correspondence with Ruiz Zorrilla, No. 16, Jan. 22, 1884, BFO 72:1678.

[65] Solms to A.A., No. 2, Jan. 4, 1884, GFO, Reel 60.

[66] Hohenlohe in Paris to A.A., No. 4, Jan. 8, 1884, GFO, Reel 60.

[67] Marginalia on Hohenlohe to A.A., No. 4, Jan. 8, 1884, and on Solms to A.A., No. 4, Jan. 7, 1884, GFO, Reel 60.

[68] Cuno von Rantzau in Friedrichsruh to A.A., Jan. 11, 1884; Hatzfeldt to Bismarck, No. 6, Jan. 13, 1884, unnumbered; Hatzfeldt to Solms, Jan. 15, 1884, A 248, GFO, Reel 60.

[69] Solms to A.A., No. 12, Jan. 16, 1884, GFO, Reel 60. Rantzau directed that a press response be made to the speech, Jan. 18, 1884, A 393, GFO, Reel 60.

[70] The king was pleased that he could show in Spain the same decisiveness as Bismarck in Germany. Solms to A.A., Nos. 15, 17, Jan. 19, 1884, GFO, Reel 60.

[71] Ibid.; Foster to Frelinghuysen, No. 153, Jan. 22, 1884, U.S. Dept. of State, Reel 99.

[72] Undoubtedly many shared the opinion of Morier that if the "Spanish demon of anarchy once more reasserts his sway, the guiltiest of the guilty . . . will have been the late President of the Ministry" and he added that the actions of the Posada Herrera government had been "right throughout" and those of Sagasta "wrong throughout." Morier to Granville, Nos. 5, 10, 15, Jan. 5, 18, 22, 1884, BFO 72:1678. Solms reported that Martos had led the "Viva el Rey!" as the Cortes dissolved and that even the Dynastic Left preferred Cánovas to the return of Sagasta. Solms to A.A., No. 10, Jan. 21, 1884, GFO, Reel 60.

CHAPTER 9. *Cánovas—Last Minister of Alfonso XII*

[1] Apparently there was no specific action changing the name of the party. The creation of new liberal parties and the joining of the Liberal Conservatives and Moderados apparently brought the changed emphasis. There was serious fear of revolution at the outset and quick action by the new government to prevent danger. The naming of the government brought the rise of Spanish credits, which had fallen to a critical point. Von Bülow in Paris to A.A., No. 17, Jan. 19, 1884; Solms to A.A., No. 16, Jan. 19, 1884, GFO, Reel 60.

[2] Fernández Almagro, *Historia política*, 1:425–26, 586–90. Cierva gives credit for the reconciliation of Cánovas and the church to Pope Leo XIII, whom he calls a "true tuteletary angel" for the monarchy, *Historia básica*, pp. 110–11. Cuenca Toribio also stresses the role of the pope in reducing tensions between state and church and his real love of Spain during the period that followed, *Estudios sobre la iglesia*, pp. 28–29, 96, 178. But throughout this ministry Cánovas had difficulty in restraining religious extremism. With Elduayen and Romero Robledo supporting a moderate position, he was still to be in difficulty in the university question noted below and in such cases as the violent Lenten address of the bishop of Plasencia in April 1885. In the latter case the government was able to get from the pope a mild rebuke of the bishop. Morier to Granville, Nos. 95, 140, Aug. 29, Dec. 10, 1884, BFO 72:1679; No. 34, April 10, 1885, BFO 72:1705. For Pidal's parliamentary gifts see his replies to government opponents in the debates on the message from the throne, June 23, July 7, 1884, *Diario*, Congreso, 2:747–53, 760–61, 1017–29. The debates reflected increased acerbity in the relations of Cánovas and Sagasta, the latter bitterly condemning Cánovas, who in reply called Sagasta "always a demagogue." *Diario*, Congreso, 2:1072–97.

[3] Foster to Frelinghuysen, No. 153, Jan. 22, 1884, U.S. Dept. of State, Reel 99. Morier also reported that the Conservatives were "irrationally reactionary" and that the king had only two more years before he confronted revolution. Morier to Granville, No. 40, March 16, 1884, BFO 72:1678. Solms said that in Spain one could not be liberal without going to revolution and could not be conservative without going to clericalism. Solms to A.A., No. 10, Jan. 21, 1884, GFO, Reel 60.

[4] Foster to Frelinghuysen, Nos. 166, 168, Feb. 8, 14, 1884, U.S.

Dept. of State, Reel 99; Lafuente, *Historia general*, 25:228–29; cf. statement of Elduayen in Cortes, July 3, 1884, *Diario*, Congreso, 2:953–58.

[5] Solms to A.A., Nos. 22, 32, 59, Jan. 26, Feb. 21, April 22, 1884, GFO, Reel 60.

[6] Lafuente, *Historia general*, 25:231–32.

[7] The German Foreign Office received separate reports from Madrid and Vienna that Zorrilla had received 250,000 francs from Freycinet, Wilson, and Clemenceau. Solms to A.A., No. 24, Jan. 24, 1884; Prince Reuss in Vienna to A.A., No. 48, Feb. 1, 1884, GFO, Reel 60. Solms warned Elduayen, who reported that precautions were being taken, but the report of a German Police Counselor Krueger still found a strong influence on the part of Pi y Margall in April 1884. Solms to A.A., No. 22, Jan. 26, 1884; Minister of Interior to Bismarck, April 11, 1884, Confidential, A 2494, GFO, Reel 60.

[8] Solms to A.A., Telegram No. 9, March 17; No. 49, March 20; No. 60, April 26, 1884, GFO, Reel 60.

[9] Lafuente, *Historia general*, 25:233; Fernández Almagro, *Historia política*, 1:428.

[10] Fernández Almagro, *Historia política*, 1:430–31. This time the French government had given Spain a warning. The commandant responsible for taking care of Mangado's band and his lieutenant colonel were promoted. Solms questioned this procedure, but Elduayen said Ruiz Zorrilla promised all soldiers promotions of two grades for a revolt and the government must give at least one for stopping a revolt. Solms to A.A., No. 65, May 2, 1884, GFO, Reel 60. For a contemporary witness's report of Mangado's actions and the influence of Zorrilla see Pirala, *Historia contemporánea*, 6:732–40.

[11] Lafuente, *Historia general*, 25:235.

[12] Lindau in Barcelona to A.A., June 28, 1884; Solms to A.A., No. 101, June 29, 1884, GFO, Reel 60.

[13] Lafuente, *Historia general*, 25:234, doubts the political aspect of the incident. Elduayen told Solms he believed it had political causation—see Solms to A.A., No. 65, May 2, 1884, GFO, Reel 60.

[14] Polizeirat Krueger in Berlin to A.A., Feb. 10, 1884, A 2187; April 11, 1884, A 2494, Confidential, GFO, Reel 60.

[15] Lafuente, *Historia general*, 25:236.

[16] Fernández Almagro, *Historia política*, 1:433–35.

[17] Bécker, *Historia de las relaciones exteriores*, 3:530–38; Foster to Frelinghuysen, No. 227, July 24, 1884, U.S. Dept. of State, Reel 101.

18 Solms to A.A., No. 187, Dec. 7, 1884, GFO, Reel 64.

19 Solms to A.A., No. 38, Feb. 27, 1884; Hohenlohe in Paris to A.A., No. 76, March 3, 1884 forwarding another letter from his Spanish "confidant," GFO, Reel 60.

20 Solms to A.A., No. 59, April 22, 1884, GFO, Reel 60.

21 Solms to A.A., No. 73, May 16, 1884, GFO, Reel 60.

22 Werther in Vienna to A.A., No. 138, May 3, 1884; Solms to A.A., No. 66, May 7, 1884, GFO, Reel 60. During his visit in Vienna Conte had reported that the king shocked his hosts by coming to early morning maneuvers in cold weather without any kind of coat. From first to last the king evidently insisted on ignoring his illness. *Recuerdos de un diplomático*, 3:489.

23 Bülow in Paris to A.A., No. 150, May 20, 1884, including another letter from his Spanish "confidant," GFO, Reel 60.

24 Solms from La Granja to A.A., No. 114, July 26, 1884, GFO, Reel 60.

25 Solms to A.A., No. 116, Aug. 15, 1884, GFO, Reel 60.

26 Solms to A.A., No. 34, Feb. 22; No. 47, March 19, 1884; Hohenlohe to A.A., No. 64, Feb. 23, 1884 with letter from Spanish confidant, GFO, Reel 60.

27 Solms to A.A., No. 28, Feb. 8; No. 59, April 22; No. 116, Aug. 15, 1884; Gutschmid, chargé in Madrid, to A.A., Nov. 15, 1884, GFO, Reel 60.

28 Lafuente, *Historia general*, 25:239.

29 In Minister of Interior to Bismarck, April 11, 1884, Confidential, A 2494, GFO, Reel 60.

30 Comment of Solms in dispatches to A.A., Nos. 59, 153, April 22, Nov. 9, 1884; but contradicted by a letter from Dr. A. Beckmann "whose daughter is engaged to a young Spanish diplomat" and spent some weeks in Madrid, July 5, 1884, in Hohenlohe to A.A., No. 209, July 13, 1884, GFO, Reel 60.

31 Solms to A.A. from La Granja, Nos. 117, 118, Sept. 4, 11, 1884, GFO, Reel 60.

32 Solms to A.A., Nos. 121, 135, Sept. 18, Oct. 8, 1884, GFO, Reel 60. Morier also found Silvela angry at not being able to appear before the cabinet as his position as ambassador to France should have allowed, and complaining of Cánovas's "domineering and despotic temper." Morier to Granville, No. 104, Sept. 22, 1884, BFO 72:1679.

33 Solms to A.A., No. 153, Nov. 9, 1884, GFO, Reel 60.

34 Solms to A.A., No. 154, Nov. 12, 1884, GFO, Reel 60.

[35] Fernández Almagro, *Historia política*, 1:437; Gutschmid to A.A., No. 164, Nov. 21, 1884, GFO, Reel 60. The London *Times* considered that Morayta's speech was "more distinguished for talent than discretion." Nov. 21, 1885.

[36] Fernández Almagro, *Historia política*, 1:437–38. The London *Times* reported the events, noting the spread of demonstrations to the provincial universities and the severity of government action. Nov. 22, 25, Dec. 3, 8, 1884. Gutschmid to A.A., Nos. 164, 168, 169, Nov. 21, 22, 24, 1884, GFO, Reel 60. Morier also criticized the brutality of the police in the matter, Nos. 130, 131, Nov. 21, 22, 1884, BFO 72:1679. See also Pirala, *Historia contemporánea*, 6:774–77.

[37] Gutschmid to A.A., Nos. 174, 185, Nov. 29, Dec. 6, 1884, GFO, Reel 60. Cánovas blamed the attitude of the London *Times* on its "Jewish editorship." The *Times* had asserted, "a little conciliation would probably have averted a state of things which has now become a scandal to the country, and has stirred up a party opposition which it may be difficult to control." Nov. 25, 1884.

[38] When Silvela made this statement in the Senate before a large audience, he received an ovation. Gutschmid to A.A., Nos. 10, 11, Jan. 10, 11, 1885, GFO, Reel 60. See *Diario*, Senado, 2:1005–10, 1015–16, Jan. 10, 1885. The speeches of Luis Silvela in the Congress of Deputies present the most convincing account of the events. Although a member of the government party, he was as a professor directly involved in the events and an eye witness of Oliver's actions. See his interpellation, Jan. 14, 26, 27, 1885, *Diario*, Congreso, 4:1656–67, 1874–86, 1897–98. The responses of the civil governor of Madrid, Raimundo Fernández Villaverde, are unconvincing, *Diario*, Congreso, 4:1667–73, 1862–74.

[39] Lafuente, *Historia general*, 25:247–50.

[40] Ibid.; descriptions also by Gutschmid to A.A., Nos. 1, 9, 18, Jan. 6, 10, 14, 1885, GFO, Reel 60.

[41] Solms (just returned from leave) to A.A., Nos. 29, Jan. 4, No. 31, Confidential, Jan. 27, 1885, GFO, Reel 60.

[42] The protocol on Sulu had not been finalized until January 1885. See Bunsen to Granville, No. 9, Jan. 19, 1885, BFO 72:1705.

[43] Bécker, *Historia de las relaciones exteriores*, 3:596–97.

[44] Ibid., pp. 598–99.

[45] Michels to Ferry, Private and Confidential letter, Oct. 9, 1884, DDF, 5:446–48.

[46] *Diario*, Congreso, 4:1691–93 (Marqués de la Vega de Armijo);

4:1699–1701 (Elduayen), Jan. 16, 1885. The Marqués had raised the question earlier in July 1884 and received similar responses. Ibid., 2:946, 958–59, 960–61, July 3, 1884. The Liberals in this period were more imperialist than the Conservatives. As early as 1881 they had attacked the Conservatives in the Cortes for having surrendered sovereign rights in Sulu and North Borneo. See speeches of Canamaque, Dec. 21, 1881, ibid., 5:2007–14, 2019–21; replies of Silvela, 2015–19, 2022–24; Cánovas, 2027, 2030, 2034–36.

[47] Elduayen's speeches noted in ch. 9, n. 46 were awkward and sought to place major responsibility for the failure to reach agreement on these matters on the Germans. Elduayen ignored the original comments of the Germans that the action of the Spanish Cortes should precede that of the German Reichstag and now spoke of "mutual and simultaneous" action.

[48] Solms to A.A., Nos. 28, 30, Confidential, Jan. 23, 27, 1885, GFO, Reel 60.

[49] State Secretary Herbert von Bismarck to Solms, Feb. 4, 1885, GFO, Reel 60.

[50] Kempermann, Manila, No. 34, Aug. 4, 1885, A 7604, GFO, Reel 94.

[51] In the GFO files are three letters from the firm of Robertson and Hernsheim, Jan. 23, May 2, May 21, 1884, A 1390, 1377, 4108, GFO, Reel 93. The Germans also learned of the voyage of the Spanish warship *Velasco* to the area on February 26, and this evidently triggered German action—Hatzfeldt to Bismarck, May 21, A 4291; to von Rantzau at Varzin, July 11, A 5673. The kaiser's approval of German action was reported by Bülow from Bad Gastein, No. 7, July 21, 1885, A 5961 and instructions sent to Caprivi, secret, *eigenhändig*, July 23, A 5955; Caprivi's response, Secret, July 29, A 6178, GFO, Reel 93. Bismarck *did* know of the Spanish expedition by August 2 but decided to go ahead with German plans—Hatzfeldt to Bismarck, A 6240/6257, Aug. 2, and Bismarck to A.A., Telegram No. 6, Aug. 4, 1885, A 6314, GFO, Reel 93. Solms reported the beginning of the excitement in Madrid on Aug. 15, 1885, No. 169, Very Confidential, GFO, Reel 92. From Morphy and Elduayen he heard that the king was very excited over the "loss" of the Carolines and bitter at Germany for having treated him so badly. Solms and Bismarck blamed Elduayen for misleading the monarch, concealing the fact that both England and Germany had specifically denied Spanish possession in 1875 without

Spanish protest. Solms to A.A., Telegram No. 58, Aug. 22, No. 174, Aug. 20, No. 179, Aug. 29, 1885. On the latter dispatch Bismarck wrote, "I think E. is lying. The king will not believe such lies." On Aug. 26, Hatzfeldt relayed to Solms Bismarck's direction to see the king and tell him Elduayen was stirring up sentiment against Germany and that for him to remain in office was not in the best interests of Germany or the king of Spain, A 7014, GFO, Reel 93.

52 Bülow to Bismarck, Karlsruhe, Sept. 14, 1885, sends to Bismarck a referat given to the kaiser by Caprivi, dated Sept. 10, 1885, summarizing the report of Captain Lieutenant Hofmeyer of the *Iltis*, A 7718, GFO, Reel 94. Bismarck's marginalia seem to recognize Spanish priority.

53 On the role of the press and Bismarck's reaction, see Solms to A.A., No. 179, Aug. 22; Lindau, Barcelona to A.A., Aug. 22, A 7003; Bismarck to Rantzau, Aug. 27, A 7025; Instructions to Solms, Aug. 27, A 6906; Solms to A.A., Telegram No. 63, Aug. 27, 1885, with marginalia suggesting Solms to take leave if the "*Unverschämtheiten*" continue; and direction that no negotiation be undertaken until things quieter, Bismarck to A.A., Telegram No. 19, Aug. 27, 1885, A 7068; Solms interview with Elduayen, No. 193, Aug. 31, 1885, GFO, Reel 92.

54 Reports on mob action of Aug. 23, Solms to A.A., Telegram No. 60, Aug. 24; No. 183, Aug. 24, 1885; Legation Secretary Bange, unnumbered, Aug. 24, 1885, GFO, Reel 92. Reports on demonstration of Sept. 4, Gwinner, German consul in Madrid to A.A., Sept. 5, 1885, A 7350, A 7585. By this time Bismarck was beginning to temper his position and directed that the demonstration be ignored—Bismarck to A.A., Telegram No. 27, Varzin, Sept. 5, 1885, A 7363, and note of Herbert von Bismarck to Kaiser, Sept. 5, 1885, relating this advice, GFO, Reel 92.

55 Opposition movements noted in Bécker, *Historia de las relaciones exteriores*, 3:612; Fernández Almagro, *Historia política*, 1:452–53; Lafuente, *Historia general*, 25:271. On September 5 Solms reported that Sagasta and his colleagues were ready to take over with an immediate declaration of war on Germany. (Bismarck noted on this news, "Don Quixote.") Solms to A.A., Telegram No. 75; Herbert von Bismarck to Otto von Bismarck, Telegram No. 20, Sept. 6, 1885, with marginal comment, GFO, Reel 92. A day later Solms heard that Martínez Campos and Jovellar were supposed to have seen the king and warn

him that the war fever could not be restrained if Sagasta came to power, but on September 7 the Liberals backed away and began to stress that they would seek a peaceful settlement. Solms to A.A., Nos. 204, 210, Sept. 6, 7, 1885, GFO, Reel 92.

[56] Plessen in London, Telegram No. 211, Sept. 11, 1885; copy of note of Lord Salisbury to Sir Edward Malet, Sept. 11, 1885, Confidential, A 7568, GFO, Reel 94.

[57] First note of kaiser's influence, report of interview by Herbert von Bismarck to Otto von Bismarck, No. 38, Aug. 28, 1885, A 7109; references to actions of Salamanca, who sent back to Germany the decoration given him by the crown prince and agitated within the "Centro Militar," Captain von Deines, Military Attaché in Madrid, Military Reports, Nos. 12, 13, 14, Aug. 25, 27, 1885, GFO, Reel 92.

[58] Series of reports from von Deines, No. 13, Aug. 27; No. 15, Aug. 28; No. 16, Sept. 2; No. 18, Sept. 7; No. 19, Sept. 14; No. 29, Nov. 18, 1885; Caprivi also wrote, Sept. 10, 1885, A 7606, Secret, to ask Consuls for reports on the strength of the Spanish navy, GFO, Reel 65.

[59] Originally offered in Note of President of Council of Ministers to Spanish ambassador in Berlin, Aug. 26, 1885, copy, A 7054. Benomar, the Spanish ambassador, added his own personal appeal to Count Hatzfeldt along with critical references to his government's actions, private letter of Aug. 27, 1885, included in Hatzfeldt to Bismarck at Varzin, No. 35, Aug. 27, 1885. Later reports Solms to A.A., Telegram No. 64, Aug. 27; No. 190, Aug. 28, 1885, GFO, Reel 92; Solms to A.A., No. 213, Sept. 8, 1885; Memo of Bismarck No. 65, Sept. 15, 1885, GFO, Reel 94.

[60] In reference to Spanish priority see ch. 9, n. 52; Solms to A.A., Telegram No. 42, Sept. 4, 1885, GFO, Reel 92; cf. report of Courcel, the French ambassador to Berlin, to Freycinet, No. 179, Confidential, Oct. 4, 1885, DDF, 6:104–5. Bismarck's directions restraining German navy, Note from Bismarck to Caprivi, copy, Sept. 2, 1885, A 7201, 7261; Bismarck to A.A., Telegram No. 31, Sept. 6, 1885, A 7418, GFO, Reel 92.

[61] Bismarck's comments made to Courcel at Friedrichsruh on Oct. 20, Courcel to Freycinet, No. 187, Confidential, Oct. 22, 1885, DDF, 6:123–31.

[62] Solms to A.A., No. 189, Aug. 28, 1885; No. 194, Sept. 1, 1885; No. 212, Sept. 5, 1885; telegrams Nos. 90, 91, Dispatch No. 218, Sept. 11, 1885; personal letter of Cánovas to GFO, Sept. 2, 1885,

copy, A 7304; GFO, Reel 92; Solms to A.A., No. 237 and private letter to Hatzfeldt, Sept. 16, 1885, GFO, Reel 93.

[63] Lafuente, *Historia general*, 25:276–77.

[64] Foster to Frelinghuysen, Nos. 166, 168, Feb. 8, 14, 1884, U.S. Dept. of State, Reel 99.

[65] German Consul in Havana to A.A., No. 3, Jan. 10, 1884; Solms to A.A., No. 94, June 18, 1884, GFO, Reel 95. Debates in *Diario*, Congreso, 2:714–32, June 21, 1884, et seq. Reports of Foster to Frelinghuysen, No. 226, July 17, 1884; No. 233, July 28, 1884, U.S. Dept. of State, Reel 101. Solms to A.A., June 25, 1884, GFO, Reel 95.

[66] Description of negotiations in Foster to Frelinghuysen, No. 299, Confidential, Nov. 25, 1884, U.S. Dept. of State, Reel 102. Bécker, *Historia de las relaciones exteriores*, 3:539–54, summarizes but without references to personalities.

[67] Foster to Frelinghuysen, No. 300, Nov. 25, 1884, U.S. Dept. of State, Reel 103. But the German consul in Havana, Raschdon, reported that this would mean considerable decline in the revenues of the islands, No. 77, Dec. 11, 1884, A 8082, GFO, Reel 95.

[68] Reed to Frelinghuysen, Nos. 278, 279, 280, 281, Dec. 29, 30, 1884, Jan. 1, 14, 1885, U.S. Dept. of State, Reel 103; von Gutschmid to A.A., No. 1, Jan. 6, 1885, GFO, Reel 60. For the Senate debates see *Diario*, Senado, 2:768–71, 776–84, 1056–75, Dec. 27, 29, 1884, Jan. 13, 1885. Final vote on charges was 114 to 5 with minorities abstaining and many of majority as well.

[69] Foster to T. F. Bayard, Nos. 305, 311, May 16, 23, 1885, U.S. Dept. of State, Reel 104. The German consul in Havana, Raschdon, reported that plantation owners in Cuba had raised a million dollars to influence Congress in Washington, but had found the money insufficient and had little trust in Spain's promises, No. 23, March 4, 1885, Unnumbered, GFO, Reel 95.

[70] Bécker, *Historia de las relaciones exteriores*, 3:557–59.

[71] Foster to Bayard, No. 388, Aug. 15, 1885, U.S. Dept. of State, Reel 104; Solms to A.A., Nos. 311, 316, 337, Oct. 21, 24, Nov. 6, 1885, GFO, Reel 71; Solms to A.A., No. 289, Oct. 9, 1885, GFO, Reel 61.

[72] In February debates on the student question found Romero Robledo so angry he blamed the military revolts of 1883 on Sagasta and Martínez Campos with the consequence that the latter resigned command of the Army of the North. Solms to A.A., No. 50, Feb. 21, 1885, GFO, Reel 60.

⁷³Pirala, *Historia contemporánea*, 6:782–83. The king added that he would be the "advocate, and convinced advocate" of the interests of Catalonia. Cf. Lafuente, *Historia general*, 25:252–56. The words of the king are repeated in Soldevila, *Historia de Catalunya*, 3:1370; and Maximiano García Venero's statement in *Cataluña: Sintesis de una región* (Madrid: Editora Nacional, 1954), pp. 194–95, that the king's reply was only courteous does not seem justified.

⁷⁴García Venero, *Cataluña*, pp. 194–95; Fernández Almagro, *Historia política*, 1:440.

⁷⁵Solms to A.A., No. 44, Very confidential, Feb. 11; No. 78, April 21; No. 81, April 23; No. 88, May 5; No. 89, May 8, 1885, GFO, Reel 60. Morier also reported the extent of the opposition and indicated the need for a cabinet change. Morier to Granville, Nos. 41, 42, 44, 45, April 28, May 4, 6, 1885, BFO 72:1705.

⁷⁶Solms to A.A., No. 96, Very confidential, May 18, 1885, GFO, Reel 60.

⁷⁷Solms to A.A., No. 113, June 15, 1885, GFO, Reel 60.

⁷⁸Solms to A.A., Nos. 122, 124, June 21, 23, 1885, GFO, Reel 61. Morier showed considerable sympathy for the opposition, speaking of Romero Robledo's "sanitary orgies." Morier to Granville, No. 60, June 21, 1885, BFO 72:1705. The reports of the American consuls in Spain showed the great reluctance of the authorities to admit the existence of cholera in each place where it appeared. Only when affairs had reached crisis stage did they give public notice. Manuel Casagemos to Asst. Secy. of State, No. 323, Sept. 10, 1884; Schenck to Asst. Secy. of State, No. 346, April 25, 1885; Nos. 352, 354, Aug. 4, 18, 1885, U.S. Consular Dispatches, Barcelona, Roll 8; Marston to Asst. Secy. of State, Nos. 263, Aug. 10, 151, Aug. 27, 161, Dec. 24, 1885, U.S. Consular Dispatches, Málaga, Roll 13.

⁷⁹Solms to A.A., Telegram No. 37, June 20; Nos. 118, 121, 123, 125, June 20, 21, 22, 23, 1885, GFO, Reel 61.

⁸⁰Solms to A.A., No. 129, June 27, 1885, GFO, Reel 61; Lafuente, *Historia general*, 25:258.

⁸¹See lengthy biographical sketch in *Enciclopedia universal ilustrada: Europeo-americana*. Cierva places Ferrán with Santiago Ramón y Cajal and Marcelino Menendez y Pelayo as the great trio of the Restoration, *Historia básica*, p. 117. See also Mariano Peset, *Muerte en España: Política y sociedad entre la peste y el cólera* (Madrid: Seminarios y Ediciones, 1972), pp. 228–30.

[82]Lafuente, *Historia general*, 25:258–59. Foster to Bayard, No. 342, July 4, 1885, enclosing report of Dr. E. de la Granja, a physician resident in Boston. An examination of Ferrán's serum by medical professors of the University of Madrid found no toxic substances in the serum although it was apparently derived from the feces of cholera victims. See *La Epoca*, June 6, 16, 1885. After the report of the commission and petitions from the province of Valencia, Romero Robledo indicated on June 23, 1885, his intention to lift the prohibition against the use of the vaccine. Apparently this was not implemented in time to make a serious trial of Ferrán's system. See *Diario*, Congreso, 11:5310–16.

[83]See Oscar Felsenfeld, chief of the Division of Communicable Diseases at Tulane University, *The Cholera Problem* (St. Louis, Mo.: Warren H. Green, 1967), pp. 145–50; the quotation derives from the less serious book by Norman Longmate, *King Cholera: The Biography of a Disease* (London: Hamish Hamilton, 1966), p. 233.

[84]Solms to A.A., Nos. 130, 132, both June 29, 1885, GFO, Reel 61.

[85]Description of visit in Pirala, *Historia contemporánea*, 6:798 and Solms to A.A., Telegrams Nos. 41, 42, July 2; No. 136, July 3, 1885, GFO, Reel 61; Morier to Granville, No. 66, July 3, 1885, BFO 72: 1706.

[86]Soldevila, *Historia de España*, 8:239.

[87]Fernández Almagro, *Historia política*, 1:445; Solms to A.A., No. 150, July 13, 1885, GFO, Reel 61. He had been civil governor of Madrid at the time of the university difficulties.

[88]Rotenhan in Paris to A.A., No. 177, Confidential, July 1, 1885; Solms to A.A., Nos. 146, 147, July 9, 10, 1885; Richard Lindau in Barcelona to A.A., unnumbered, July 10, 1885, A 5735; July 12, 1885, A 5818; Solms to A.A., No. 153, July 17, 1885; von Deines, Military Report No. 10, July 23, 1885, GFO, Reel 61.

[89]Von Deines to A.A., Military Report No. 22, Sept. 24, 1885, GFO, Reel 61.

[90]Solms to A.A., No. 293, Confidential, Oct. 6, 1885, GFO, Reel 61.

[91]Lafuente, *Historia general*, 25:262, 285.

[92]Solms to A.A., No. 293, Confidential, Oct. 6, 1885, GFO, Reel 61.

[93]Solms to A.A., No. 298, Very confidential, Oct. 12, 1885, GFO, Reel 61. A telegram sent by Cánovas to Count Benomar in Berlin told him, "You may affirm on your honor, if it is necessary, that at the

moment there is no illness." The only difficulty was a severe bronchitis with intermittent fever! Telegram, Oct. 17, 1885, GFO, Reel 61.

94 Solms to A.A., No. 329, Oct. 31, 1885, GFO, Reel 71.

95 Solms to A.A., No. 344, Nov. 14, 1885, GFO, Reel 71.

96 Solms to A.A., No. 355, Confidential, Nov. 20, 1885, GFO, Reel 71.

97 Solms to A.A., Telegram No. 139, Nov. 24, 1885; No. 358, Nov. 24; No. 360, Nov. 25; Telegrams Nos. 140, 141, Nov. 25; No. 359, Nov. 25; No. 362, Nov. 25; No. 367, Nov. 26; No. 386, Very confidential, Nov. 30, 1885, GFO, Reel 71. The effect of the secrecy which attached to the illness is reflected in Bunsen's report to the marquis of Salisbury of the king's "sudden illness." No. 143, Nov. 24, 1885, BFO 72:1706.

98 Solms to A.A., No. 368, Nov. 26, 1885, GFO, Reel 71. This lengthy report followed Solms telegram No. 139, Nov. 24, and Bismarck's telegram to A.A., No. 81, Nov. 25, 1885, which had the kaiser's personal direction to hasten the signing of the protocol on the Carolines. GFO, Reel 71.

CHAPTER 10. *Retrospect and Judgment*

1 *Cambó, 1876–1918* (Barcelona: Editorial Alpha, 1952), p. 47.

2 Comellas, *Historia de España moderna*, p. 408. His biography of Cánovas is heavily based on that of Fernández Almagro.

3 *Historia de España*, 8:119. Soldevila honors Cánovas for tolerating opposing opinions, pp. 146–47; criticizes him for opposing universal suffrage, p. 156, and for the lack of a firm foreign policy, p. 228, and most severely castigates his Cuban policy, pp. 363–67.

4 "Vieja y nueva política," *Obras completas*, 1:281–82.

5 Cierva, *Historia básica*, pp. 107–8. Cierva, however, does count Cánovas as "one of the foremost statesmen of his time" and "one of the foremost statesmen of all times in Spain." He pays tribute to his liberalism in spite of the conservative title and finds that he along with Sagasta, "the keystone of liberalism," and the king, "the first king of Spain who knew how to be constitutional," made possible a successful restoration, but one which did not solve Spain's economic and social problems. *Historia del Franquismo: Orígenes y configuración* (Barcelona: Planeta, 1975), pp. 22–38.

⁶ See the essays in Cánovas del Castillo, *Problemas contemporáneas*, for example, and the "discursos" in the various collections and anthologies.

⁷ The bibliography indicates the very significant scope of Cánovas's historical work. Gregorio Marañon y Posadillo, himself an able historian, paid tribute to Cánovas's high achievements in this area. See his commentary, e.g., in *El Conde-Duque de Olivares: La pasión de mandar*, 4th ed., (Madrid: Espasa-Calpe, 1959), pp. 411–12.

Selected Bibliography

DOCUMENTARY MATERIALS

France, Ministère des Affaires Étrangères, Commission de Publication des Documents Relatifs aux Origines de la Guerre de 1914. *Documents Diplomatiques Français, 1871–1914*. 1st ser., 1871–1900. 16 vols. in 17. Paris: Imprimerie Nationale, 1929–59. (Cited DDF.)

Germany, Auswärtiges Amt (Foreign Office). *Die grosse Politik der europäischen Kabinette, 1871–1914. Sammlung der diplomatischen Akten des Auswärtigen Amtes im Auftrage des auswärtigen Amtes.* Edited by Johannes Lepsius, Albrecht Mendelssohn Bartholdy, Friedrich Thimme. 2d ed., 39 vols. in 54. Berlin: Deutscheverlagsgesellschaft für Politik und Geschichte, 1924–26. (Cited GP.)

Germany, Auswärtiges Amt (Foreign Office). Unpublished records on microfilm (cited GFO) with following series designations:

I.a.B.o. (Spanien), 30. "Acta betr. die Verhältnisse der Insel Cuba." Reel Nos. 94–95.

I.a.B.o. (Spanien), 36. "Acta betr. die eventuelle Intervention der Mächte in Spanien." Reel No. 92.

I.a.B.o. (Spanien), 37, 40. "Schriftwechsel mit der Gesandtschaft zu Madrid sowie mit anderen Missionen und fremden Kabinette über die inneren Zustände und Verhältnisse Spaniens." Reel Nos. 48–61.

I.a.B.o. (Spanien), 37 adh. "Die Lage der Protestanten in Spanien." Reel Nos. 56–57.

I.a.B.o. (Spanien), 38. "Acta betr. die Aufenthalt des Prinzen Alfons von Asturien in Berlin." Reel No. 57.

I.a.B.o. (Spanien), 39. "Acta betr. das Verlangen der spanischen Regierung auf Auslieferung des Infanten Alfonso von Bourbon und Este." Reel No. 57.

I.a.B.o. (Spanien), 44. "Militär- und Marine-Angelegenheiten Spaniens." Reel Nos. 64–65.

I.a.B.o. (Spanien), 47. "Reise des Koenigs Alfonso von Spanien nach Deutschland, Oesterreich, Belgien und Frankreich." Reel No. 69.

I.a.B.o. (Spanien), 48. "Französische-spanische Beziehungen." Reel No. 69.

I.a.B.o. (Spanien), 49. "Annäherung Spanien an Deutschland, Mission Sr. Kaiserl. und Koenigl. Hoheit des Kronprinzen nach Spanien." Reel No. 70.

I.a.B.o. (Spanien), 51, "Differenz mit Spanien wegen der Carolinen-Inseln." Reel Nos. 92–93.

I.a.B.o. (Spanien), 51. "Rückgabe preussischer Orden seiten spanischer Staats-angehöriger (Angelegenheiten Salamanca). Austritt der deutschen Offiziere aus dem militär-politischen Madrider Klub 'Centro Militar.'" Reel No. 93.

I.a.B.o. (Spanien), 55. "Das spanische Königshaus." Reel No. 71. (Reels 92–95 are portions of materials held by the University of Michigan, Ann Arbor; all other reels are portions of Doc. Film 3547, U.S. National Archives, Washington, D.C.)

Great Britain. Unpublished Records of the British Foreign Office, Public Records Office, London. (Cited BFO.)

Spain, Cortes. *Diario de las sesiones de Cortes*. Congreso de los diputados, 1875–85. Senado, 1875–85 (in part). Madrid: Imprenta y Fundición de los hijos de J. A. García, 1876–86. (Cited *Diario*.)

Spain, *Gaceta de Madrid* (Official Bulletin of the State).

United States, Department of State. Dispatches from U.S. Ministers to Spain. Doc. Film 436, Microcopy No. M. 31, Reels 64–105. (Cited U.S. Dept. of State.)

Dispatches Addressed to the Department of State by United States Consular Representatives Abroad (all cited U.S. Consular Dispatches with city concerned):

Microcopy T357, Alicante.
Microcopy T121, Barcelona.
Microcopy T217, Málaga.
Microcopy T422, Port Mahón.

NEWSPAPERS

Barcelona, *La Correspondencia de Barcelona*.
London, *Times*.
Madrid, *El Diario Espanol*.

Selected Bibliography

Madrid, *El Globo*.
Madrid, *El Imparcial*.
Madrid, *El Mundo Político*.
Madrid, *El Pabellón Nacional*.
Madrid, *La Epoca*.
Madrid, *La Iberia*.
Madrid, *La Política*.

PRINTED WORKS

Abad de Santillán, Diego. *Historia del movimiento obrero español*. Madrid: Editorial ZYX, 1967.

Aguado, Emiliano. *Don Manuel Azaña Diaz*. Barcelona: Ediciones Nauta, 1972.

Alonso, José Ramón. *Historia política del ejercito español*. Madrid: Editora Nacional, 1974.

Angelon, Manuel. *Isabel II. Historia de la reina de España*. Madrid: Librería Española, 1860.

Armiñan, Luis de. *Weyler*. Madrid: Editorial "Gran Capitán," 1946.

Ballesteros y Beretta, Antonio. *Historia de España y su influencia en la historia universal*. Vol. 11. Barcelona: Salvat Editores, 1956.

Bécker, Jerónimo. *Historia de las relaciones exteriores de España durante el siglo XIX: Apuntes para una historia diplomática*. 3 vols. Madrid: Editorial Voluntad, 1926.

———. *Historia de Marruecos: Apuntes para la historia de la penetración europea, y principalmente de la española, en el Norte de África*. Madrid: Jaime Ratés Martín, 1915.

———. *Relaciones commerciales entre España y Francia durante el siglo XIX*. Madrid: Jaime Ratés Martín, 1910.

Benoist, Charles. *Cánovas del Castillo: La restauration rénovatrice*. Paris: Plon, 1930. Spanish edition: *Cánovas del Castillo: La restauración renovadora*. Madrid: Ediciones Literarias, 1931.

Bergamini, John D. *The Spanish Bourbons: The History of a Tenacious Dynasty*. New York: G. P. Putnam's Sons, 1974.

Bermejo, Ildefonso Antonio. *Historia de la interinidad y guerra civil de España desde 1868*. 3 vols. Madrid: R. Labajos, 1875–77.

Bertelson Repetto, Raul. *El senado en España*. Madrid: Instituto de Estudios Administrativos, 1974.

Borrego, Andrés. *Datos para la historia de la revolución, de la interinidad y del advenimiento de la restauración*. Madrid: Imprenta de la Sociedad Tipográfica, 1877.

Brandt, Joseph A. *Toward the New Spain*. Chicago: University of Chicago Press, 1933.

Bravo Morata, Frederico. *Historia de Madrid*. 3 vols. Madrid: Fenicia, 1970.

Cabezas, Juan Antonio. *Concepción Arenal o el sentido romántico de la justicia*. Vidas españolas e hispanoamericanas del siglo XIX, vol. 59. Madrid: Espasa-Calpe, 1942.

Cacho Viu, Vicente. *La institución libre de enseñanza*. Vol. 1, *Origenes y etapa universitaria, 1860–1881*. Madrid: Ediciones Rialp, 1962.

Campoamor, Ramón de. *Cánovas*. Madrid: Luis Navarro, 1884.

Cánovas del Castillo, Antonio. *Apuntes sobre la historia de Marruecos*. Madrid: Victoriano Suárez, 1913.

———. *Bosquejo histórico de la casa de Austria en España*. Madrid: Librería General de Victoriano Suárez, 1911.

———. *De la casa de Austria en España: Bosquejo histórico*. Madrid: Imprenta de la Biblioteca Universal Económica, 1869.

———. *Discursos leidos ante la Real Academia de Ciencias Morales y Políticas en la recepción pública del Excmo. Señor . . . el domingo 5 de Junio de 1881*. Madrid: Imprenta de Manuel Ginés Hernández, 1881.

———. *El Solitario y su tiempo: Biografía de D. Serafín Estébenez Calderón y crítica de sus obras*. 2 vols. Madrid: A. Pérez Dubrull, 1883.

———. *El teatro español*. Madrid: Editorial Ibero-Americana, n.d.

———. *Estudios del reinado de Felipe IV*. 2 vols.

———. *Estudios literarios*. 2 vols. Madrid: Imprenta de la Biblioteca Universal Económica, 1868.

———. *Historia de la decadencia de España desde el advenimiento de Felipe III al trono hasta la muerte de Carlos II*. 2d ed. Madrid: J. Ruiz, 1910.

———. *La campana de Huesca: Crónica del siglo XII*. Madrid: Imprenta de la Biblioteca Nueva, 1854.

———. *Matias de Novoa. Monografía de un historiador español desconocido*. Madrid: Miguel Ginesta, 1876.

———. *Problemas contemporáneas*. 3 vols. Madrid: Pérez Dubrull (vols. 1, 2) and M. Tello (vol. 3), 1884–90.

Cánovas del Castillo, Emilio, comp. *Cánovas del Castillo: Juicio que mereció a sus contemporáneos españoles y extranjeros. Recopilación hecha por su hermano Emilio de gran parte de lo escrito y publicado con motivo de su muerte*. Madrid: M. Romero, impresor, 1901.

Cardell y Pujalte, Carlos. *La casa de Borbón en España*. Madrid: Agemundo, 1954.

Carr, Raymond. *Spain, 1808–1939*. Oxford: Oxford University Press, 1966.

Cavanillas, Julian Cortes. *María Cristina de Austria: Madre de Alfonso XIII*. Madrid: Ediciones Aspas, 1944.

Challice, Rachel. *The Secret History of the Court of Spain During the Last Century*. London: John Long, 1909.

Christiansen, Eric. *The Origins of Military Power in Spain, 1800–1854*. Oxford: Oxford University Press, 1967.

Cierva, Ricardo de la. *Historia básica de la España actual, 1800–1975*. Barcelona: Editorial Planeta, 1974.

————. *Historia del Franquismo. Orígenes y configuración*. Barcelona: Planeta, 1975.

Clarke, H. Butler. *Modern Spain, 1815–1898*. Cambridge: Cambridge University Press, 1906.

Comellas, José Luis. *Cánovas*. Barcelona: Ediciones Cid, 1965.

————. *Historia de España moderna y contemporánea, 1474–1974*. Madrid: Ediciones Realp, 1974.

"Conservador, Un." *Ecos de ultratumba: Cánovas como juzgaría la actual situación*. Barcelona: Tobella & Costa, 1903.

Conte, Augusto. *Recuerdos de un diplomático*. 3 vols. Madrid: Gongora, 1901–3.

Corwin, Arthur F. *Spain and the Abolition of Slavery in Cuba, 1817–1886*. Austin: University of Texas Press, 1967.

Creux, V. C. *Antonio Cánovas del Castillo: Sa carrière, ses oeuvres, sa fin. Étude biographique et historique*. Paris: F. Levé, 1897.

Cuenca Toribio, José Manuel. *Estudios sobre la iglesia española del XIX*. Madrid: Ediciones Rialp, 1973.

Díaz-Playa, Fernando. *Historia de España en sus documentos: El siglo XIX*. Madrid: Instituto de Estudio Político, 1960.

————. *La sociedad española: Desde 1500 hasta nuestros días*. San Juan, P.R.: Ediciones de la Torre, 1968.

————. *La vida española en el siglo XIX*. Madrid: Afrodisio Aguado, 1952.

————. *Otra historia de España*. Barcelona: Plaza & Janes, 1972.

Duberman, Martin. *James Russell Lowell*. Boston: Houghton Mifflin, 1966.

Espadas Burgos, Manuel. *Alfonso XII y los orígenes de la restauración*. Madrid: C. S. I. C., Escuela de Historia Moderna, 1975.

Espina, Antonio. *Cánovas del Castillo*. Madrid: Pegaso, 1947.

Estévez y Romero, Luis. *Desde el Zanjón hasta Baire: Datos para la historia política de Cuba*. Habana: Tipografía La Propaganda Literaria, 1899.

Estibaliz Ruiz de Azua y Martínez de Ezquerecocha, María. *El sitio de Bilbao en 1874: Estudio del compartimiento social de una ciudad en guerra*. *Historia general del señorio de Bizcaya*, supplement 4. Bilbao: Editorial La Gran Enciclopedia Vasca, 1976.

Fabié, Antonio María. *Cánovas del Castillo: Su juventud, su edad madura, su vejez*. Barcelona: Gustavo Gili, 1928.

Fabié y Escudero, Antonio. *Biografía del excmo. señor D. Pedro Salaverría*. 2 vols. Madrid: Imprenta de Fortanet, 1898.

Felsenfeld, Oscar. *The Cholera Problem*. St. Louis, Mo.: Warren H. Green, 1967.

Ferandis, Manuel, and Caetano Beirao. *Historia contemporánea de España y Portugal*. Barcelona: Editorial Labor, 1966.

Fernández Almagro, Melchor. *Cánovas, su vida y su política*. Madrid: Ediciones Ambos Mundes S.S., 1951.

———. *Historia política de la España contemporánea*. 2 vols. Madrid: Pegaso, 1956.

Field, Henry M. *Old Spain and New Spain*. New York: Charles Scribner's Sons, 1888.

Figueroa, Agustín de. *La sociedad española bajo la restauración*. Madrid: Ediciones Aspas, 1945.

Foner, Philip S. *A History of Cuba and Its Relations with the United States*. New York: International Publishers, 1962.

———. *The Spanish-Cuban-American War and the Birth of American Imperialism, 1895–1902*. 2 vols. New York and London: Monthly Review Press, 1972.

Francos Rodríguez, José. *En tiempo de Alfonso XII, 1875–1885*. Madrid: Renacimiento, 1917.

Fuess, Claude M. *The Life of Caleb Cushing*. New York: Harcourt, Brace, 1923.

García-Nieto, María Carmen, Javier María Donezar, and Luis López Puerta. *Restauración y desastre, 1874–1898*. Bases documentales de la España contemporánea, vol. 4. Madrid: Guadiana, 1972.

García Venero, Maximiano. *Alfonso doce: El rey sin ventura*. Madrid: Ediciones S. C. L., 1960.

———. *Cataluña: Sintesis de una región*. Madrid: Editora Nacional, 1954.

————. *Historia de los movimientos sindicalistas españoles, 1840–1933.* Madrid: Ed. del Movimiento, 1961.

Gómez Chaix, Ruiz. *Ruiz Zorrilla: El ciudano ejemplar.* Vidas españolas e hispanoamericanas del siglo XIX, vol. 41. Madrid: Espasa-Calpe, 1934.

Gómez Llorente, Luis. *Aproximación a la historia del socialismo español hasta 1921.* Madrid: Editorial Cuadernos para el Diálogo, 1972.

González-Blanco, Edmondo. *Ideario de Cánovas.* Madrid: Ediciones Jasón, 1931.

Griñal Peralta, Leonardo. *Antonio Maceo: Análisis carácterológico.* La Habana: Editorial Trópico, 1936.

Herr, Richard. *Spain.* The Modern Nations in Historical Perspective. Englewood Cliffs, N.J.: Prentice-Hall, 1971.

Holt, Edgar. *The Carlist Wars in Spain.* Chester Springs, Pa.: Dufour Editions, 1967.

Houghton, Arthur. *Les origines de la restauration des Bourbons en Espagne.* Paris: Plon, Nourrit et cie., 1890.

Hughey, John David. *Religious freedom in Spain: Its Ebb and Flow.* London: Carey Kingsgate Press, 1955.

————. "Spanish Governments and Protestantism, 1868–1931." Ph.D. dissertation, Columbia University, 1951. University Microfilms, 113. Ann Arbor, Mich.: University Microfilms, 1952.

Hume, Martin A. S. *Modern Spain, 1788–1898.* New York: G. P. Putnam's Sons, 1900.

Ibáñez Marín, José, and the Marqués de Cabriñana [Julio Urbina y Ceballos]. *El general Martínez Campos y su monumento.* Madrid: Establecimiento Tipográfico "El Trabajo," 1906.

Izquierdo Hernández, Manuel. *La historia para todos: Historia clínica de la restauración.* Introduction by Dr. G. Maranon. Madrid: Editorial Plus-Ultra, 1946.

Jarnés, Benjamin. *Castelar, hombre del Sinaí.* Vidas españolas e hispanoamericanas del siglo XIX, vol. 45. Madrid: Espasa-Calpe, 1935.

Johnson, William Fletcher. *The History of Cuba.* 3 vols. New York: B. F. Breck & Co., 1920.

Jover Zamora, José María, ed. *El siglo XIX en Espana: Doce estudios.* Barcelona: Planeta, 1974.

Kern, Robert W. *Liberals, Reformers and Caciques in Restoration Spain, 1875–1909.* Albuquerque: University of New Mexico Press, 1974.

Klinger, Wallace R. "Spain's Problem of Alliances: Spanish Foreign

Policy from the Conference of Madrid, 1880 to the Mediterranean Agreement of 1907." Ph.D. dissertation, University of Pennsylvania, 1944.

Knight, Franklin W. *Slave Society in Cuba during the Nineteenth Century*. Madison: University of Wisconsin Press, 1970.

Labra y Cadrona, Rafael María de. *La crisis colonial de España, 1868–1898: Estudios de política palpitante y discursos parlamentarios*. Madrid: A. Alonso, 1901.

————. *La reforma política de ultramar: Discursos y folletos de . . . , 1868–1900*. Madrid: A. Alonso, 1901.

Lafuente y Zamalloa, Modesto. *Historia general de España desde los tiempos primitivos hasta la muerte de Fernando VII por don Modesto Lafuente, continuada desde dicha época hasta la muerte de don Alfonso XII, por don Juan Valera en colaboración con d. Andrés Borrego, d. Antonio Pirala y d. José Coroleu, y hasta la mayor edad de don Alfonso XIII por don Gabriel Maura y Gamazo*. Vol. 25. Barcelona: Montaner y Simón, 1922.

Lara y Pedrajas, Antonio de. *D. Antonio Cánovas del Castillo: Estudio crítico*. Madrid: Hijos de M. G. Hernández, 1901.

Latimer, Elizabeth Wormeley. *Spain in the Nineteenth Century*. Chicago: A. C. McClurg and Company, 1898.

Lema, Salvador Bermúdez de Castro y O'Lawlor, Marqués de. *Cánovas o el hombre de estado*. Vidas españolas e hispanoamericanas del siglo XIX, vol. 25. Madrid: Espasa-Calpe, 1931.

————. *De la revolución a la restauración*. 2 vols. Madrid: Editorial Voluntad, 1927.

————. *La política exterior española a principios del siglo XIX*. Madrid: Editorial Reus, 1935.

Lida, Clara E. "Agrarian Anarchism in Andalusia: Documents on the Mano Negra." *International Review of Social History* 14, no. 3 (1969): 315–51.

————. *Anarquismo y revolución en la España del XIX*. Madrid: Siglo Veintiuno Editores, 1972.

————. *Antecedentes y desarrollo del movimiento obrero español, 1835–1888: Textos y documentos*. Madrid: Siglo XXI de España, 1973.

————. *La mano negra: Anarquismo agrario en Andalucía*. Algarte, Vizcaya: Zero, 1972.

————. "Orígenes del anarquismo español, 1868–1884." Ph.D. dissertation, Princeton University, 1968.

Linares Rivas, Aureliano. *La primera cámara de la restauración: Retratos y semblanzas*. Madrid: J. C. Conde, 1878.

Selected Bibliography

Livermore, Harold V. *A History of Spain*. London: G. Allen, 1958.

Llanos y Torriglia, Felix de. *Francisco Silvela*. Madrid: Editorial Purcolla, 1946.

Llorca Vilaplana, Carmen. *Isabel II y su tiempo*. Alcoy: Editorial Marfil, 1959.

Longmate, Norman. *King Cholera: The Biography of a Disease*. London: Hamish Hamilton, 1966.

Lozoya, Juan Contreras López de Ayala, Marqués de. *Historia de España*. Vol. 6. Barcelona: Salvat Editores, 1967.

Luz, Pierre de. *Isabel II, reina de España*. Translated by Gabriel Conforto Thomas. Madrid: Editorial Juventud, 1940.

McGlinchee, Claire. *James Russell Lowell*. New York: Twayne Publishers, 1967.

Marañón y Posadillo, Gregorio. *El Conde-Duque de Olivares: La pasión de mandar*. 4th ed. Madrid: Espasa-Calpe, 1959.

Martí, Casimiro. *Orígenes del anarquismo en Barcelona*. Centro de Estudios Históricos Internationales, Series B, 1. Barcelona: Editorial Teide, 1959.

Martí, José. *Obras completas*. 74 vols. Edited by Gonzalo de Quesada y Miranda et al. La Habana: Trópico, 1936–53.

Martínez Cuadrado, Miguel. *Elecciones y partidos políticos de España, 1868–1931*. 2 vols. Madrid: Taurus, 1969.

Martínez de Campos y Serrano, Carlos, Duque de la Torre. *España bélica: El siglo XIX*. Madrid: Aguilar, 1961.

Medio, Dolores. *Isabel II de España: Biografía*. Madrid: Editorial sucesores de Rivadeneyra, 1966.

Meléndez Meléndez, Leonor. *Cánovas y la política exterior española*. Madrid: Instituto de Estudios Políticos, 1944.

Mesa, Roberto. *El colonialismo en la crisis del XIX español*. Madrid: Editorial Ciencia Nueva, 1967.

Moreno Echevarría, José María. *Isabel II: Biografía de una España en crisis*. Madrid: Ediciones 29, 1973.

Mousset, Alberto. *La política exterior de España, 1873–1918*. Introduction by the Conde de Romanones. Madrid: Biblioteca Nueva, 1918.

Muni, Fernando de León y Castillo, Marqués del. *Mis tiempos*. 2 vols. Madrid: Lib. de los sucesores de Hernando, 1921.

Navarro y Rodrigo, Carlos. *Un período de oposición*. Madrid: Imprenta de los Hijos de J. A. Garcia, 1886.

Nevins, Allan. *Hamilton Fish: The Inner History of the Grant Administration*. New York: Dodd, Mead and Company, 1936.

Nido y Segalerva, Juan del. *Historia política y parlamentaria del excmo. sr. d. Antonio Cánovas del Castillo.* Madrid: Prudencio P. de Velasco, 1914.

Nogués, Emilio J. M. *Historia crítica de la restauración bourbónica en España: Veinticinco años de historia contemporánea.* 3 vols. Barcelona: La Enciclopedia Democrática, 1895–97.

Ochando, T. *El general Martínez Campos en Cuba: Reseña político-militar de la última campaña, noviembre de 1876 a junio de 1878.* Madrid: Imprenta de Fortanet, 1878.

Orrego Luco, A., et al. *Al insigne Cánovas del Castillo.* Barcelona: Imprenta Barcelona, 1897.

Ortega y Gasset, José. *Obras completas.* Vol. 1, 1902–16, 2d ed. Madrid: Revista de Occidente, 1950.

Ortega y Gasset, Manuel. *"El Imparcial": Biografía de un gran periódico español.* Introduction by Juan Pujal. Zaragoza: Librería General, 1956.

Ortega y Rubio, Juan. *Historia de la regencia de María Cristina Habsbourg-Lorena.* 3 vols. Madrid: Felipe González Rojas, 1905.

Oyarzun, Roman. *La historia del carlismo.* Madrid: Alianza, 1969.

Pabón y Suárez de Urbina, Jesús. *Cambo, 1876–1918.* Barcelona: Editorial Alpha, 1952.

———. *La otra legitimidad.* 2d ed. Madrid: Prensa Española, 1969.

Parent, M. Celine Esther, Sister. "Caleb Cushing and the Foreign Policy of the United States, 1860–1877." Ph.D. dissertation, Boston College, 1958.

Parry, E. Jones. *The Spanish Marriages, 1841–1846: A Study of the Influence of Dynastic Ambition upon Foreign Policy.* London: Macmillan, 1936.

Payne, Stanley G. *Politics and the Military in Modern Spain.* Stanford, Calif.: Stanford University Press, 1967.

Pérez Galdós, Benito. *Episodios nacionales Série Final: Cánovas.* Madrid: Editorial Hernando, 1943.

Peset, Mariano. *Muerte en España: Política y sociedad entre la peste y el cólera.* Madrid: Seminarios y Ediciones, 1972.

Pidal, Alejandro. *Velada en memoria de d. Antonio Cánovas del Castillo: Celebrada en el ateneo de Madrid, la noche del 9 de noviembre de 1897, discurso.* Madrid: Hijos de M. G. Hernández, 1897.

Pino, Francisco de. *El excmo. señor don Manuel Becerra: Apuntes biográficos.* Madrid: Sucesores de Rivademyra, 1885.

Pirala y Criado, Antonio. *Historia contemporánea: Segunda parte de la*

guerra civil. Anales desde 1843 hasta el fallecimiento de don Alfonso XII.
6 vols. Madrid: Felipe González Rojas, 1893–95.

Pons y Umbert, Adolfo. Cánovas del Castillo. Madrid: Hijos de M. G.
Hernández, 1901.

———. Lecturas constitucionales en la España del siglo XIX: Discurso leido
ante las seis academias reunidas en la de ciencias exactas, físicas, y naturales
para commemorar la "Fiesta del Libro" el día 23 de abril de 1933. Madrid:
Gráfica Mundial, 1933.

Portell Vilá, Herminio. Historia de Cuba en sus relaciones con los Estados
Unidos y España. 4 vols. Miami, Fla.: Minemosyne Publishing, 1969.

Portuondo y Barceló, Bernardo. Voto particular sobre la reforma social de
Cuba. Madrid: Impr. à cargo de J. J. de los Heros, 1879.

Ramos Oliveira, Antonio. Politics, Economics and Men of Modern Spain,
1808–1946. London: Victor Gollancz, 1946.

Répide, Pedro de. Isabel II, Reina de España. Vidas españolas e hispanoamericanas del siglo XIX, vol. 20. Madrid: Espasa-Calpe, 1932.

Rivas Santiago, Natalio. Estampas del siglo XIX: Episodios históricos. Páginas de mi archivo y apuntes para mis memorias. Tercera parte del "Anecdotario Histórico Contemporáneo." Madrid: Editora Nacional, 1947.

———. Estampas del siglo XIX: Narraciones contemporáneas. Páginas de mi
archivo y apuntes para mis memorias. Septima parte del "Anecdotario Histórico Contemporáneo." Madrid: Editora Nacional, 1953.

Robinson, Richard A. H. The Origins of Franco's Spain: The Right, the
Republic and Revolution, 1931–1936. Newton Abbot: David & Charles,
1970.

Rodezno, Tomás Domínguez Arévalo, Conde de. Carlos VII, Duque
de Madrid. Vidas españolas del siglo XIX, vol. 4. Madrid: Espasa-
Calpe, 1929.

Romano, Julio. Weyler, el hombre de hierro. Vidas españolas e hispanoamericanas del siglo XIX, vol. 44. Madrid: Espasa-Calpe, 1934.

Romanones, Alvaro Figueroa y Torres, Conde de. Amadeo de Saboya,
el rey efímero: España y los orígenes de la guerra Franco-Prusiana de 1870.
Vidas españolas e hispanoamericanas del siglo XIX, vol. 46. Madrid:
Espasa-Calpe, 1935.

———. Doña María Cristina de Habsburgo Lorena: La discreta regente de
Espana. Vidas españolas e hispanoamericanas del siglo XIX, vol. 34.
Madrid: Espasa-Calpe, 1933.

———. Sagasta o el político. Vidas españolas del siglo XIX, vol. 7.
Madrid: Espasa-Calpe, 1934.

Rubí, Valeriano Weyler y Nicolau, Duque de. Mi mando en Cuba,

Selected Bibliography

10 febrero 1896 a 31 octubre 1897: Historia militar y política de la última guerra separatista durante dicho mando. 5 vols. Madrid: F. González Rojas, 1910–11.

Salom Costa, Julio. *España en la Europa de Bismarck: La política exterior de Cánovas, 1871–1881.* Madrid: C. S. I. C., Escuela de Historia Moderna, 1967.

Sevilla Andrés, Diego. *Constituciones y otras leyes y proyectos políticos de España.* 2 vols. Madrid: Editorial Nacional, 1969.

————. *Historia política de España, 1800–1973.* 2 vols., 2d ed. Madrid: Editora Nacional, 1974.

Soldevila, Ferrán. *Historia de Catalunya.* 2d ed., vol. 3. Barcelona: Editorial Alpha, 1962.

————. *Historia de España.* Vols. 7, 8. Barcelona: Ediciones Ariel, 1963–64.

Solervicens, Juan Bta., ed. *Cánovas: Antología.* Madrid: Espasa-Calpe, 1941.

Tallada Pauli, José M. *Historia de las finanzas españolas en el siglo XIX.* Madrid: Espasa-Calpe, 1946.

Tapia, Enrique de. *Francisco Silvela, gobernante austero.* Madrid: Afrodisio Aguado, 1968.

Tebar, Pedro E. de. *Las segundas Cortes de la Restauración. Semblanzas parlamentarias.* Madrid: Senado, 1880.

Terrachet Sauca, Enrique. *La agonía de los Fueros, 1844–1878, a través de los acuerdos de la Deputación Foral y Juntas Generales de Guernica. Historia general del Señorío de Bizcaya,* vol. 9. Bilbao: Editorial La Gran Enciclopedia Vasca, 1973.

Thomas, Hugh. *Cuba, the Pursuit of Freedom.* New York: Harper & Row, 1971.

Tuñon de Lara, Manuel. *El movimiento obrero en la historia de España.* Madrid: Taurus, 1972.

————. *La España del siglo XIX.* Paris: Librería Española, 1968.

Ullman, Joan Connelly. *The Tragic Week: A Study of Anticlericalism in Spain, 1875–1912.* Cambridge: Harvard University Press, 1968.

Varela Ortega, José. "Los amigos políticos: Funcionamiento del sistema caciquista." *Revista de Occidente,* 2d ser., vol. 43 (Oct., Nov., Dec., 1973), pp. 45–74.

Vicens Vives, Jaime. *Approaches to the History of Spain.* Translated and edited by Joan Connelly Ullman. Berkeley: University of California Press, 1967.

Vicens Vives, Jaime, with Jorge Nadal Oller. *An Economic History of*

Selected Bibliography

Spain. Translated by Frances M. López-Morillas. Princeton, N.J.: Princeton University Press, 1969.

Villaspesa Calvache, Vicente. *El funesto caciquismo y algo de su terapéutica*. Almería and Madrid: J. Fernández Murcia, 1908.

Villa-Urrutia, Wenceslao Ramírez, Marqués de. *El general Serrano, Duque de la Torre*. Vidas españolas del siglo XIX, vol. 1. Madrid: Espasa-Calpe, 1929.

Ward, G. H. B. *The Truth about Spain*. London: Cassell & Co., 1911.

Weyler y López de Fuga, Valeriano. *En el archivo de mi abuelo: Biografía del Capitan General Weyler*. Madrid: Industrias gráficas, 1946.

White, George F. *A Century of Spain and Portugal, 1788–1898*. London: Methuen, 1909.

MISCELLANEOUS

Diccionario de historia de España. Germán Bleiberg, ed. 2d ed., 3 vols. Madrid: Revista de Occidente, 1968–69.

Enciclopedia universal ilustrada: Europeo-americana. Madrid: Espasa-Calpe, 1905–30.

Esperabe y Arteaga, Enrique. *Diccionario enciclopédico y crítico de los hombres de España*. Madrid: Artes Gráficas, n.d.

Ossorio y Bernard, Manuel. *Ensayo de un catálogo de periodistas españoles del siglo XIX*. Madrid: J. Pacios, 1903.

Sánchez Alonso, B. *Fuentes de la historia española e hispanoamericana: Ensayo de bibliografía sistemática de impresos y manuscritos que ilustran la historia política de España y sus antiguas provincias de ultramar*. 3d ed., 3 vols. Madrid: Selecciones Gráficas, 1952.

Index

Adalbert of Bavaria, Prince: visit of Alfonso XII, 17
Agarrobillo, el: scene of Black Hand killing, 144
Aguirre de Tejada, Manuel: minister of overseas territories under Cánovas, 165; reactionary position, 166
Albacete, Salvador: budget for Cuba, 118–19; minister of overseas territories under Martínez Campos, 122; commissioner for Cuban tariff negotiations with United States, 185
Albareda, José Luis (Constitutionalist deputy, editor of the *Revista de España*): critic of government action in Mahón, 62; minister of development under Sagasta, 128; educational reforms, 128–29; criticism from right, 132; criticism of Camacho, 142; opposition to Constitution of 1876, 229n41
Alcoy: religious incident at, 92–93
Alfonso de Borbón y Austria d'Este (brother of pretender Carlos VII), 15, 40, 80
Alfonso XII, king of Spain
—assessment of reign, 194–96
—comparison with present king (Juan Carlos I), vii, 197–98
—early life: childhood, 4; exile, 4, 6; education, in Paris, 6; in Vienna, 6; in England, 17, 18, 19, 213n57
—favor for Catalonia, 25, 187, 274n73
—personal life and character: illness and death, 1, 88, 155, 170–71, 172, 176, 191–93, 268n22, 275–76n93; first marriage, María de las Mercedes, 7, 88–92, 208n24; description, 25–26; romantic adventures, 43–44, 102, 149, 154, 161, 188, 192–93, 226n70; Elena Sanz, 102; second marriage, María Cristina, 102–3, 115; Adela Borghi, 165; supposed illegitimacy, 230n61; speaking ability, 254n27

—plans for army reforms, 134, 135, 138, 154, 188
—relations with Austria, 156, 177, 262n44
—relations with England, 19, 259n18
—relations with Germany: Germanophilism, vii, 7, 171; visit to Germany, 1874, 17; on rumors of German ambitions in Spain, 18; role in alliance negotiations, 79; marriage of sister, 147; conversations with Solms, 147–48, 149–50, 151, 153–54, 183–84, 192–93, 201–4; visit to Prussian maneuvers, 151, 156–57; repercussions, 157–58; reception of Crown Prince Frederick William, 160; assessment of by German police agent, 171–72; assessment by Bismarck, 183; on Yap question, 183–84, 270–71n51; assessment by Hatzfeldt, 262n40
—restoration: abdication of mother, 6; news of Sagunto, 24; reception in Marseilles, 25; reception in Barcelona, 25; reception in Valencia, 25; reception in Madrid, 25, 215n2
—role during Cánovas's first cabinet: program of Sandhurst Manifesto, 19, 26; confirmation of cabinet, 27; support by Romero Robledo, 28; support by Carlist general Cabrera, 41; in danger at Lácar, 41; triumphal tour in northern Spain, 42; liberal sentiments, 43; popular support, 48; in background, 82, 101; names life senators, 83–84; visit in northern Spain, 88; assassination attempt against, 101–2
—role during Martínez Campos and second Cánovas cabinets, 122–23, 250n68
—role during Posada Herrera cabinet: liberalism, 162; role in fall of ministry, 162–63
—role during Sagasta cabinets: reason for change in government, 122–23, 126; final arbiter of politics, 127; greater

Index

Alfonso XII (*continued*)
freedom, 129; support by Democratic Dynastic party, 132; liberalism, 133–34; invitation to Russian Jews, 134; visit to fleet in northern Spain, 134; support for Sagasta, 142; 1883, year of triumph and disillusion, 144; fall of Sagasta, 158; support of Martos, 259n*13*
—role during third Cánovas cabinet: stricter controls, 163, 170; unhappiness, 164–65; recognition of legitimacy by pope, 169; critical of Cánovas, 170, 176; visit to earthquake zones, 176–77; dispirited, 188; concern for cholera, 188, 190
Almirall, Valentí: father of Catalan nationalism, 137
Alonso Martínez, Manuel (Center party leader): leadership of Constitutional dissidents, 61; defense of Constitution of 1876, 61; criticism of action at Mahón, 62; opposition to Senate nominations, 85, 86; criticism by Romero Robledo and press, 95; inability to gain leadership of Center party, 99; Fusionist grouping, 122; minister of grace and justice under Sagasta, 128; proposed judicial reforms, 135–36, 141; resignation, 142; character, 229n*44*; mentioned, viii, 94
Álvarez Bugallal, Saturnino (Liberal Conservative deputy): removed from attorney generalship, 87; hostility to Romero Robledo, 244n*15*
Alzugaray, Ricardo: attorney general, 87
Amadeo I of Savoy (Spanish king), 5, 6, 10, 11, 18, 28, 38
Anarchism: under First Spanish Republic, 11; sympathy for, 33; in South, 65, 98, 144–45; French support, 80
Andalusia: anarchism in, 144–45
Antequera, Juan, Rear Adm.: minister of navy under Cánovas, 165; resignation opposing naval reforms, 190–91
Anton, Prince: head of Hohenzollern family, 78
Antonelli, Cardinal (papal secretary of state): circular to Spanish bishops, 38
Aragon: Carlist influence in, 1874, 13
Arenal, Concepción: advocacy of prison reforms and women's rights, 98–99, 197
Army, Spanish
—comparison with German army, 216n*32*

—proposed reforms, 134, 138, 149, 153, 155, 159, 256n*37*
—role in politics: and events leading to Sagunto, 21, 23–24; republican officers, 34, 104, 105, 152–53; revolts, 104, 152–53, 168, 261nn*38, 39*; and support of Martínez Campos, 121; influence on fall of Cánovas, 121–23, 126; mentioned, 3–4, 8
—role of king in relationship to, 123, 126, 134, 135, 138, 154–55, 188
—role of Martínez Campos in assuring loyalty, 128, 141, 172–73
—significance of Gen. López Domínguez in, 141, 159
Aurioles, Pedro Nolasco: from Constitutional dissident to Liberal Conservative, 52
Austria, relations with: Alfonso XII in Vienna, 6; favor for Alfonso XII, 17–18; support for religious toleration, 35; support for restoration, 68; choice of María Cristina, 102–3; visit of Alfonso XII, 156, 262n*44*; advice to Alfonso, 177
Ávila, Bishop of: criticism of Morayta's speech, 173
Azcárate, Gumersindo de (professor at University of Madrid): protest against Orovio's control measures, 37; member of Democratic-Progressive party, 131

Badajoz: military rising at, 1883, 152
Bad Homburg: Prussian maneuvers at, 151
Balaguer, Victor (Catalan deputy): opposition to tariff, 137; directive committee of Dynastic Left, 141
Balmes, Jaime: philosophy, 216n*7*
Barcelona: reception for Alfonso XII, 25; harsh administration of Ibáñez de Aldecoa, 97; opposition to commercial treaty with France, 136–37; congress of workers, 145; king's visit, 1883, 155; conditions in, 1878, 240n*80*; conditions in, 1882, 255n*35*
Basilewsky Palace: exile headquarters of Isabella II, 5, 10, 89
Basque provinces: strength of Carlism, 2, 11, 13; loss of fueros, 42–43; unrest in, 97; settlement under Cánovas, 241–42nn*83, 85*
Beatrice, Archduchess of Este: gift of palace in Venice to pretender, 139

Index

Cánovas del Castillo (*continued*)

—in opposition: debate on gambling houses, 133; critic of tariff changes, 137; religious conservatism, 140, 142; role in formation of Dynastic Left, 141, 257n43; Commission on Social Reforms, 159; opposition to universal suffrage, 160

—internal policies of first cabinet: Constitutionalists as official opposition, 54–55; managed elections, 55; dominant position, 63–64, 82, 84; controversy over Senate, 82–87; opposition to Center party, 87; king's first marriage, 89–90; press and electoral laws, 96–97; problems in Catalonia and Basque provinces, 97–98, 241n83; party divisions, 105–11

—judgments on, 67–68, 183, 191, 196–97, 228n37, 276n5

—last ministry under Alfonso XII: reactionary cabinet, 163, 165–68, 266n3; difficulties with United States, 166, 177, 184–86; difficulties with Great Britain, 166, 177, 186; army disciplinary measures, 167, 168, 173, 191; difficulties with Italy, 169; favor from pope, 169, 254n21, 266n2; university controls, 175; controversy over Carolines, 177–83; improved relations with France, 178; problems with Catalonia, 186–87; cholera epidemic, 189–90; cabinet changes, 190–91

—personal relations with Alfonso XII, 1, 26, 82, 89, 150, 161, 163, 170, 190, 192, 226n70

—role during Martínez Campos government: influence on formation, 111–12; promised support, 113; opposition to tariff reforms, 114–16

—role in respect to Constitution of 1876: concept of "internal constitution," 44–47, 56, 227n1; alliance with dissident Constitutionalists, 48, 52, 59, 62; compromise on religious matters, Article 11, 53–54, 58, 60, 62–63, 216n7

—second ministry: abolition of slavery in Cuba, 117–18; economic reforms in Cuba, 118–21; fall of ministry, 122–25; accomplishments, 127

Cantonalist movement: in southern Spain, 11, 13, 17, 28, 29

Capriles, Enrique: Spanish officer at Yap, 180, 181

Cárdenas, Francisco de: minister of grace and justice under Cánovas, 27; out of ministry, 53

Carlism: origin and strength in Basque provinces, 2; in Navarre, 3; nature of, 3; in Catalonia and Valencia, 3; defeat, 1839, 3; relation of Francisco de Asís to, 5; revival after 1868, 11; strength during Serrano government, 13–14; French aid, 16, 209n38; seizure of German ship and reprisals, 17, 211n46; war against, 20–21, 27, 35, 40–41, 224n55; end of war, 42; continuance of "Tradition," 42, 97, 139–40, 169

Carlos V: first Carlist pretender to Spanish throne, 2

Carlos VII: Carlist pretender after 1868, 13, 17, 38, 42, 89, 97, 139, 167, 191, 241n84

Caroline Islands: dispute over Yap, 177–84, 191

Cartagena: end of cantonalist movement at, 13

Cassola, Manuel, Gen.: support of Martínez Campos, 121

Castañeira, Antonio de (subgovernor of Mahón): incident of August 19, 1876, 59–60

Castelar, Emilio: last president of First Spanish Republic, 11, 13; support for Serrano, 20; in Cortes during restoration, 29, 95–96, 162; role in *Virginius* affair, 69–70; opinion on Cánovas and Sagasta, 131; Democratic Possibilist, 131; cause of bad relations with Italy, 169; friend of Morayta, 173

Castro, Alejandro: minister of foreign affairs under Cánovas, 27; resignation, 53

Catalonia: Cánovas civil governor, 1858, 9; under republic, 11; Carlist control, 13; Martínez Campos, captain general, 22, 28; reception of Alfonso XII, 25; Alfonso XII's respect for, 25, 187, 274n73; campaign of Martínez Campos in, 42; treatment at end of Carlist war, 42–43; expansion of textile factories, 65; difficulties in Barcelona, 97; industrial growth, 97–98, 252n86; would-be assassin from, 101–2; opposition to Cuban tariff reforms, 114, 124, 248n53; anti-

Index

Maldonado Macanaz, Joaquín: supervisor of public instruction, 37

Mangado, Hinginio, Capt.: abortive revolt, 168, 267n10

Marfori, Carlos: favorite of Isabella II, 44, 206n12, 207n13

Margarita (wife of pretender): entertainment by Isabella II, 89

María Cristina de Borbón (mother of Isabella II): regent, 2; at Alfonso XII's first wedding, 90; death, 103

María Cristina of Hapsburg-Lorraine (second wife of Alfonso XII): Conte's negotiations for marriage, 102; love for Alfonso XII, 103, 149, 243n10; description and wedding, 103, 243n8; concern for role of army, 154; pregnancy, 156, 170, 193, 243n10, 259n16

María de la Paz, Infanta (sister of Alfonso XII): marriage, 147; visit of Alfonso XII, 156; illness and operation in Madrid, 170

María de las Mercedes (daughter of duke of Montpensier): meeting with Alfonso XII, 7; marriage, 89–91, 208n24 death, 91–92, 238–39nn51, 53; description, 91, 238n49; miscarriage, 102; contrast with María Cristina, 103

María de las Mercedes (daughter of María Cristina): recognized as successor to throne, 129

Marianas Islands: German and Spanish interest in, 180

Martínez Campos, Arsenio, Gen.: pronunciamiento at Sagunto, 21, 23–24; relations with Cánovas del Castillo, 21, 23, 28, 42; military career, 22–23, 42, 225nn62, 63, 65: in Cuba, 71, 99–100, 106–11, 244n22, 245n23; ministry, 112–16, 246n32, 247n46, 249n60, 249–50n66; debate over reforms, 117–22, 124–25, 252n99; origin of Fusionists, 122; minister of war under Sagasta, 128, 138, 141, 148, 152; resignation, 158, 253n3; and Yap controversy, 181, 271n55; mentioned, viii, 36, 46, 105, 273n72

Martínez Campos, Miguel (brother of Gen. Arsenio M. C.): on Hispanic-Colonial Bank loan, 251n88

Martín Herrera, Cristóbal: Committee of Thirty-Nine Notables, 52; minister of grace and justice, 62; minister of overseas territories, 84; defense of entry into Liberal Conservative party, 86–87

Martos, Cristino: abstention from politics under Cánovas, 29; meeting with Serrano and Ruiz Zorrilla, 104, 217n16; criticism of law for abolition of slavery in Cuba, 118; organization of Democratic-Progressive party, 130; desertion of Dynastic Left, 169; support of Alfonso XII, 259n13

Memorial de Greuges: list of Catalan grievances, 187

Merry y Colon, Francisco. See Benomar, Francisco Merry y Colon, count of

Michels, Baron de (French ambassador): betterment of relations with Spain, 171, 264n55

Moderado party: representation in Cánovas cabinet, 27; character, 27, 216n7, 221nn41, 42; role during early restoration, 36–38, 48, 52–54; relations with Martínez Campos, 36, 112, 221nn41, 247n35; Senate members, 83; opposition to king's marriage to María de las Mercedes, 90; divisions, 99, 105, 122, 139–40; tendency to merge with Conservatives, 164, 166; rehabilitation of Isabella II, 169

Molíns, Mariano Roca de Togores, first marquis of: minister of navy, 25, 27

Montero Ríos, Eugenio: in Democratic-Progressive party, 131; directive committee of Dynastic Left, 141

Montpensier, Duke of: marriage to sister of Isabella II, 3; leadership of Alfonsist cause, 7, 10, 208n23; significance during Serrano government, 12, 17, 20; at death of Alfonso, 193, 203–4

Morayta, Miguel (professor of universal history at University of Madrid): controversy over speech, 173–75

Moreno (cardinal archbishop of Toledo): controversy over pastoral letter, 132–33

Moreno Nieto, José: opposition to government, 244n15

Moret y Prendergast, Segismundo: member of Democratic-Dynastic party, 131; directive committee of Dynastic Left, 141–42; ministry of interior and reform project, 159, 162, 167

Morier, Sir Robert (British ambassador to Spain): report of reactionary position of Cánovas, 266n3

Index

Index

BAY OF BISCAY
ATLANTIC OCEAN
LA CORUÑA
Santiago de Compostela
Lugo
GALICIA
Pontevedra
Vigo
Tuy
RIO MIÑO
RIO SIL
Ovense
ASTURIAS
Llanes
Covadonga
CANTABRIAN MOUNTAINS
SANTANDER
LEÓN
LEÓN
Carrión
RIO CARRION
Santo Domingo de la Calzada
BURGOS
Najera
RIO PISUERGA
OLD CASTILE
Braganza
Zamora
VALLADOLID
RIO DUERO
OPORTO
RIO DOURO
RIO DUERO
SALAMANCA
PORTUGAL
SEGOVIA
Riofrío
Ávila
SIERRA DE GUADARRAMA
Escorial
RIO HENARES
MADRID
SIERRA DE GATA
SIERRA DE GREDOS
Aranjuez
RIO TAJO
Talavera
RIO TAJO
TOLEDO
RIO TEJO
SPAIN
NEW CASTILE
Torres Vedras
ESTREMADURA
Ciudad Real
LA MANC
Valdenpeña
LISBON
BADAJOZ
RIO GUADIANA
RIO GUADIANA
Nares de Tolosa
SIERRA MORENA
Bailén
CÓRDOVA
RIO GUADALQUIVIR
ANDALUSIA
HUELVA
SEVILLE
RIO GUADALQUIVIR
GRANADA
SIERRA NEVADA
Cape St. Vincent
SAN LÚCAR
MÁLAGA
CÁDIZ
Algeciras
GIBRALTAR (United Kingdom)
Tarifa
Strait of Gibraltar
TANGIER
MEDIT
SPANISH
42° N LAT.
40° N LAT.
38° N LAT.
36° N LAT.
8 W LONG.
6° W LONG.
4° W LONG.